This is the first book-length study of Oscar Wilde's *Salome*, a play now regarded as central to his artistic achievement. Often drawing on little-known sources, the authors provide a detailed stage history of this controversial work, and its transformation into opera, dance and film, with such major innovators as Max Reinhardt, Richard Strauss, Sergei Diaghilev, Peter Brook, Salvador Dali, Lindsay Kemp and Steven Berkoff contributing to *Salome*'s contemporary reputation. Beginning with Sarah Bernhardt's aborted production of 1892, the book surveys *Salome*'s principal realisations in the European theatre, including Lugné-Poe's Parisian première of 1896, Reinhardt's Berlin productions of 1902–3, attempts at presentation in pre-revolutionary Russia and the play's impact on the English stage between 1911 and 1990. A separate chapter explores a wealth of further interpretations, including Aubrey Beardsley's challenging illustrations, Strauss's operatic version, the exotic dances realised by Maud Allan and Ida Rubinstein and the provocative films by Alla Nazimova and Ken Russell.

WILDE

SALOME

PLAYS IN PRODUCTION

Series editor: Michael Robinson

PUBLISHED VOLUMES

WILDE

SALOME

*

WILLIAM TYDEMAN AND STEVEN PRICE
University of Wales, Bangor

CAMBRIDGE
UNIVERSITY PRESS

CAMBRIDGE UNIVERSITY PRESS
Cambridge, New York, Melbourne, Madrid, Cape Town, Singapore, São Paulo

Cambridge University Press
The Edinburgh Building, Cambridge CB2 8RU, UK

Published in the United States of America by Cambridge University Press, New York

www.cambridge.org
Information on this title: www.cambridge.org/9780521454230

First published 1996

A catalogue record for this publication is available from the British Library

Library of Congress Cataloguing in Publication data
Tydeman, William.
Wilde – Salome / William Tydeman and Steven Price.
p. cm. – (Plays in production)
Includes bibliographical references and index.
ISBN 0 521 45423 9 (hardback). – ISBN 0 521 56545 6 (paperback)
1. Wilde, Oscar, 1854–1900. Salome. 2. Wilde, Oscar, 1854–1900 –
Stage history. 3. Wilde, Oscar, 1854–1900 – Audio adaptations.
4. Wilde, Oscar, 1854–1900 – Film and video adaptations. 5. Salome
(biblical character) – In literature. I. Price, Steven. II. Title.
III. Series.
PR5820.S23T9 1996
822'.8–dc20 96-43082 CIP

ISBN 978-0-521-45423-0 hardback
ISBN 978-0-521-56545-5 paperback

Transferred to digital printing 2008

CONTENTS

ILLUSTRATIONS

GENERAL PREFACE

Volumes in the series Plays in Production take major dramatic texts and examine their transposition, firstly on to the stage and, secondly, where appropriate, into other media. Each book includes concise but informed studies of individual dramatic texts, focusing on the original theatrical and historical context of a play in relation to its initial performance and reception followed by subsequent major interpretations on stage, both under the impact of changing social, political and cultural values, and in response to developments in the theatre generally.

Many of the plays also have been transposed into other media – film, opera, television, ballet – which may well be the form in which they are first encountered by a contemporary audience. Thus, a substantial study of the play text and the issues it raises for theatrical realisation is supplemented by an assessment of such adaptations as well as the production history, where the emphasis is on the development of a performance tradition for each work, including staging and acting styles, rather than simply the archaeological reconstruction of past performances.

Plays included in the series are all likely to receive regular performance and individual volumes will be of interest to the informed reader as well as to students of theatre history and literature. Each book also contains an annotated production chronology as well as numerous photographs from key performances.

Michael Robinson
University of East Anglia

ACKNOWLEDGEMENTS

Our warmest thanks go to our General Editor, Michael Robinson, and Victoria Cooper of Cambridge University Press, for their support and advice; our colleagues at the University of Wales, Bangor: Sylvia C. Ellis; Linda Jones; W. Gareth Jones; Catrin Haf Williams; Andrew Plowman, who translated much of the material relating to Max Reinhardt; Katherine Thomson, who performed the same service with regard to works in Russian; our Departmental secretaries, Michelle Harrison and Gail Kincaid, and the staff of the Information Services unit.

Further afield, we must thank Simon Bailey, Archivist at Oxford University; Richard Allen Cave of London University; Joel H. Kaplan, University of Birmingham; Richard Mangan and the Mander and Mitchenson Collection; Anthony Pearson, University of Glasgow; Glanville Price of the University of Wales, Aberystwyth; Paul Raven, formerly of the University of Warwick; Lucy Reford, Oxford University Press; Laurence Senelick of Tufts University, Medford, Mass., USA; Ian Small, University of Birmingham; John Stokes at the University of Warwick; Glynne Wickham, formerly of the University of Bristol.

We are also grateful to all those who assisted us in our archival researches at the Reinhardt Archive, Binghamton; the Fonds Rondel, Bibliothèque de l'Arsenal, Paris; and in London, the staff of the British Library, the Theatre Museum, Covent Garden, the National Theatre, the Witt Library at the Courtauld Institute, and the University of London Library, Senate House.

A NOTE ON NAMES

In the original French text of his play Wilde christened his heroine 'Salomé', using that form as the title of his work. With the publication of the English text she became anglicised into 'Salome'. In the course of her many transmutations she has been referred to by both names; we have decided to refer to both work and character as 'Salome' throughout. By the same token, Wilde spelt Iokanaan with an initial 'I'; others (including Strauss) have preferred the form 'Jokanaan'. In this case we have made no attempt to regularise the spellings adopted.

INTRODUCTION

It is only in recent decades that Oscar Wilde's one-act drama *Salome* has attained what many see as its rightful degree of prominence in the Wildean canon. More castigated than complimented on its first published appearance in French in 1893 and in English translation the following year,[1] denied public presentation in Britain until 1931, *Salome* frequently suffered during its early existence from being adjudged a work reflecting the extravagant lifestyle and outrageous attitudes of a writer who after May 1895 had to endure the stigma of an exposed and convicted homosexual. The subsequent cult of overt, self-conscious masculinity which dominated the last years of Queen Victoria's reign rejected all art that its adherents characterised as *outré*, decadent, morbid, unnatural, perverted and unwholesome: *Salome* seemed tailor-made for disapprobation on precisely such grounds. Yet even when Wilde's reputation recovered sufficiently to assume that of a 'tragic genius', the instability of *Salome*'s critical popularity and the infrequency of its theatrical realisation often left his most experimental play isolated as an apparent aberration among the complete works.

Yet for the more dispassionate observers of his own day, Wilde's exotic symbolist sidelight on a popular biblical incident might not have stood out quite so signally from amongst his dramatic *oeuvre* as a flagrant anomaly, had they examined its stage predecessors more carefully. His two ventures into territories unfamiliar to the average contemporary playgoer, prior to the success of *Lady Windermere's Fan* in 1892, did something to prepare them for the emotional and linguistic intensity, if not the superb theatrical concentration, Wilde achieved in the handling of the traditional scriptural legend of the involvement of the Jewish princess in the martyrdom of St John the Baptist.

His first dramatic essay, *Vera; or the Nihilists*, a spirited if stagey political melodrama written in 1880 and first presented in New York in August 1883, had for its heroine a Russian woman of the people who joins the Nihilists to free her country from the oppression of its detested Tsarist regime. In Vera herself we encounter the pent-up ardour and the unleashed fury of a Salome and this is not the sole anticipation of the later piece. In the elder Tsar's role we meet something of the grim humour, sadism and nervous energy displayed in that of Herod. It has also been claimed that Vera's climactic act of sacrifice in allowing the power of human love to triumph over vindictive desires – or in this instance the desire for liberty in the abstract as opposed to regard for the sentient individual – anticipates future works in which the sovereign potency of love overcomes baser feelings.[2] However, in the case of Salome the realisation strikes the heroine too late to save a life.

A similar case can be made for *The Duchess of Padua*, Wilde's grandiose Jacobean-inspired tragedy of revenge subsumed in love, completed in Paris in March 1883 and eventually staged in New York under the title of *Guido Ferranti* early in 1891. Here, too, passion, vengeance and remorse constitute key ingredients in a Shakespearean pastiche which has a certain borrowed lustre, but which lacks true originality of tone or purpose. Although the fervent reciprocal feelings which develop between the youthful revenger Guido and Beatrice, the unhappily married wife of the elderly tyrant Duke, seem far removed from the virginal Salome's abortive wooing of the unresponsive Iokanaan, both relationships founder on incompatibilities of temperament and attitude, which death alone can resolve. Even closer to the heart of *Salome* is the Duchess's terrible reaction to her lover's harsh, judgmental, if temporary repudiation of her, following her murder of the Duke. Like Salome, sexually humiliated by a man's priggish response to her declaration of devotion, Beatrice reacts by denouncing Guido for the killing, and allows

him to go virtually to the scaffold before she acknowledges the fact
of their love, and they die together, much as Salome dies cradling
the Baptist's severed head in her arms.

Katharine Worth also finds, in both *Vera* and *The Duchess*,
devices which anticipate what is usually referred to today as 'total
theatre'.[3] Originating in large measure in Richard Wagner's notion
of the *Gesamtkunstwerk*, whose principles were embraced by the
French symbolist poets, 'total theatre' strives to orchestrate sound,
light, movement, costumes and décor, speech, music, and dance,
blending visual and aural effects to create one whole and indivisible
staged entity. Wilde was undoubtedly a dedicated proponent of the
concept; in his essay 'The Truth of Masks', which, as 'Shakespeare
and Stage Costume', first appeared in the *Nineteenth Century* for
May 1885, defending the stage as 'the meeting-place of all the arts',
he emphasised the importance in the playhouse of such concepts as
'the unity of artistic effect', 'harmony in the scene as a picture', and
the necessity for 'one single mind directing the whole production'.[4]
But while *Vera* and *The Duchess of Padua* may on occasion employ
such devices as symbolic verbal and scenic leitmotifs in embryonic
form, they never receive the sustained artistic attention Wilde lavished on *Salome* while modulating in a thoroughgoing and sophisticated way the techniques of what have since become theatrical
commonplaces.

This feature of his work was certainly in accordance with
Wilde's aim in *Salome* to embody the literary principles evolved and
espoused by that anti-realist group of influential French writers and
theorists known as the *Symbolistes*, several of whom Wilde knew personally. Richard Aldington once argued that Wilde was writing
symbolist verse 'years before the symbolist movement began',[5] and if
we apply Edmund Wilson's succinct if narrow definition of symbolism as 'an attempt by carefully studied means – a complicated
association of ideas represented by a medley of metaphors – to com-
municate unique personal feelings',[6] then Wilde's early sub-
Arnoldian poems may be deemed mildly symbolist. But in many

ways Wilde's verse falls far short of the genuine originality of subject and invention, the verbal daring and dexterity, the ability to invest ordinary objects and events with the intangible, indefinable, suggestive mystery of being characteristic of the best work of Baudelaire, Verlaine, Rimbaud and Mallarmé. Only in *Salome* does he truly succeed in matching the highest achievements of his French symbolist mentors.

The ideals of symbolism were less easily achieved on stage than on the printed page: the evocation of delicate personal sensations and emotions, the intimations of other spheres of existence, which the movement desiderated as suitable subjects for treatment, were insubstantial, transient, fragile. Though dedicated to that unification of all the arts in one aesthetic experience which theatre is uniquely capable of delivering, the symbolists found the essential concreteness and tangibility of practical playhouse drama a deterrent to the realisation of dreams which were essentially best animated and experienced in the privacy of the individual consciousness. Thus, of those of the symbolist persuasion, the only playwright to achieve durable success (prior to Paul Claudel to whom fame came much later) was the Flemish writer Maurice Maeterlinck.

Acclaimed since as the precursor of Beckett and of Artaud's Theatre of Cruelty, Maeterlinck, with his strange, disturbing, mystical dramas, was originally greeted with ridicule and suspicion, and even today his plays remain little known to the general public.[7] Yet in June 1898 J. T. Grein, journalist and stage entrepreneur, who was to mount a production of *Salome* in extremely controversial circumstances in 1918, wrote reviewing Mrs Patrick Campbell's production of *Pelléas et Mélisande*: '[t]here is, in fact, no French writer of our days who succeeds, with such simplicity of material, in obtaining such marvellous effects, and there is scarcely a French poet whose verse equals Maeterlinck's prose in the rhythm, the cadence, the music of its language'.[8]

However, Grein begins his review with the observation that

Maeterlinck's style 'lends itself particularly to caricature, and his method in its infantile simplicity is an easy prey to ridicule', and so closely did Wilde capture in *Salome* the terse, repetitious, incantatory, *faux naif* cadences of Maeterlinck's first published play *La Princesse Maleine* (1889), to whose English translation William Heinemann had invited him to write an introduction, that many have believed it to be little more than straightforward parody.[9] But it seems more likely that Wilde, by mirroring the *Princesse*'s hesitant, melodic, patterned prose, conjuring up mysterious invisible forces at work on human lives, and capturing Maeterlinck's brooding atmosphere of menace and anguish, was engaging in the sincerest form of flattery.

Peter Raby and others have demonstrated the links between *La Princesse Maleine* (which never received public production in its author's lifetime) and *Salome*, both in verbal and visual terms.[10] The first scene is set in the moonlit garden of a castle, while a noisy betrothal-feast takes place off-stage; two sentinels comment on various ominous portents seen in the heavens – a comet with a fiery tail, a reddening moon. Soon the bride-to-be, Princess Maleine herself, appears, a child-woman as Salome is often felt to be, though in Maleine's case a far more lost and vulnerable figure, fleeing in fear from the banquet where quarrelling has broken out. Next from the hall erupts her putative father-in-law, a drunken monarch surrounded by his entourage, fiercely forbidding the espousal and promising to wage war on Maleine's people; his son is to marry another. But sadly Maleine has already conceived a deep obsessional passion for the lost bridegroom she has only met fleetingly, and her father imprisons her in a dark tower for her obstinacy. Eventually she escapes, seeks out and finds her beloved, but caught in the web of destiny Maleine's fate, like that of the obsessed Salome, is violent death.

Certainly, aspects of Maeterlinck's first act bring Wilde's play very much to mind despite the considerable differences between the Belgian's medievalised fairy tale and the Irishman's scriptural legend, but setting aside the points of immediate contact, 'Maeterlinck's insistent use of colour, sound, dance, visual description and visual effect offered Wilde a theatrical vocabulary more complete and more innovative than anything the London stage could demonstrate'.[11]

The connection was tacitly acknowledged shortly after Wilde completed *Salome*, when both *La Princesse Maleine* and Wilde's piece were considered for production by Paul Fort's Parisian Théâtre d'Art, a short-lived attempt to establish a theatre company dedicated to the performance of stage pieces of a symbolist tendency. Though neither play was presented, their affinities seem recognised in this gesture, even if Wilde's precise degree of indebtedness to the Belgian master is constantly under review.

There is one other possible link between Wilde, *Salome* and the Théâtre d'Art. Before its premature demise (or transmogrification into Lugné-Poe's Théâtre de l'Oeuvre), during the period in late 1891 when Wilde was resident in Paris and working on *Salome*, Fort's group staged on the evening of 11 December a remarkable programme of stage experiments which included a dramatisation based on the Song of Solomon or the Song of Songs from the Old Testament by Paul-Napoléon Roinard.[12] Several of his Paris associates being involved with the company, there is at least a possibility that advance discussions of this adaptation reached Wilde's ears and alerted him to the dramatic relevance of this rich scriptural text with its sharply etched erotic imagery, lyric simplicity of expression, patterned repetitions and periphrastic elaboration. The apocalyptic speeches of Iokanaan often consist of inflated scriptural pastiche of the kind Wilde uses in *Vera* or *The Duchess*, but in the seductive speeches of Salome herself particularly, Wilde deploys the register and cadences of one of the most melodious books of the Bible far more authentically: 'Thy body is white like the snows that lie on the mountains, like the snows that lie on the mountains of Judaea, and come down into the valleys. The roses in the garden of the Queen of Arabia are not so white as thy body', for example, might easily be a quotation from the Authorised Version's rendition of the Song of Songs. Wilde's diction has often been labelled as synthetic or derivative, but at such moments it soars away from both its Maeterlinckian and its scriptural origins.[13]

Wilde also contrived to incorporate into the texture of his dialogue entirely characteristic passages of his own, so that neither the elevated nor the plangent becomes monotonous. In the exchanges involving Herod and Herodias, the Jews and the Nazarenes, one finds the brilliantly orchestrated conversational cut-and-thrust of the four social comedies:

HEROD: Concerning whom did he speak?
FIRST NAZARENE: Concerning Messias who has come.
A JEW: Messias hath not come.
FIRST NAZARENE: He hath come, and everywhere he worketh miracles.
HERODIAS: Ho! ho! miracles! I do not believe in miracles. I have seen too
   many. (*To the Page.*) My fan!

Even within a short compass Wilde's theatrical instincts were always alive to the importance of not being too earnest for too long.

Several previous accounts, including that of Gustave Flaubert in 'Hérodias' (1877), had introduced Salome into the action almost casually or late in its development. By launching forth *in medias res* Wilde not only achieved the attendant increase in concentration and rapidity of action as is customary, but also provided for an immediate focus on his eponymous protagonist with the Young Syrian's opening words, 'How beautiful is the Princess Salome tonight!' As a result her arrival is keenly anticipated from the beginning.

Moreover, the lack of a conventional preliminary exposition, along with the absence of digression or diversion, enables Wilde to give to his treatment of the Salome theme the intense yet brief burst of jewel-like illumination similar to that which the French symbolist painter Gustave Moreau was able to bestow on two of his celebrated portrayals of the princess exhibited at the Paris Spring

Salon of 1876. Whatever his Maeterlinckian affiliations in terms of verbal structures and textures, Wilde rarely resorts to the slow trance-like vagueness of the Belgian. Much in *Salome* is dynamic, clear-cut, hard-edged, brilliant: however Wilde intended his princess to be dressed, there is a bejewelled nakedness about the play that bears her name.

Like several of those handling the Salome story, including Jules Laforgue in the posthumous *Moralités Légendaires* (1887), Wilde in some respects can be viewed as debunking its chief figures, much as his fellow-Irishman Shaw deflated the great ones of history (Julius Caesar and Napoleon Bonaparte among them) by exposing their human foibles. Wilde reveals his princess to be proud and beautiful but also stubborn and self-willed; Iokanaan is selfless in his denunciations but almost neurotically ascetic; Herod is worldly-wise and shrewd, but superstitious and weak-willed.

Despite the play's brevity Wilde's Salome emerges as a far more complex creation than is the case in other literary treatments in which she features. She begins as the cool, chaste, aloof figure Stéphane Mallarmé had presented in his 'Hérodiade' (1866), self-absorbed until the Baptist awakens her latent sexuality. Evading her stepfather's lustful advances, she also has no time for the devoted Young Syrian except as someone to be exploited in order to obtain a sight of the prophet. At the start of the play she is associated with the moon when Narraboth proleptically speaks of it as 'a princess who has little white doves for feet. You would fancy she was dancing', and later she herself seems to identify with the planet which 'has never abandoned herself to men'.

Initially seen as an untainted victim of Herod's lust, with her insistence on the appearance of Iokanaan Salome is transformed first into a young woman instantaneously engulfed by sexual desire, and then, finding herself rebuffed, into a cruel and vindictive preda-tor whose destruction of the Baptist is presaged in the suicide of the Young Syrian. Tradition and other versions of the material had pos-tulated a Salome in love with the Baptist, but Wilde's originality lies in having his princess overcome with pure physical desire for Iokanaan's body rather than moved by admiration for his fine character or fearless preaching. Frustrated, insulted, rejected, Salome exacts the terrible revenge that her wilfulness, in demanding to see the prophet, has precipitated in the first place.

One result is that Wilde's Salome is no longer made the instrument of her mother's destructive designs on the Saint as in many other versions; she pursues her own vendetta, not that of Herodias. Instead of being a mere innocent manipulated by her mother, the daughter relegates the parent to a subordinate role. Now, rather than urging Salome to execute the dance in order to entrap Herod into dispatching Iokanaan, Herodias seeks to prevent the performance for fear it will stimulate the Tetrarch's desire for her daughter even further. Another variation on a familiar theme is Wilde's handling of Herod: here his agreement to grant the dancer anything she asks *precedes* the performance and is quite casually formulated. But some have argued that Wilde erred in having Herod make the 'rash promise' prior to Salome's exhibition, and so deprived the dance of its main motive, namely the seduction of Herod. Wilde's Tetrarch is already 'won over' before the music begins, so that all his stepdaughter's dance achieves is to prevent him from reneging on his sworn oath. We are given no indication of the moods of the dance or of Herod's responses to them. Indeed, in 1906 the American dancer Ruth St-Denis felt the dance to be nothing more than an 'intermezzo' in Wilde's script: she sought to create a far tenser version in which the entire action depended on Herod's response to Salome's gyrations, rather than appear in a dance which in her opinion arose from no more than a *fait accompli*. As an admirer wrote at the time, 'it's necessary that the audience already knows in advance that the resolution of the conflict [between Herodias and John] *depends* on the dance, so that it follows its intensifying stages in a state of *dramatic* tension'.[14]

Down the years Wilde's play has been faulted on a number of other counts; some have even questioned its claim to the title of play, arguing that there is a better case for treating it as a prose poem. But despite its affinities with certain kinds of verse, to most readers and certainly almost all spectators its dramatic *raisons d'être* can scarcely be called in question, for it is rich in those qualities which make for effective drama: colour, contrast, conflict, reversals of expectation, several major *coups de théâtre*. But it may still be argued that these excellences are overlaid by a baroque plethora of elaborate talk, a charge which even some of Wilde's society comedies also had levelled against them.

Some have not even cared for the quality of the talk: W. B. Yeats, who was to follow his fellow-countryman's lead in at least two of his own dramas, had reservations about the piece. In a letter of 6 May 1906 he informed a correspondent, T. Sturge Moore, that in *Salome* '[t]he general construction is all right, is even powerful, but the dialogue is empty, sluggish and pretentious. It has nothing of drama of any kind, never working to any climax but always ending as it began'.[15] On the other hand, while there is something self-conscious in the prodigality of effect, it gives to *Salome* an artistic unity hard to accomplish by other means.

Perhaps more sustainable is the charge that so short a piece cannot really afford to indulge in three separate sequential crises – an evocative dance, an impassioned speech of farewell and a visibly violent death. One question for a would-be director to resolve is whether to ensure that each of these high points makes an equal impact, or whether their competition will reduce the force of each one. Does nothing succeed like excess, or is the playwright here not loading every rift with an embarrassment of ore?

Perhaps Wilde should at least be indicted for his failure to make clear his artistic purposes in contriving the Dance of the Seven Veils, to the secret of which he suggested that only his illustrator-friend Aubrey Beardsley was privy.[16] Since in Wilde's case the dance is not the pivot on which the entire dénouement balances, it would have been helpful to know whether Wilde wished it to represent in physical form the apogee of Salome's erotic hold over the male sex in the person of Herod, or had in mind something more ambivalently orientated, less literal, more stylised and abstract, possibly a dance lamenting Iokanaan's repudiation of her newly awakened desires. Freedom to interpret Wilde's laconic stage direction may be felt to leave a director with too important a decision to make unaided by the author.

The following pages are devoted to considering these and other issues connected with Wilde's play, both in the light of what we can discover concerning *Salome*'s evolution as a dramatic script, and in the light of almost a century of being brought to life, initially on the boards of its original home, the theatre, but subsequently through the transforming agency of other powerful media: the graphic arts, the operatic stage, modern ballet and the cinema screen.

CHAPTER ONE

BEGINNINGS

The intertextual history of the Salome story is so complex as to make any account of Wilde's precise influences highly problematic.[1] Like the majority of his contemporaries, he was of course familiar with the salient features of the Gospel accounts, which he certainly consolidated by reading both ancient and modern historians. Yet their impact on him was immeasurably intensified by the zeal with which those contemporary French artists whom he viewed as his aesthetic mentors and frequently sought to emulate annexed the chief characters and situations in the service of the principles of *symbolisme* and *décadence*. His treatment was preceded by those of Mallarmé, Moreau, Flaubert, Huysmans and Laforgue, to name only the most important of them; small wonder that as Katharine Worth has observed, 'French airs play all round *Salome*.'[2]

However, despite the abundance of putative candidates for the roles of Wilde's literary foster-fathers, theatrical stimuli to composition were also present. Commentators have perhaps been too ready to accept Wilde's denial that his piece had been composed with the magnetic personality of Sarah Bernhardt, France's greatest actress of the day, in his sights. Kerry Powell in particular has argued persuasively that by writing *Salome* in French Wilde not only hoped, when performances in Britain were mooted, to elude the restraining hand of the British Lord Chamberlain's Examiner of Plays (known to be more liberal in his attitude towards dramatic works in a foreign tongue), but to reserve for the title-role the one actress who in his view had the necessary histrionic panache and vocal distinction to succeed in it.[3] At the same time, this interpretation seems at odds with Wilde's alleged quest for a leading actress who was also an accomplished dancer, and with the testimony of some of his friends.

Whatever weight we attach to Powell's thesis, Wilde's considered decision to compose the piece in 'a tongue that is not my own'[4] is entirely explicable, given the popularity of the Salome theme with Gallic authors and painters, and his desire to pay homage to several of them. Appropriate too is the simultaneity of its publication (at Wilde's own expense) in Paris as well as in London in February 1893. Nor was it merely a happy accident that the play should have received its world première at Aurélien Lugné-Poe's Parisian Théâtre de l'Oeuvre three years later: early plans for performance appear to have had a French goal in view, whatever view Wilde took of *Salome*'s chances on the English stage. In every sense *Salome* appeared under French auspices.

Yet the debts Wilde owed to his Gallic precursors should not be over-emphasised. French in atmosphere, language and treatment *Salome* may be, but its subject-matter has its roots in Wilde's own academic as well as imaginative preoccupations. At Dublin and Oxford he had read with great success for degrees in Classics; in anecdotes and conversations he was frequently found drawing on considerable knowledge of biblical literature and history, in particular the years covered by the New Testament narratives and those post-Messianic centuries dominated by the early Christian Fathers. The best of his early poems were classical in inspiration; even as early as 1878 he had been inspired in composing the Newdigate Prize poem *Ravenna* to muse on the fate of this ancient capital of the western Roman Empire, and a large proportion of his writings is replete with scriptural echoes and allusions, for example much of *A House of Pomegranates* and *De Profundis*. While *Salome* is in some measure the heiress to European traditions, Wilde's choice of a biblical subject whose treatment would derive some of its resonance from a collision of conflicting ideologies, Roman, Judaic and Christian, suggests a dimension of intellectual continuity which too often goes unrecognised.

Remarkably, the protracted emergence of *Salome* apparently left no detectable traces among Wilde's formal utterances or extant writings. In their absence we are forced to glean what enlightenment we can concerning the play's evolution and composition from casual allusions, codicological evidence and from not necessarily reliable remarks culled from the assorted memoirs of Wilde's contemporaries.

According to the writer's own account, given to an interviewer from the *Pall Mall Budget* and published on 30 June 1892,[5] the piece had been written in Paris 'some six months ago', but there can be little doubt that he had envisaged a work on the subject of Salome for a far longer period. In 1890 Wilde informed Edgar Saltus, an American author then preparing a work on Mary Magdalen, that he intended to write something featuring Salome,[6] and they agreed to 'pursue the wantons together'. In his autobiography, *Self and Partners*, Sir Charles Holmes (recalling a discussion at the Chelsea home shared by Charles Ricketts and Charles Shannon) identified its original conception as 'a fantastic *jeu d'ésprit*'.[7] A later glimpse of the piece in its embryonic state is furnished by W. Graham Robertson, the chosen designer for *Salome*'s abortive stage appearance in 1892. In his 1931 autobiography Robertson remembered how on one occasion Wilde read aloud to him from some notes 'the first few pages of "Salome"', which suggests a period predating the completion of the full text. At this juncture, the artist undiplomatically mistook what Wilde read to him for a humorous parody of Maeterlinck, only to be crisply informed of his error.[8] Yet Robertson's impression coincides with that conveyed by Holmes, and Jean Cocteau also recalled that 'Aubrey Beardsley's charmingly pretty sister told me that "Oscar" himself never intended his "Salome" to be taken too seriously.'[9] It seems possible, then, that Wilde gradually came to see that what had originated as a Maeterlinckian pastiche or a piece of burlesque had in fact serious dramatic potential.[10]

At what point Wilde determined that the Salome theme

should assume dramatic form is unclear; certainly, by 27 October 1891 (just at the start of Wilde's stay of some eight weeks in Paris), Wilfrid Scawen Blunt could write in his celebrated diaries: 'I breakfasted with [George Nathaniel Curzon], Oscar Wilde and Willy Peel, on which occasion Oscar told us he was writing a play in French to be acted in the [Comédie] Français[e]. He is ambitious of being a French Academician. We promised to go to the first representation, George Curzon as Prime Minister.'[11] However, the notion that Wilde had firmly decided on a work in theatrical form (or indeed that he had yet committed his ideas to paper) by the time he came to spend from late October to the week before Christmas 1891 in Paris, is partly called into question by the not necessarily accurate testimony of a young Parisian acquaintance, the Guatemalan Enrique Gomez Carrillo, published in an article in the important art and literary review *La Plume* (Paris) in 1902.[12] Carrillo's evidence, if reliable, does not suggest that at this point Wilde was firmly committed to treating Salome as the subject of a play, or to a single interpretation of her appearance and motivation, veering perhaps between Gustave Moreau's voluptuous bejewelled courtesan and Mallarmé's fiercely chaste virgin. Carrillo also describes how he witnessed Wilde's encounter with the sculpted head of a decapitated woman at the home of the celebrated poet, columnist and pederast Jean Lorrain,[13] where the bust apparently reminded the Irishman of the strange tale of a Hebrew princess who offered her philosopher-lover the head of an apostle as an act of homage, but finding her gift spurned, sent to her beloved the same evening her own severed head on a golden dish. Here, in the image of a woman reacting to her lover's indifference and her own frustration by sacrificing *herself* for love, was a counterweight to Wilde's princess who would wreak terrible vengeance on one who had awakened yet repelled her passionate overtures. According to Carrillo, Wilde, urged by the company to elaborate on this fable, apparently embarked on a prose work to be entitled *The Double Beheading*, but later destroyed what he had written and planned the composition of a poem in its place.

However, given that Wilde appears to have mentioned Salome as a *dramatic* subject to Curzon, Blunt and Peel before he even met Carrillo in Paris, it is possible that the latter's memories, however graphic, are inaccurate. Wilde must have considered it at least viable that a drama could be created with Salome at its centre; one wonders if he ever seriously wavered in his choice of genre, as Carrillo implies. Yet it may be that it was only as a result of the types of experiences that Carrillo describes, as well as through recounting different treatments of the legend to rapt Parisian auditors on a number of occasions, that Wilde began to clarify the dramatic potential of his chosen theme in his own mind.

Certainly one account of the composition of the piece, as relayed by Vincent O'Sullivan,[14] would bear out such a theory. This testimony has Wilde telling the tale of Salome to an enthralled group of young French writers, then returning to his lodgings, where he begins to record in a conveniently empty notebook the words with which he had been regaling his admiring audience. Breaking off, he betakes himself to the Grand Café, where he informs the leader of the orchestra, 'I am writing a play about a woman dancing with her bare feet in the blood of a man she has craved for and slain. I want you to play something in harmony with my thoughts.' Having received due stimulation from some 'wild and terrible music', Wilde by his own account 'went back and finished *Salome*'.[15]

While the theatrical orientation of the piece may never have been seriously in question, what was clearly far harder to resolve was the question as to which of several possible treatments of theme and character best accorded with Wilde's conception of his subject. Yet the manuscript evidence for the development and progress of Wilde's text suggests that once he embarked, he deviated little from his chosen route. But even here experts disagree as to the precise status of what survives and what it can tell us unequivocally of *Salome*'s emergence into print.

The three versions of *Salome* which all exist in holograph form confirm late autumn 1891 as the main period of the play's ultimate composition, during which time its progress was no doubt reviewed and discussed with members of Wilde's Parisian circle, including the minor symbolist poet Stuart Merrill, Adolphe Retté, and Pierre Louÿs, the author friend of André Gide. What is presumably the first extant draft, written (and its errors lightly corrected) in Wilde's distinctive hand, is contained in a half-leather notebook purchased in Paris, almost certainly the blank notebook alluded to by Vincent O'Sullivan above, now in the Bodmer Library, Geneva.[16] Another notebook bound in black cloth (now in the Harry Ransom Humanities Research Center at the University of Texas) holds another early draft of the text, and is unambiguously inscribed 'Paris, November '91'. What appears to be a later copy still is contained in two notebooks of British provenance now in the Rosenbach Foundation Museum, Philadelphia. One of these versions (either the Texas or the Philadelphia draft) must have been that submitted to Pierre Louÿs in December, accompanied by an extant letter stating that the drama was not yet completed or corrected, but that the manuscript supplied an adequate idea of the construction, theme and dramatic movement.[17]

Clyde de L. Ryals has suggested that the Philadelphia version is of particular value in recording both the amendments proposed by Louÿs and his corrections to the Irishman's striking but idiosyncratic French.[18] Ryals states that where Louÿs's alterations concerned points of grammar, and in particular the use of the subjunctive, Wilde accepted them. Wherever his friend proposed other changes, 'Wilde in nearly every case refused to adopt them, and he crossed out Louÿs's interlinear emendations . . . What remains, therefore, is *Salome* almost entirely as Wilde wrote it.'

But there is evidence that others almost certainly involved in the compositional stages of *Salome*. Ellmann, while recording (with no evidence to back the claim) that corrections and changes at the proof stage were made not only by Louÿs but also by Merrill and Retté,[19] fails to consider the possibility that they were actively involved in vetting the text at an earlier stage. We know from Wilde's letter to his Parisian publisher Edmond Bailly that proofs were sent to Marcus Schwob and Louÿs,[20] and it is possible that Merrill and Retté received and commented on them too. But their role almost certainly went beyond this.

In his edition of Wilde's letters, Sir Rupert Hart-Davis suggests that there may well have been yet another intermediate draft version of the play, now lost, since both Merrill and Retté seem to have handled one. In his *Souvenirs sur le Symbolisme*, originally published in *La Plume*[21] and later issued posthumously, Stuart Merrill claims that he had a hand in the composition stage:

> One day Oscar Wilde handed me his drama which he had composed extremely rapidly, at the first attempt, in French, and asked me to correct the more obvious errors. It was no easy matter to persuade Wilde to accept all my corrections. He wrote French as he spoke it, that is to say with an air of whimsicality, which, if it gave spice to his conversation, would have produced a deplorable effect in the playhouse . . . I therefore corrected *Salome* as best I could. I recall that the majority of the characters' declamations began with the expletive: 'Well! [enfin]'. I had quite enough of striking out enfins! But I soon realised that good old Wilde had only limited confidence in my taste, and I commended him to the care of Retté. The latter continued my task of correction and emendation. But Wilde ended up mistrusting Retté as much as he did me, and it was Pierre Louÿs who finally smoothed off the rough corners in the text of *Salome*.[22]

Merrill's recollections seem precise enough to be true, and they are certainly supported by Retté's account in *Le Symbolisme, Anecdotes et Souvenirs* (1903), where he states that Merrill approached him with the claim that Wilde wished the two men to 'take out the anglicisms which are too explicit'. Although some argued that the idiosyncrasies of Wilde's French constituted one of the play's charms, Wilde was evidently insistent, as Retté makes clear:

> He brought me the manuscript of *Salome*. I remember that during this visit he stated that he would like to see the role of Salome played

by an actress who was also a first-class dancer. For more than an hour he imagined all the possibilities of this idea and held me spell-bound . . . I pointed out a few marginal corrections. I made Wilde cut out a lengthy speech by Herod in which he listed precious stones. For his part Merrill suggested a few slight alterations. Next *Salome* passed into the hands of Pierre Louÿs who also changed a few sentences. It is this text which was printed.[23]

If these accounts are substantially true, there seems little doubt that Wilde received advice on and assistance with one at least of the extant manuscript drafts of *Salome*, not merely from Louÿs, as Ryals states, but from Merrill and Retté too. Nor do we need to accept Hart-Davis's postulated lost version in order to do so: the Texas and/or the Philadelphia texts could obviously have been the subject of more than one reviser's suggestions. While it is quite possible that Louÿs at least was involved with both drafts and proofs (though neither his set nor that sent to Marcel Schwob survives), Retté and Merrill probably only handled the draft holograph version(s). At all events, according to Ellmann,[24] the piece received its author's finishing touches at Torquay during the last days of December 1891 and early January 1892.

Whether or not Wilde envisaged live stage production for his play from the outset can never be resolved. Hints that he may have done so may be found in the preceding paragraphs, not least in the discussion with Blunt and Curzon, in Retté's remark that Wilde wanted the part given to an actress who was also a first-class dancer, and in Powell's belief that Wilde intended from the start that Sarah Bernhardt should play the princess. Certainly Robert Ross's firm assertion that the piece was never meant for stage presentation cannot go unchallenged. It is again significant that André Salmon recounted how Wilde and Stuart Merrill, during Wilde's time in Paris, attended a performance at the Moulin Rouge where they watched a Romanian entertainer dance on her hands, just as Flaubert's Salome does in *Trois Contes*. Wilde is said to have tried to make contact with the acrobat, stating that he wished to cast her in a play he was writing in which she would dance on her hands, 'as in Flaubert's story'.[25] The dancer was never traced.

There is also evidence that shortly after the play was completed, a presentation was at least under consideration by the Théâtre d'Art in Paris, an experimental stage venture then in the hands of the young poet Paul Fort (with whom and Louÿs Wilde seems to have lunched at least once during his Parisian stay of 1891).[26] Stuart Merrill was not only one of Wilde's Parisian contacts, but was acting at the time as Fort's manager. Though the project to stage Wilde's piece never came to fruition, *La Bataille* for 9 February 1892 informed its readers that *Salome* would be one of the plays presented during the next season at the theatre,[27] and this may account for Merrill's and Wilde's visit to the Moulin Rouge. The fact that the Théâtre d'Art shelved the presentation may have led Wilde to transfer his hopes once more to 'the divine Sarah'.

Certainly Bernhardt's interest in undertaking the piece, once completed, was not slow to kindle. In mid-May 1892 she arrived in London to appear at Richard D'Oyly Carte's short-lived Royal English Opera House (now the Palace Theatre), at the junction of Shaftesbury Avenue and Cambridge Circus, in a repertory season of French-language plays which included Sardou's *Cléopâtre*, *La Tosca* and *Fédora*, Dumas *fils's La Dame aux Camélias*, and Racine's *Phèdre*. Encountering Wilde at a gathering hosted by Henry Irving, she suggested that he should write a piece for her to star in; allegedly the response came pat: 'I have already done so.'[28] On studying the proffered text, she ignored both Wilde's semi-flippant warning that the leading role was that of the moon, and her own impression that Herod rather than his step-daughter was the principal figure, and decided to appear in it. Her reported remarks were highly commendatory: according to an unidentified interview of 8 July, she found it heraldic, fresco-like, demanding for its realisation no rapidity of movement but stylised hieratic gestures.[29]

To accommodate Sarah's latest wish a space had to be found in the agreed English Opera House programme, and rehearsals were scheduled to begin in the second week of June. It is unclear what the casting was to be, but it is likely that Bernhardt's leading man Albert Darmont, whose roles that season already included Mark Antony, Baron Scarpia and Hippolyte, was to play Herod. It is a reasonable conjecture that Jane Méa (Octavia in *Cléopâtre*, Queen Marie Caroline in *Tosca*, and Aricie in *Phèdre*) was earmarked for Herodias, and that Fleury, Cavaradossi to Sarah's Tosca and Armand Duval in *La Dame aux Camélias*, would have undertaken the role of Iokanaan.[30]

The décor was placed in the hands of W. Graham Robertson, who in *Time Was* recalls a prior discussion with Wilde on the design scheme appropriate to *Salome*:

> Wilde had written the play in French, but with no particular actress in his mind, and he and I had often talked over its possible production together.
>
> 'I should like,' he said, throwing off the notion, I believe, at random, 'I should like everyone on the stage to be in yellow.'
>
> It was a good idea and I saw its possibilities at once – every costume of some shade of yellow from clearest lemon to deep orange, with here and there just a hint of black – yes, you must have that – and all upon a pale ivory terrace against a great empty sky of deepest violet. 'A violet sky,' repeated Oscar Wilde slowly. 'Yes – I never thought of that. Certainly a violet sky and then, in place of an orchestra, braziers of perfume. Think – the scented clouds rising and partly veiling the stage from time to time – a new perfume for each new emotion!'
>
> 'Ye–es,' said I doubtfully, 'but you couldn't air the theatre between each emotion, and the perfumes would get mixed and smell perfectly beastly and – no, I don't think I care for the perfume idea, but the yellow scheme is splendid.'[31]

In the event there proved to be insufficient time to mount the play in the imaginative and challenging manner it so obviously required:

Bernhardt and her designer were forced to accept and adapt whatever came readily to hand, in this instance the costumes and settings imported for Sardou's *Cléopâtre*. Bernhardt recognised this as a compromise and promised to stage the piece worthily at some future date. In the meantime,

> [t]he Cleopatra dresses proved very useful and all was going well.
> For Sarah I had designed a golden robe with long fringes of gold,
> sustained on the shoulders by bands of gilt and painted leather
> which also held in place a golden breastplate set with jewels. On
> her head was a triple crown of gold and jewels and the cloud of
> hair flowing from beneath it was powdered blue.[32]

This last detail might have caused the mildest friction between author and leading lady; Wilde pointed out that his text specified that it was Herodias's hair which was 'powdered with blue', but Bernhardt claimed this distinguishing trait for her own. Wilde and his designer yielded on the point, and Robertson was subsequently to compare favourably the overall effect created with later attempts to clothe or unclothe the princess: 'This dress, stately, almost priestly, and indeed partly suggested by the sacerdotal robes of Aaron, seemed to me to express that royal "Salomé, fille d'Hérodias, Princesse de Judée", but when I saw the play given as an opera, Salome ran in and out of her palace half-naked, in the flimsy muslins of an Eastern dancing-girl.'[33] It seems clear from the designer's account that Sarah planned to execute the Dance of the Seven Veils herself. She certainly refuted Robertson's assumption that she would employ a veiled stand-in to perform before Herod as would some future impersonators of Strauss's operatic heroine.

But whatever *coup de théâtre* Bernhardt had in mind will never be known, for the entire project was brought to a premature halt by Edward F. Smyth Pigott, the Examiner of Plays, who, after some two weeks of rehearsals had elapsed, refused to grant the piece a licence on the entirely traditional grounds that the play involved the depiction of biblical figures on the English stage. Robertson indicts Wilde for his thoughtlessness in failing to realise that the chances of *Salome* being granted a licence were too slim to justify his allowing Bernhardt to become involved; Powell believes the author acted in good faith, and had genuine grounds for assuming a play in French starring Bernhardt would pass through the barrier of officialdom. Whatever the truth, perhaps the prospect of seeing his vision of the perfect Salome materialise on stage overruled Wilde's doubts, and persuaded him to ignore possible obstacles to his dream's fulfilment. According to Robertson, Sarah had no idea that objections might be raised to her proposed presentation, and felt some indignation towards Wilde as a result, even if it was tempered with sympathy. But Bernhardt, too, was celebrated for the impulsive nature of her decision-making, and it is perhaps too simple to blame Wilde alone for ignoring what Pigott's decision would almost certainly prove to be.

Matters dragged on a little longer. When *Salome* was published in French in February 1893, *The Times* asserted in its review that the piece had been expressly written for Bernhardt to perform, and Wilde strongly rejected the notion, remarking in passing:

> The fact that the greatest tragic actress of any stage now living saw in my play such beauty that she was anxious to produce it, to take for herself the part of the heroine, to lend the entire poem the glamour of her personality, and to my prose the music of her flute-like voice – this was naturally, and always will be, a source of pride and pleasure to me, and I look forward with delight to seeing Mme Bernhardt present my play in Paris, that vivid centre of art, where religious dramas are often performed. But my play was in no sense of the words written for this great actress.[34]

Nothing more appears to be known of the Paris production Wilde alludes to; he may indeed have been indulging in wishful thinking to boost his spirits after the brush with the censor. However, at the time of his downfall Wilde tried to get Robert Sherard to negotiate with Bernhardt for the purchase of the rights to *Salome*, but nothing came of it.[35] When actress and author eventually re-encountered each other in Nice after a performance there of *La Tosca*, Lugné-Poe had already presented *Salome* in Paris. But Wilde never wavered from fidelity to his original vision, telling Leonard Smithers that Bernhardt was 'the only person in the world who could act Salome'.[36] She seems never to have grasped any further opportunity to do so.

CHAPTER TWO

EARLY STAGE PRODUCTIONS
IN EUROPE

Although *Salome* is not one of the most frequently performed of Oscar Wilde's plays, for reasons of censorship as well as of perceived difficulties in realising its dramatic potential, it would nevertheless be impossible to give a full account of all the major productions over the years in a book of this scope. Rather than offer a piecemeal guide to as many performances as possible, we have first of all sought to give a detailed account of the earliest attempts to stage the play in France, Germany, England and Russia. In each case a distinctive style of performance developed, often as a result of the tensions between censorship and the theatrical traditions of the country concerned. We have then attempted to trace the history of the play on the English stage throughout the twentieth century, an approach which allows for a reasonably detailed account of a wide range of productions in a variety of styles. A selective production chronology will be found in the Appendix.

THÉÂTRE DE L'OEUVRE, PARIS, FEBRUARY 1896

The first performance of Wilde's *Salome* was staged by the Théâtre de l'Oeuvre in Paris on 11 February 1896. The date and company are significant. Between 1887 and 1894 the main focus for theatrical innovation in Paris had been André Antoine's Théâtre Libre, which was predominantly associated with the propagation of naturalism.[1] The very success of the Théâtre Libre, however, led to the creation of a spate of theatrical movements and counter-movements in the early 1890s, many associated with the 'idealist reaction' against naturalism's rationalist and materialist foundations. Paul Fort's Théâtre d'Art, for example, which was at one stage considering *Salome* for production, regarded itself as 'totally symbolist', and in 1891 was the first to stage *L'Intruse* and *Les Aveugles* by Maurice Maeterlinck. Only Maeterlinck seemed able to negotiate the inevitable contradiction of Fort's purism: a symbolism which privileged aesthetic mood and scenic design over the corporeal presence of the actor, who was frequently reduced to a static, dimly lit reciter of verse, could not in any serious sense be termed dramatic. Fort's self-defeating project soon collapsed for reasons which also informed much of the early criticism of Wilde's *Salome*, of which Max Beerbohm quipped, 'I almost wonder Oscar doesn't dramatise it.'[2]

The Théâtre de l'Oeuvre, founded in October 1893 by Aurélien Lugné-Poe, in many ways represented a continuation of the symbolist project, but Lugné-Poe soon recognised the need for a broader repertoire and a more flexible approach. Between 1893 and 1895, for example, the company staged plays by Maeterlinck, Strindberg and Hauptmann; while 1896 saw the première not only of Wilde's *Salome* but of Alfred Jarry's explosively original *Ubu Roi*. The world première of *Salome* therefore took place at a wholly appropriate venue: sympathetic to symbolist principles and aesthetics, theatre and play both seemed nevertheless to acknowledge that symbolism in its pure form turns against itself and becomes a dramatic impossibility.

In his autobiography, published long after the event, the director recorded the circumstances under which *Salome* came to be produced.[3] The case of Wilde was one in which sections of the Parisian intelligentsia felt themselves to be demonstrably more enlightened than their English counterparts. On a visit to London following Wilde's trial, Lugné-Poe had been surprised by 'the apathetic stupor by which the intellectual or artistic society seemed struck', an example of the 'pitiless' behaviour of 'our puritanical neighbours . . .

towards a writer who a few weeks earlier had been the favourite of all
the clubs, of all the London salons, and who was still the artist of the
day. His fall was atrocious . . . But in Paris Wilde remained
esteemed.' According to the director he found Wilde's friends More
Adey and Robert Ross still too upset to assist in any supportive
movement, and his decision to perform *Salome* was therefore taken
without any preliminary authorisation. The legal status of the production became highly complicated:

> [W]e too were threatened with legal action, which was only commer-
> cial this time, and on French soil. Indeed, English law stipulates that
> criminals – and Wilde was a criminal – are to be in a state of tutelage,
> guardianship, in all their affairs; and by virtue of international
> conventions on literary protection, we were threatened with a ban
> through the intermediary of a legal official operating at the request of
> an English judge. Such an intervention, therefore, could make things
> awkward for me. Nevertheless, in Paris, the Oeuvre was still a private
> theatre, and I took the risk.[4]

The world première of *Salome* was therefore conducted under the
threat of punitive legal measures either before or after the performance, although the director's judgement proved sound and no
action was finally taken. Lugné-Poe's legal ingenuity and friendship
with Wilde were further demonstrated the following February,
when he arranged for the protection under French law of the French
text of the play.

Such problems with the law, as well as a concern to avoid
hostile publicity, led the director to keep his preparations for the
play secret. Advance announcements made reference only to
Raphaël, a three-act play by Romain Coolus, who was the dramatic
critic of *La Revue Blanche*, and it was made known only at the last
minute that this play would be followed by a performance of Wilde's
shorter piece.[5] As one reviewer remarked, the surprise performance
avoided 'even the suspicion of an out-of-place *cabotinnage*'.[6] This
word, which means something along the lines of 'theatricality', here
seems to imply 'sensationalism', and indicates therefore Lugné-Poe's

concern to avoid publicising a production which could create a scandal in the aftermath of Wilde's trial and conviction. The project was further troubled by severe practical problems in mounting the production. The plays were to be performed at the Comédie-Parisienne (later known as the Athénée), but the venue was barely safe. Demolition work had been proceeding all around the theatre, which was the only building still standing like a fortress surrounded by trenches ten to fifteen metres deep, and the police were on the point of banning the performance because of the risk of fire or accident. (These fears proved well founded, for one of the dresses caught fire backstage during the performance and had to be doused by Lugné-Poe, still dressed as Herod, and some of his friends.) Nevertheless the architect was persuaded to construct a temporary passage twelve metres long connecting the theatre to the Rue Boudreau, and to provide a tolerable auditorium, although cast and crew remained hampered by cramped and inadequate facilities and by lack of equipment. To make matters worse, John the Baptist's head, which had been lent to Lugné-Poe by Paris's wax museum, the Grévin, fell off the platter and smashed during the last night of rehearsals, and the separate pieces of the prophet had to be glued back together for the performance, with the director compensating the museum afterwards. This was a proleptic mishap: in each of the first two London productions, in 1905 and 1906, Max Beerbohm considered the performance to be seriously weakened when the artificiality of the head became too apparent to the audience. Remarkably the audience at the Comédie-Parisienne seems to have remained oblivious to the various backstage disasters.

It is by now impossible to reconstruct the performance with any accuracy. The major Parisian theatrical archive at the Fonds Rondel contains only the programme and a few reviews, most of which are rather uninformative exercises in rhetoric, while the director's own account concentrates on the frankly comic misfortune which pursued him in his efforts to mount the play.

Individual performances can be described only in general

terms. Lugné-Poe considered Lina Munte's performance as Salome to be a triumph, and his response was matched by that of reviewers. The director's own portrayal of Herod was held by Jean de Tinan in the *Mercure de France* to be the best representation of the figure he had seen, combining a 'suppleness and dynamic [*nerveuse*] precision of intonations and attitudes' with 'a concern for the physically beautiful [*le plastique*]'.[7] Herodias was played by Mme Barbieri, Iokanaan by Max Barbier, whose physical size and resonant voice enabled him to dominate the stage when necessary.

The most controversial casting decision concerned Herodias's Page. In the text this male figure is jealous of the attention Salome receives from the Young Syrian, Narraboth (played in Paris by a M. Lerey), with whom the Page is evidently in love. This is the closest the play comes to an unveiled homosexuality, but possibly for this very reason Lugné-Poe obscured the meaning in assigning the role to Suzanne Després (according to all accounts, although the actress is named in the programme as Suzanne Auclair, who also appeared as Rita in *Raphaël*). Tinan observed that at the moment when the Page bemoans the Young Syrian's death with the words 'Il était mon frère et plus qu'un frère', the actress spoke 'so exquisitely that no-one dreamed, charmed as one was, that this was the dangerous passage'.[8] There is a possibly deliberate ambiguity in Tinan's following remark that 'il a peut-être tout sauvé, ce petit page, avec sa jolie voix et sa beauté timide', in which the pronoun 'sa' may be either male or female, creating an uncertainty as to whether the pretty voice and timid beauty which may have rescued everything belonged to the male character or to the female actor.

This casting decision appears to have upset Wilde. His literary executor, Robert Ross, wrote in 1905 in a private letter to Gwendolen Bishop concerning the projected first London production that

> I may venture to express a hope that none of the male parts will
> be taken by a lady, as that entirely ruined the original production in
> France. The artist who sustained [*sic*] the role of Salome should also,
> if I may be allowed to say so, abstain from introducing in the dancing

scene anything in the nature of Loie Fuller's performances. You will excuse my mentioning these points, as I do not pretend to be an expert on dramatic productions, but I remember very well the author's instructions to Sarah Bernhardt, and his constant conversations to me when I was describing to him the production of it in France while he was still in prison.[9]

The first sentence here can only refer to the Page, although it is worth mentioning that in Paris Herodias's seven slaves were all played by women as well.

The programme was designed by Toulouse-Lautrec, whose lithograph featured a portrait of Romain Coolus on one page, and on the facing page Wilde, with a misty Westminster and Tower of London in the background. On the whole Lugné-Poe could also feel satisfied with the critical response, although Wilde's French biographer stated that '[i]n spite of good reviews its success was mitigated [*sic*] because the production was lacking in splendour'.[10] In any case, approval was by no means unanimous: the *Journal des Débats* considered it 'a mediocre work' and 'excruciatingly boring',[11] while according to Gertrude Jasper an argument, which broke out in the intermission following *Raphaël*, between Maeterlinck, attacking Wilde, and Rodolphe Darzens defending him, became so intense that it nearly ended in a duel.[12] Perhaps Maeterlinck's reaction was occasioned by Wilde's imitative style.

These responses, and Lugné-Poe's concern to avoid gossip by preparing the play in secret, go some way towards qualifying the popular view, propagated by Lugné-Poe himself and by many of the play's French reviewers, that Wilde was being championed by the French while being destroyed by the English. To be sure, the supportive voices were far more audible in Paris than in London. Tinan, for example, wrote of Lina Munte's performance that 'not to have been there, not to have seen his *Salome* more beautiful and more terrible than he had imagined, was for Oscar Wilde the most cruel misfortune for which an artist would have been inconsolable'.[13] In many cases, however, reviewers were unable to resist a somewhat patronising air which contributed to that teleological construction of Wilde as martyr which has been prominent in critical responses to the author ever since. So, for instance, Segard remarked in the course of his favourable account in *La Plume* that Wilde, 'whom people pity even more than they blame, was an admirable artist and a poet'.[14] In view of the commonplace assumptions about the differing attitudes of French and English circles towards Wilde, it is worth recording the more cynical and reductive response of the critic of the *Journal des Débats*: 'When the curtain came down, the audience greeted the author's name with terrific applause. Is it the case, then, that the shameful affair, and the conviction that we all know about, was necessary for Oscar Wilde's talent to turn into genius?'[15]

MAX REINHARDT'S PRODUCTIONS, 1902–1904

Although a production of *Salome* was contemplated in Naples in late 1897, with Eleanora Duse in the title-role,[16] the play was not in fact performed again until 15 November 1902 at the Kleines Theater, Berlin, as part of a private matinée double bill with *Bunbury (The Importance of Being Earnest)*, in a production directed by Friedrich Kayssler and Hans Oberländer under the supervision of the twenty-nine-year-old Max Reinhardt.[17]

A milestone in Reinhardt's career and in the history of the play, *Salome* gave Reinhardt the opportunity to mount a non-realistic, luxurious production, although his conception of the play was initially cramped by the limitations of the venue, and did not really come into its own until he was able to present the piece publicly at the larger Neues Theater the following year. Reinhardt's previous work had been largely in the field of realism: as a young actor in 1890 he had been taught by Maximilian Streben and Emil Bürde, and later at the Salzburg Stadttheater he performed many roles, all in broadly realistic plays; while Otto Brahm's company at Berlin's

Deutsches Theater, which Reinhardt had joined in February 1894, favoured an almost photographic realism. His interest in direction developed as he experimented with revue-style material and short plays at a hotel in the Unter den Linden, which became the Kleines Theater in 1902, the same year in which he left the Deutsches Theater to concentrate on his directorial career. The double bill of *Salome* and *Bunbury* was the first important production at the renamed Kleines Theater.

As with the Théâtre de l'Oeuvre's production, then, *Salome* was being mounted in conscious opposition to realistic and naturalistic schools of drama, although the rivalry was evidently friendly, for some of Reinhardt's former colleagues at the Deutsches Theater collaborated in staging the play.[18] For his first major experiment in symbolism, Reinhardt, like the Symbolists themselves, was indebted to Wagner's ideas of the *Gesamtkunstwerk*, the 'total art-work',[19] and the Maeterlinckian repetitions of Wilde's text and the frequent displacement of language by sound, movement and dance, led Reinhardt to a quasi-operatic form of production which directly influenced Richard Strauss, who attended the opening night.[20]

Critics in England and on the Continent would subsequently point to the success of this production, as well as to Lugné-Poe's pioneering gesture six years previously, as evidence of an enlightened theatrical policy on the Continent, in contrast to the persisting ban in Britain. But in fact *Salome* fell foul of a new decree in Germany forbidding the representation of biblical characters on stage, despite the similarities between Wilde's play and Hermann Sudermann's *Johannes* (1898), which the censor had passed for performance after the decree came into effect. The Kleines Theater's *Salome* had to be a private affair, and was attended by the official representative of the censor.[21] One reviewer implied that the play had been banned simply because it had been written by Wilde.[22]

An article published in Berlin's *Deutsche Zeitung* the following February helps to clarify the question of censorship.[23] Outside Prussia the play could be performed without interference (as happened in Hamburg and Stuttgart, for instance), and the Prussian ban started to appear ridiculous when a number of private performances were staged. Those attending at the Kleines Theater did so by invitation only, but the Lessing Society charged members standard theatre prices for a production mounted on the anniversary of Schopenhauer's birthday. The Neues Theater contested the ban and finally gained permission for its public performance on 29 September 1903.[24] As in other countries in which a ban on public performance was enforced, the text itself was readily available. In Germany Hedwig Lachmann's translation was published by Insel Verlag of Leipzig in 1902, in an edition illustrated by Markus Behmer in the style of Beardsley.[25]

Reinhardt employed as designers the artist Lovis Corinth, who had previously painted a representation of Salome, and the sculptor Max Kruse. The work of this pair was so impressive that some felt them to be the real stars, their talents wasted on an inferior play.[26] Their set designs gestured towards historical accuracy, but were offset by interpretive lighting, by orchestrated patterns of colour in the costumes, and by the music of Max Marschalk and Friedrich Bermann. According to one account, Marschalk subsequently wrote some new introductory music for the public performance at the Neues Theater in September 1903. His score was 'Bacchanalian', featuring 'southern dance rhythms' and an 'oriental motif' upon which Bermann composed elaborations.[27]

Inevitably, given the very long run of Reinhardt's *Salome* at a number of different venues, there were many changes in the cast, with actors often dropping out, often to reappear later, while it seems that understudies occasionally performed as well. Hence only the most important performances and changes are worth recording in any detail. Initially, at the Kleines Theater, the title-role was taken by Gertrud Eysoldt, with Emanuel Reicher as Herod, Luise Dumont as his wife, and co-director Friedrich Kayssler as Iokanaan. Reinhardt himself played an ancient Jew. Max Eisfeldt replaced Kayssler for the first public performance on 29 September at the

Neues Theater. On 14 September 1904, the occasion of the hun-
dredth performance of the run, Eysoldt was still playing Salome,
although both before and afterwards the part was frequently taken
by Tilla Durieux who, confusingly, played Herodias on this com-
memorative occasion. Ludwig Wüllner was the new Herod.

It was Wüllner who received the most entertaining reviews.
His predecessor, Reicher, was a subtle actor who had received splendid notices for his performances at both the Kleines and the Neues
Theaters. Wüllner, on the other hand, had acquired a good reputation as an actor in the provincial theatre of Meiningen between 1889
and 1895,[28] but was now making a return to acting after an absence
of many years, during which he had become a well-known
Liedersänger (concert-hall singer). Some enjoyed his declamatory
approach,[29] but one reviewer took a very different line on Wüllner's
vocal performance, discerning a disproportion between his massive
body and 'sweet' voice.[30] Whatever the truth of the matter, even
those who responded favourably tended to think that his exaggerated gestures could become distracting.[31] Some felt that in his
attempts to make his performance distinct from Reicher's he had
made the role crude and boring, 'the old father-figure from
comedy',[32] out of joint with the rest of the piece.[33] One critic
described his Herod as a 'shallow king of the provincial theatre',
which would put audiences off going to see his forthcoming
attempts at King Lear and Manfred,[34] while another found himself
dreading what Wüllner was going to do to Faust.[35]

Such strong preferences were less commonly expressed about
the actresses who played Salome. Gertrud Eysoldt was described in
one review as a Pre-Raphaelite figure,[36] which suggests an attempt to
integrate her appearance with certain familiar Victorian iconographies of the feminine. According to one reviewer, Tilla Durieux
enacted the dance brilliantly, the only flaw in her performance being
a tendency to become too strident in the heat of passion.[37]

Towards the end of the run Durieux sometimes instead performed the role of Herodias, in an evidently striking fashion, for one

critic commented on how she 'strips the last masks off Herodias, going to the limits of what is possible',[38] although another critic was dissatisfied and thought that the actress, who had projected a 'pure' and 'feminine' personality in an earlier role, was miscast as the 'diabolical woman', rolling her eyes and shaking her body in a futile attempt to produce a 'daemonic' effect.[39] Of those actresses more frequently cast in this role, Hedwig Wangel was thought to have less impact than Luise Dumont.[40] As Iokanaan, Friedrich Kayssler was somewhat stereotypical, with pale thin body, long black hair and burning red lips, while Max Eisfeldt cut a younger, more sober figure.

There were in addition several other *Salome*s which played all over Germany between 1902 and 1905. A performance at Munich was seen by Claude Phillips, who on 25 August 1903 wrote to Robert Ross that *Salome*

> is the *great* success of the moment all over Germany. Salome was wonderfully played by a young Jewess, Lili Marberg. It is a brilliant piece of work, showing more grip and concentration than I had seen in anything else [Wilde] did. And yet it leaves – in my mind, at anyrate [*sic*] – a certain impression of shallowness, of something too *voulu* [contrived] in its fascinating horror. The main episode is certainly inexpressibly revolting – even to me. And yet these dear, stolid, unprejudiced Germans look on placidly . . . They give the text intact, including certain words which I am sure Paris wouldn't stand.[41]

As late as May 1905 German audiences were still being treated to Wilde's play, with Ida Roland and a Herr Stehrüch as the principals,[42] but interest appeared to be fading. *Salome*, which was now expected to constitute the whole evening's entertainment, was thought by some to be too slow, while the casting of Wüllner had perhaps pushed the production too far towards the realms of comedy.

The most detailed accounts of Reinhardt's *Salome* tend to be of the visually spectacular first public performance of 29 September 1903 at Berlin's Neues Theater. This was a large venue; and whereas

Plate 1 Setting for Max Reinhardt's production, Neues Theater, Berlin, 1903.

at the Kleines Theater *Salome* had run for about an hour,[43] now Reinhardt was able to mount a more lavish, ninety-minute production, an 'artistic revelation' surpassing anything else in the Berlin theatre at the time.[44] The set (plate 1) was spectacular:

> The painted backdrop, which so often proves theatrically disturbing, has given way to a starry night sky, which arches over the whole stage, and creates the effect of reality. The moon shines its pale beams down on to the terrace of the royal palace, the scene of the drama, here and there casting fleeting patches of light. Footlights and border lights are switched off; yet despite, or precisely because of this, peculiar lighting effects are achieved. On the spectator's right, a reddish light streams from the Tetrarch's banqueting hall (in which a feast is taking place) through the arched door, which appears covered in copper tiles, and throws its light on to the lion which flanks the entrance door. On the

left stands an imposing arched gate, from whose pillars torches cast a glow on to the armaments of the guards. Moonlight floods the white stone walls around the dungeon, in whose depths the prophet John languishes in captivity. Everything is immersed in a semi-darkness, anticipating the coming events.[45]

This mood of foreboding was intensified by the visible presence of the executioner throughout the play, standing by a wall at the back of the stage.[46]

The cistern was located upstage. The arched gate to the spectator's left was supported by Syrian winged lions; the banqueting hall to the right was surrounded by white walls decorated with paintings.[47] The terrace was replete with palm-trees and carpets, such luxury being central to the meaning of the production, since 'the many repetitions and moody demands of the women gradually destroyed the attraction of the court, and the sensual palace became a robber's den'.[48] The sensuality was heightened by the costume designs, a 'symphony of colour',[49] with the women wearing tightly fitting outfits and rings on their feet.[50]

Also evident from these accounts is Reinhardt's fascination with the possibilities of lighting, in which he was undoubtedly influenced by Adolphe Appia. He was now able to deploy the new Fortuny system of indirect lighting, playing against a high cyclorama.[51] At the Neues Theater this allowed for a range of subtle effects, not only in setting the scene but in interpreting the action. For instance, when Salome addressed the head as if it were a living person, Herod saw this as a crime against some unknown god, and as if in sympathy the stars disappeared and a cloud covered the moon.[52] Reinhardt also decided to use a spotlight to indicate the moon as a source of direct light.[53] This use of direct light may have been contrary to Wilde's intentions, since the author had suggested privately that the source should remain unseen,[54] although Reinhardt would not have been aware of this.

The nature of the dance remains a little obscure, but some clues are to be found in reviews of a number of different performances. Prior to the dance Salome allowed Herod to remove her sandals and massage her with ointment. She was illuminated by a flickering greenish light, and, assisted by the slaves, removed veil after veil until she was left in a transparent garment. During the dance, Herod averted his eyes,[55] an unusual interpretation which, when combined with the veiling of the moon when Salome addressed the head, suggests that Reinhardt was keen to establish Herod as a man fully aware that both his own and Salome's actions ran contrary to natural law. In turn, this suggests a slightly cautious, conservative interpretation of the events of the play consonant both with Lugné-Poe's decision during his earlier production to mask the homosexual subtext and with the timid London production which was to follow in 1905.

Indeed, there is some evidence to suggest that the artistic conservatism in Berlin extended to an attempt to divert attention from the erotic charge of the dance. According to a somewhat elliptical account of the dance at the Kleines Theater, it was depicted not as the climactic moment but as a 'scenic ballad of extreme power'.[56] Another spectator at the Kleines Theater agreed that the dance was not the climax. Instead, it was

> the final scene of *Salome* [which] remains unforgettable. In the foreground, the hot prostitute Salome, her narrow predator's head surrounded by wild, flowing, reddish-blonde locks, who again and again strokes and kisses the bloodstained head of John. Next to her Herod's Roman guards, swinging their shields threateningly, about to carry out the sentence which their master, horrified by such an excess of criminal desires, has imposed on his wife's child.[57]

The audience at the first public performance gave the piece a curious reception. Icy hissing, apparently for the play itself, was followed by friendly applause for the performers and also, it seems, for director and designers.[58] Entrenched attitudes to the author also loomed large in the critical reception of the play, which was of course receiving its first performance since Wilde's death. In Paris

the response had been complicated by the recognition that the performance was in some sense a gesture of solidarity with an artist cur-
rently languishing in an English prison. His death in 1900 invited
subsequent critics to speak with the voices of judgement on a closed
chapter, while the sense of an ending is felt, also, with the passing of
the anxieties associated with the *fin de siècle*. It is only with these two
almost simultaneous endings that the teleological construction of
Wilde as tragic hero could begin in earnest. In Paris in 1896 his
stature could still be diminished, even by the most sympathetic
commentators, to that of misguided martyr; but by 1902 he was the
representative of an age.

While several critics exploited the perspective of a kind of
post-apocalyptic certainty to condemn the author in predictable
ways, others were more generous. An extraordinary article in the
Berliner Tageblatt found in Wilde 'the tired but superior scorn of the
decadent', at whose core 'lies a melancholy longing; melancholy
because it is powerless, and knows that it will have no fulfilment'.[59]
If in the context of the play this immediately suggests the passion of
Herodias's Page for the Young Syrian, and of the Young Syrian for
Salome, for this critic there were analogous relationships between
Herod's court and the coming of Christ, and between Wilde's deca-
dence and the new order to come. Wilde 'wanted to build a world,
and yet he knew everything around him was crumbling'. Similarly,

> Iokanaan only appears as the chorus, as the prophetic voice of the
> time to come. The way that the coming of this time is suggested by
> Wilde is of great – but perhaps too stylised – artistry. The soldiers,
> Jews, Nazarenes, Tetrarch, and Tigellinus, who all find each other's
> beliefs ridiculous, show how everything which was once considered
> great and important is now falling apart . . . The poet was closer to
> the ruling culture than to the great revolution, whose name the
> creature from the desert proclaims.

In this remarkable account, Wilde is placed in a self-conscious relation to Herod's court, the play's 'ruling culture'. The time to come is

now, in 1902, the time past, and decadence is seen to have died along
with Wilde and his era. Furthermore, the *Berliner Tageblatt*'s critic
could now also read Wilde proleptically, in relation to a new age:
'now, all at once, his art is bearing new blossoms; he is being translated, and people are trying to "save" him, and he is being played in
the theatre . . . The dead Oscar Wilde remained forgotten, until yes-
terday afternoon.' In a potent manoeuvre, these images of rebirth
begin to associate Wilde not with Herod but with Christ. As the same
critic remarked of Herod's response to the prophecies of Iokanaan:
'Dead people shouldn't rise again. It disrupts law and order.'

In many ways this production was about beginnings, not only
of the Kleines Theater and Reinhardt's directorial career, but also of
the revaluation of Wilde and, perhaps, of the possibilities of 'total
theatre'. Many of the newspapers recognised it as an event of
unusual significance, and there was much interest in the attendance
of the most important progressive artists in Berlin. The production
was also seen by the dancer Maud Allan and the composer Marcel
Rémy, who later collaborated on *The Vision of Salomé*, while Allan
was subsequently to appear as Salome in an ill-fated production of
Wilde's play in London in 1918.

BIJOU THEATRE, LONDON, MAY 1905

Reinhardt had demonstrated the significance of the symbolist influence on Wilde's work, while providing at the Neues Theater a professional, large-scale, high-budget production which enabled the
piece to be viewed not as a curiosity but as a theatrical event.
Meanwhile, the London stage lagged behind, stifled by a residual
gentility in performance style which the theatrical revolutions on
the Continent had been unable to disturb, while as far as *Salome* was
concerned the censor's ban ensured that the early London productions could only be small-scale affairs mounted by private clubs, in
the face of almost universal hostility from the press.

The first performances of the play in London, for example, were staged on 10 and 13 May 1905 by the New Stage Club at the Bijou Theatre in Archer Street, Westbourne Grove, a venue far removed from the major West End theatres. The production was largely boycotted by the press, although the *Daily Chronicle* was among the few to send a correspondent. The club, in the person of Mrs Gwendolen Bishop, had contacted Wilde's executor, Robert Ross, regarding the performance rights (which in fact were held by the Official Receiver; surviving correspondence between Mrs Bishop and Charles Russell and Co. establishes that a fee of ten guineas was paid for the two performances).[60] It was in the course of his reply to this letter, on 6 April, that Ross expressed his reservations about the Lugné-Poe and Loie Fuller productions.

Such reservations may imply that Ross envisaged a style and level of production somewhat exceeding the capabilities of the New Stage Club; if so, the letter he received from Laurence Housman on 3 May gave a clearer picture of the current state of affairs, and anticipated the critical response: 'I am lending some garments and ornaments for "Salome"[.] I fear she herself will be bad: but Herod, I hear, is very good, and I hope my friend [Herbert] Alexander will acquit himself well.'[61] Such remarks, which expose some of the amateurishness of the Bijou's efforts, cannot altogether have inspired confidence, and it seems clear that while the New Stage Club had managed to engage some talented actors, and despite the best efforts of the stage-manager, Florence Farr, their priority was the staging of a text previously unperformed in England, and not the mounting of a fully realised theatrical production. In other words, this was precisely the kind of performance one might have expected from a private club with limited means, primarily inspired by extra-theatrical concerns.

There was, for example, no music, in marked contrast to Reinhardt's productions. Consequently the emphasis on the changing phases of the moon, and the beating of mighty wings, appeared as merely peculiar rather than as manifestations of a synthesising poetic imagination. As even a reviewer hostile to the play acutely noted, these are motifs which

> run through the piece, and which could only be made effective by music. Indeed *Salome* ought to have a musical accompaniment throughout, something vague and melancholy and persuasive, which might make us dream, even though it were a dream full of mysterious threats of looming danger and imminent death. We never for one moment can dream, or, at all events, we could not last night.[62]

The *Chronicle* recognised in the production a fusion of styles which at first seems appropriate, the play being 'treated solemnly, dreamily, phlegmatically, as a sort of cross between Maeterlinck and a "mystery play"'.[63] However, the reviewer actually thought this style damaged the play, contributing to a 'lack of natural life and vigour', so that 'beneath this pall of solemnity on the one hand and lack of real exaltation on the other, the play's beauties of speech and thought had practically no chance whatever'.

Reviewers, finding the action slow and the language prolix, tended to agree that the play was better read than staged, while few apart from Beerbohm found much to say about the acting. With deliberate perversity one writer found himself in sympathy with Tigellinus (played by C. L. Delph) on the grounds that he looked bored throughout.[64] The performance of Housman's friend Herbert Alexander as the young Syrian Captain went unremarked, but Housman's fears regarding Millicent Murby's Salome proved well founded. In a publicity still she looks stiff and mannered, dressed unimaginatively in a toga.[65] Disappointingly, but not surprisingly, the surviving accounts of the dance are sketchy, but according to one witness it was 'very weird, very Eastern, and certainly not . . . very entrancing'.[66] Beerbohm, more perceptively, found the style of acting inappropriate: Salome remained resolutely 'a young English lady in the twentieth century', and Louise Salom's Herodias was 'not a day older nor a degree less ladylike than her daughter', although the *Chronicle* thought better of Salom's performance.[67]

The response to Robert Farquharson's Herod was more mixed. The *Chronicle* thought he 'gave what appeared to be a sort of semi-grotesque portrait of one of the late Roman emperors', and incongruously portrayed Herod as a 'doddering weakling', while another reviewer thought he 'seemed a caricature of Osric, Slander, Andrew Aguecheek rolled into one, crowned with roses'.[68] Beerbohm, on the other hand, shared Housman's enthusiasm for an actor who was in the event to play Herod in several significant London productions:

> Here, indeed, was Herod himself, incarnate [*sic*] from out of the pages of the play – a terrible being, half-dotard, half-child, corrupt with all the corruptions of the world, and yet not without certain dark remnants of intellect, of dignity . . . Mr Farquharson's performance was especially laudable in that he never let his minute expression of Herod's self in all its hideousness interfere with his musical delivery of the elaborate cadences. He performed two tasks in perfect fusion. Passages that might have been merely beautiful he made dramatically hideous, without loss of their beauty. Passages that might have been merely hideous he made beautiful, without loss of their appropriateness. Of course he played all the other people off the stage, figuratively. Literally, they remained there, I regret to say.

Farquharson's performance was, for Beerbohm, the one redeeming feature of a shabby production, but it was nevertheless a production which provoked the critic's early and crucial recognition of the precariousness of the theatrical illusion in *Salome*. While one reviewer complained that 'the stage was on occasions so dark that the action was obscure',[69] Beerbohm felt that at the climactic moment the problem at the Bijou Theatre was quite the reverse:

> It seems to me . . . very obvious that the severed head of John the Baptist ought not to be very obvious to the audience. Salomé, when she receives it from the executioner, ought to remain at the back of the stage, in as dark a shadow as can possibly be thrown on her. In the Bijou Theatre, Salomé brought the head briskly down to the

footlights, and in that glare delivered to it all her words and kisses. This was wrong, not merely because it intensified our physical disgust, but also because it destroyed all our illusion. Even though we looked away, we were aware that this was not the head of the prophet, but simply a thing of painted cardboard – a 'property', prepared with much labour and ingenuity. And the fact that we knew it to be no more than this did not make us one whit the less uncomfortable. Indeed, an unpleasant thing that proclaims itself a 'fake' is worse than an unpleasant thing that illudes us. Cold cardboard lips kissed passionately by a young lady, on the pretence that they are the cold real lips of a man murdered at her behest, are really a more horrid spectacle for us than they would be if we believed for the moment that in truth Salomé was kissing the lips of John the Baptist.

Such remarks tend to support the logical view that *Salome* requires for its successful staging something of the symbolism of the Lugné-Poe and Reinhardt productions. They also suggest that the physical limitations of the fringe theatres at which Salome was first performed in London inevitably prohibited the exploitation of such techniques, since the kind of illusion for which Beerbohm called could hardly be met by shallow stages and inflexible lighting.

KING'S HALL, COVENT GARDEN, LONDON, JUNE 1906

Similar conclusions about theatre in general had already been reached by the artist Charles Ricketts, who was the motivating force behind the next London production of *Salome*, performed as the second half of a double bill with Wilde's *A Florentine Tragedy* on 10 and 18 June 1906 by the Literary Theatre Society at the King's Hall in Archer Street, Covent Garden.

Ricketts is a pivotal figure in the stage history of the play, and in many respects the King's Hall production represents a lost opportunity. His involvement with *Salome* began shortly after the play's publication, and before Bernhardt's attempt to perform the piece in London. He had been approached by Wilde to design a projected production in Paris, probably under the direction of Lugné-Poe. This plan fell through, although both Lugné-Poe and Ricketts were subsequently to stage the play independently. Fortunately the ideas shared by Wilde and Ricketts have been preserved both in sketches and in Ricketts's published reminiscences, and the artist's subsequent designs for productions in London in 1906 and in Japan in 1919 reveal how he evolved and elaborated upon the ideas developed in his conversations with the author.

Ricketts's experiences with *Salome* exposed important differences between British and European traditions of staging, and the ways in which these differences contributed to the striking discrepancy between the play's success in Europe and failure in London. In his theoretical essay, 'The Art of Stage Decoration', Ricketts tends to define the principles of design negatively, contrasting the suffocating physical restrictions of British theatres with the freedom available to continental artists like Wagner and Reinhardt to develop their ideas within more generous staging areas. Ricketts's interest in the means by which the scenic artist creates the illusion of space, of which we shall see many in his designs for *Salome*, should therefore be seen at least in part as an attempt to make a virtue of necessity. The King's Hall, however, was inadequate to his needs even by London standards.

Many years after the event, Ricketts recalled his formative discussions with Wilde:

> I proposed a black floor – upon which Salome's white feet would show; this statement was meant to capture Wilde. The sky was to be a rich turquoise blue, cut across by the perpendicular fall of strips of gilt matting, which should not touch the ground, and so form a sort of aerial tent above the terrace. Did Wilde actually suggest the division of the actors into separate masses of colour, to-day the idea seems mine! His was the scheme, however, that the Jews should be in yellow, the Romans were to be in purple, the soldiery in bronze green, and

John in white. Over the dress of Salome the discussions were endless: should she be black 'like the night'? or– here the suggestion is Wilde's – 'green like a curious poisonous lizard'? I desired that the moonlight should fall upon the ground, the source not being seen; Wilde himself hugged the idea of some 'strange dim pattern in the sky'.[70]

A still later account, published shortly after Ricketts's death, repeats this description almost verbatim, and must therefore have been constructed from the same notes or from the essay itself. This makes the small but significant changes somewhat curious. In the later version, Ricketts relates that the turquoise of the sky was to be green, not blue; the colour-scheme for the Romans and soldiery is not mentioned, but he now adds that Herod and Herodias were to be in 'blood-red'; the gilt matting is specified as Japanese; an additional possibility for Salome's costume was to have it 'silver like the moon', while the detail which is supposed to have 'captured' Wilde is more strikingly rendered: 'I proposed a black floor, upon which Salome's feet could move like white doves.'[71]

These minor but puzzling variations are symptomatic of a general difficulty in reconstructing precisely which ideas Ricketts finally favoured and executed. For example, two surviving illustrations, one by Wilde and the other by Ricketts, apparently record what the two artists visualised at this early date in the play's history, but it is unclear how precisely Ricketts adhered to these designs when he came to stage *Salome* some twelve years later. Wilde's sketch (plate 2) focuses attention on the placement of cistern and staircase in relation to the stage as a whole, and the emphasis on these relations re-emerges in Ricketts's first illustration (plate 3a). This sketch, which the Witt Library dates at 1896 but Richard Allen Cave has dated at *c.* 1893–94, shows the cistern placed upstage right, with the staircase, only partially revealed, extending upstage left. That both artists focused their attention on cistern and staircase suggests a concern clearly to demarcate each major character's area of authority upon the stage, thereby establishing a visual emphasis upon power and transgression.[72]

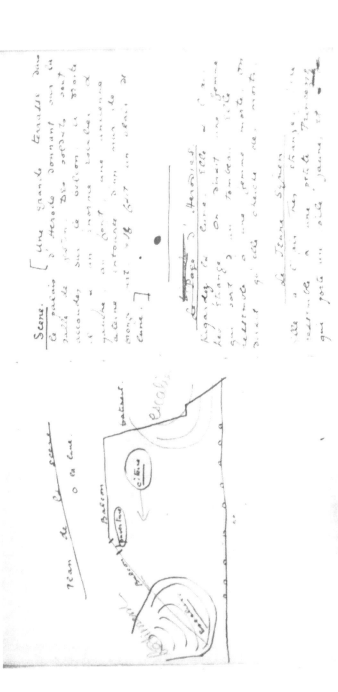

Plate 2 Wilde's own sketch of a setting for *Salome*.

Other elements of Ricketts's sketch recall the ideas discussed with Wilde, although again there are subtle differences. The gilded strips of matting, with further drapes for the canopy, form the 'aerial tent', except that the strips extend to the floor, and so could also give the impression of pillars, a possibility explored in Ricketts's work on the play in 1906 and again in 1919. Moreover, the large moon drawn on the canvas at the back of the stage would appear to give precisely the kind of visual indication of lighting source Ricketts specifically wished to avoid, and does not appear in later illustrations. Whether the watercolouring, which was superimposed upon the photograph by the poet Gordon Bottomley's wife, accurately records Ricketts's wishes is unclear. As Cave notes, instead of the black floor and turquoise sky envisaged by Ricketts and Wilde, both here have a noticeably greenish tinge. Nevertheless, Cave thinks this a deliberate attempt to capture Wilde's demand for 'a wall of green bronze' around the cistern, and he is certainly right to emphasise how closely this early sketch approximates the ideas Ricketts developed with Wilde.

So, while there are numerous inconsistencies between Ricketts's two published accounts of the discussions with Wilde, and also between them and his roughly contemporaneous sketch, a consistent pattern of emphases does emerge. The stage is almost bare save for the cistern and the staircase. This arrangement creates discrete areas of influence, while the partially concealed staircase is designed to give the illusion of great scale, and this, together with the 'aerial tent', makes the design firmly non-realistic and ahistorical. The written accounts of the desired lighting suggest ideas similar to those of Adolphe Appia, who had certainly become a major influence on Ricketts by the time the latter's *Pages on Art* was published in 1913.

Sadly, although at least some of these ideas were incorporated into the Literary Theatre Society's production, the project as a whole was undermined by lack of time, space and money, and also by the ill-defined and changing nature of Ricketts's role, which contributed to the tensions within a cast and company of uneven quality.

The Society had developed from an idea conceived in January 1901 by Ricketts and his friend Thomas Sturge Moore for a theatre 'in which the scenery would be done on a new decorative, almost symbolic principle', and was to provide Ricketts with his first practical experience in stage design.[73] This idea came to fruition some years later, with the first production, *Aphrodite Against Artemis*, being performed on 1 April 1906, followed by the double bill of Wilde plays in June. Many of those involved in staging the latter had also worked on the Bijou Theatre's production the previous year: Robert Farquharson repeated his role as Herod, C. L. Delph, who was Tigellinus at the Bijou, played the First Nazarene, while Florence Farr acted Herodias. Gwendolen Bishop, who had taken on many of the organisational responsibilities at the Bijou but had not taken an acting role, was now to play Bianca in *A Florentine Tragedy*.

From the start, the production was beset with problems. Ricketts's frustrations with the small stage were inevitable, since as noted he was unhappy with the limited space available even in the largest London theatres:

> All our stages are ludicrously shallow; behind their imposing pro-
> sceniums they are so lacking in depth that the action has to be ham-
> pered by overcrowded scenery, which in its turn is too near the
> footlights for any illusion of beauty or reality to be possible . . .
> [T]he scenery should begin where it usually has to end, namely,
> twenty or twenty-five feet away from the proscenium.[74]

Dissatisfied with the venue, Ricketts had at one point contacted George Alexander to ask if the St James's might be available, but on 12 April Alexander informed him that even a matinée performance of the notorious work might disrupt the play then running (Pinero's *His House in Order*), and cited the stupidity of the public as a reason.[75] He suggested trying the Royal Court instead, but in the end Ricketts had to settle for a Covent Garden venue described by Robert Ross as an 'odd locality chosen for an illicit entertainment, on which the critics again fell with exacerbated violence'.[76] Ricketts's hopes for his leading lady were likewise dashed: it was initially thought that either Constance Collier or Mrs Patrick Campbell might take the role, but neither was available,[77] and Ricketts appears to have been not altogether happy with Letitia Darragh, who finally played Salome at the King's Hall.

One of the more important consequences of the continuing disorganisation was that Ricketts was forced to assume more and more control over the proceedings. In less straitened circumstances this might have led to the happy result of a production supervised, co-ordinated and designed by an artist knowledgeable of and sympathetic to Wilde's intentions. Indeed, Ricketts approved in principle of such arrangements, even remarking of stage design generally that there is 'no rule save that one designer should control the entire production, from the scenery to the smallest property';[78] but regrettably so much of the work was rushed, improvised and amateurish that it cannot be regarded as the realisation of the properly Wildean conception of the piece which might have been possible with more time and resources.

Ricketts's diary for the month or so preceding the performance reveals that personal squabbles added to his mounting anxieties as he embarked on increasingly frantic attempts to complete the preparations in time. The entry for 10 June records both the rather shambolic final preparations, and some details of the performance itself:

> Turned up at four, nailed up scenery, dressed and dined at six, placed furniture, supervised dresses: train of Salome lost . . . rehearsed taking of head with Miss Darragh, who grew nervous; stood by the limelight man, the most absolute idiot I have met in my life. Audience enthusiastic. Three calls at the end of the *Florentine Tragedy*, four at the end of *Salome*. Herod almost collapsing after the curtain was down. Dance begun too soon, over too soon. Salome missed covering the head of St John with veil.[79]

This account broadly matches the response of others who witnessed the performance. It is clear that those aspects of the production over which Ricketts had the greatest control are those which represented the greatest advance on the previous year's effort at the Bijou. Reviewers were unanimously impressed by the costumes: Max Meyerfeld, for example, was delighted by their 'marvellous harmony of blue and green and silver'.[80] In May Ricketts had sent Ross details of some of the dresses and sets: 'Salome, dressed in a mist rising by moonlight, with a train of blue and black moths. Herodias, in a peacock train of Dahlias and a horned tiara. Herod, is robed in silver and blue lined with flame decorated with griffons, sphinxes and angels. The scene is all blue on blue.'[81] Salome's train, the one which infuriatingly went astray on the night, had forty-two blue foil and velvet butterflies.[82] The Page's costume was 'black with silver scales (the back of a silver tissue) with orphreys [ornamental borders] of Angels and apples!'[83]

Michael Field (Katherine Bradley and Edith Cooper) was greatly impressed by the artist's designs: 'The curtain up! – At once, what we came for. Eastern luxury in moonlight. A picture painted by Titian or Delacroix . . . no, only by Ricketts himself. Never has the stage been so wonderfully used – the picture painted by a great painter, with all the masses, lights, sparkle, glow, atmosphere of a masterpiece to set the human passion it symbolises.'[84] Unfortunately, however, the precise nature of this stage design seems impossible to establish with confidence. The painter had quit in the last week of rehearsal, and whether Ricketts's illustrations of this period provide an accurate account of what was really presented at the King's Hall remains unclear. All of his designs for *Salome* represent modifications of the original plan conceived with Wilde in the early 1890s. Sketches for the 1906 production maintain the scenic structure recorded in the sketch of *c.* 1893–94, but with several significant changes (plate 3b). The staircase has been replaced by the low cushions of Herod's throne. The central drapes have been

Plates 3a and 3b Stage designs for *Salome* by Charles Ricketts:
(a) *c.* 1893–94; (b) King's Hall, Covent Garden, 1906.

removed, more clearly dividing the stage into two distinct areas focused on the cistern and the throne. In place of the moon the backdrop shows instead part of a wall, stage right, which slopes away into the distance and finally joins the upper part of a tall pillar, which consequently appears in the middle of the canvas. This painting gives the desired effect of great scale, with the stage more clearly representing a terrace with a precipitate drop at the back. Cave thinks it helps to create an effective separation between the ordinary, public, political world outside, and the private world within which compromises it; but it is hard not to think that to have the pillar rather than the moon as the focal point of the backcloth detracts from the necessary symbolic emphases of the play, while, for this production at least, demanding too much compensatory technical excellence in lighting if the repeated references to the moon are not to become comically incongruous. The later, finished illustration offers a few changes of emphasis, especially in bringing the throne further downstage and in supplying a low wall at the back to reinforce the impression of a high terrace, while the pillar is now detached, which if anything increases the peculiar insistence upon it.

Although Cave remains undecided whether these designs represent what was actually mounted, the evidence suggests that Ricketts finally adopted a much simpler design closer to his ideas of 1894 than those in the 1906 drawings. None of the surviving accounts mentions the pillar, which would have been one of the first things to catch the eye. Given that the scene-painter quit on 5 June, and the first performance was on 10 June, it is possible that the new painter and Ricketts, who was by now embroiled in the rehearsals, were unable to complete in time the ambitious design captured in the pencil illustrations.

Again, there is a curious lack of comment concerning the terrace. Beerbohm stated only that the scenery and dresses were 'beautiful' and 'dramatically appropriate – just enough conventionalised to be in harmony with the peculiar character of the play'.[85] Likewise Roger Fry, who saw the second performance on 18 June, says nothing about a terrace but notes 'the staging with ideas of colour that surpassed belief. I've never seen anything so beautiful on the stage',[86] and Ricketts's most recent biographer mentions only a 'starlit sky'.[87] While inconclusive, these remarks do not suggest the presence of anything so realistically representational as the walls and pillar which make their first appearance in the 1906 designs. The strongest evidence that Ricketts had reverted to his earlier ideas comes from the only really hostile account of the set, that of Max Meyerfeld, who states categorically that '[t]he stage was left ridiculously bare, and never for a moment produced the illusion of the terrace outside Herod's banqueting hall. Not even the cistern out of which the Prophet rises was discoverable.'[88] Since this account can hardly be squared with the surviving illustrations of 1906, it would appear that Ricketts discovered too late that the designs were impracticable, either because of the small playing area or because of the limited time and resources available. In our view, however, something resembling the 1894 sketch serves the play better than the more elaborate later version.

As for the acting, Michael Field's account gives a good impression of the manner in which performance style could have been integrated with the stage design, while also suggesting that the inadequate period for rehearsal finally thwarted the attempt:

> All the actors stand and keep their positions long, giving their
> speeches as chords in the *Moonlight Sonata*. The whole play is full
> of harmony and 'leit motifs', of evocations, and all this character is
> brought out by gesture and timbre of voice. The Herod is a most
> Flaubertian study, but so individualised that it is out of the tone of the
> music that Oscar weaves dramatically. It is somewhat too clever; but
> consistent and engrossing, as the sombre eyes grow hollow and the
> wanton mouth grows slack under the reddest red of the rose crown. In
> the red of this rose crown the highest note of the scarcely emerging,
> yet basal blood-red of the picture is struck for us – the red that
> couches in the shadow of the precious blue of the moon.
>   The other characters are in the tone of the imaginative rhetoric

by which the play reaches us. Salome is a pale, exacting virgin – thirsting for tragedy.[89]

For many, however, the King's Hall production showed little advance on that of the Bijou Theatre. Ricketts pasted into his diary an unidentified review which is broadly typical: 'Mr Robert Farquharson repeats, with exaggerations, his singularly unpleasant, emasculated Herod. Mr Lewis Casson was dignified as Iokanaan, but Miss Darragh's Salome was even more colourless than the Salome of Bayswater. Neither voice nor gesture conveyed the least idea of emotion, and the dance, the success of the Continental performance, became a very gentle Sandow exercise.'[90] Much of the 'Englishness' remained, Meyerfeld considering that 'The Dance of the Seven Veils was executed with all the propriety of a British governess',[91] but Beerbohm considered Darragh's a better Salome than Millicent Murby's. Unlike Florence Farr, whose Herodias, being 'much too pleasant' and 'sympathetic', perhaps reminded Beerbohm of the shortcomings at the Bijou, Darragh seemed to him a 'genuine tragedian', able 'to purge somewhat our physical disgust through spiritual terror', although he too found her 'rather modern, rather occidental'.

Letitia Darragh's mistakes during the dance, which Ricketts mentioned in his brief account of the performance, reveal a considerable amount not only about the lack of rehearsal but about additional problems with the stage and the lighting. It must have been particularly galling for Ricketts that the episode with Iokanaan's head, which had occasioned Beerbohm's displeasure in 1905, should have gone so badly wrong again. Beerbohm restated the problem:

> The stage-management was faulty only in the final scene; and that, alas, is the scene where perfection is most needed. Not even the quality of Miss Darragh's acting could wholly purge our physical disgust. It is obvious that Salome ought to be in the far background, and in deepest shadow, while she holds in her hands the head of the prophet. This would not merely militate against physical disgust. It

would aid illusion. When we distinctly see the head, we are conscious of its unreality, however realistically it be made. And our consciousness of its unreality does not make it one whit the less unpleasant.

Ricketts can hardly have been unaware of the difficulty. Indeed, Cave has suggested that if Ricketts's finished pencil drawing of his set design for the 1906 production does accurately record what was staged, then the heavier concentration of curtains around the cistern, as compared to that in the rough sketch, would cast greater shadows over this section of the stage, and so may indicate one method by which he sought to overcome the difficulties of staging this climactic moment, which he was anxiously rehearsing with Darragh almost up until the last minute.[92] It is just possible, too, that this would explain Meyerfeld's curious remark about the invisibility of the cistern, although it is still hard to see how he could have failed to recognise that design as representing a terrace.

Whatever the truth of the matter, Ricketts and Beerbohm were in agreement that the closing moments damaged the production. The failure of the ending resulted from the difficulties Ricketts had faced throughout the preparations: too small a stage, poor lighting, uneven acting, rushed rehearsals. But in matters of design his was perhaps the most sympathetic staging the play had yet received, rivalling Reinhardt's work in conception if not in execution.

Thirteen years later, in 1919, Ricketts described himself 'reconstructing *Salome* for a proposed production by the Shochiku Theatrical Company, Tokyo', and was reminded that in a dream he had years ago,

> Sada Yacco had performed *Salome* in a Japanese version of the play; that, with strange muttered soliloquies she had descended a staircase haunted by her guilty passion for Herod; that John, a bound prisoner behind a wattle, had made ardent love to her till, in Japanese fashion, she had pushed the wattle back upon him with sudden birdlike cries

interrupted by the terrific entrance of Kawakami as Herod with a con-
vulsed mask, feet turned in, in a slow deliberate descent of the stairs,
supported by a hesitating Herodias. I saw the dance, rapid, vivid,
trance-like, the head thrust over the wattle, and Salome's suicide after
a slow muttered speech spoken to space or to the audience she did not
see.[93]

Sada Yacco was the leading actress of the Japanese Court Company
and visited London in 1900 and 1901, being seen by Ricketts on
several occasions.

Ricketts doubted whether the production would resemble this
vision – he observed ruefully that 'the Japanese Salome, whose
photo I have seen, wears Maud Allan pearls in her hair' – and indeed
his own designs were very much a 'reconstruction' of his earlier work
on the play. Gordon Bottomley, to whom Ricketts showed the
Japanese designs, described

Herodias wearing a robe of black and yellow that suggested not only
a tigress but a tigress 'burning bright' with searing flame, Herod's
rich apparel and black beard and hair being given a sinister touch of
unfathomed depravity by a coronal of innocent pink roses in his hair,
the Jews' large patterned dresses, beards and pointed high caps
marking them off sharply from the Romans: the scene a fragment
of a high colonnade against a dark luminous night.[94]

An extant painting shows that the stage design was an elaborate variation on Ricketts's already established ideas. The sunken cistern
upstage right and throne downstage left remain in position, as does
the canopy. The major difference is that the vertical drapes have now
been replaced by realistic pillars, a particularly huge example extending from the top of a flight of stairs, this construction slightly left of
upstage centre having been substituted for the column of the earlier
version. Another staircase ascends into darkness upstage left.
Although Ricketts added touches of oriental detail, then, his final
design for *Salome* remained very much in the pattern established in
that conversation with Wilde over twenty-five years before.

KOMMISSARZHEVSKAYA THEATRE, ST PETERSBURG, OCTOBER 1908

The various attempts to stage the play in Russia in the period preceding and even during the Russian revolution of 1917 resulted in part from the 'flourishing cult of Wilde among the Russian symbolists and decadents at the beginning of the twentieth century'.[95] No fewer than six Russian translations appeared between 1904 and 1908, as the play's apparent stance against Church and dogma made it attractive to the prevailing revolutionary spirit in art and politics;[96] and in retrospect there may have been something in *Salome*'s prophetic depiction of the catastrophes awaiting an old, corrupt and collapsing order which appealed to the Russian *Zeitgeist*.

In April 1907 the Moscow Art Theatre's co-founder, Vladimir Nemirovich-Danchenko, projected a double bill of Wilde's play alongside Byron's *Cain*, but was thwarted by the censor. Possibly the MAT's interest in the play had some influence on the decision by Vera Kommissarzhevskaya's theatre company in St Petersburg to attempt a staging of the play the following year. Certainly Kommissarzhevskaya's director, Nikolai Evreinov, had consciously distanced himself from the psychological realism which underpinned the work of Konstantin Stanislavsky, Nemirovich-Danchenko's collaborator at the MAT, and perhaps he aimed to demonstrate this distance by offering a completely different approach to the same play.

But *Salome* was in any case a perfectly natural project for Evreinov, for he was deeply interested in both Wilde and Beardsley: in 1912 he published a monograph on the latter, while he displayed his fondness for Wilde in his taste in clothes, being 'dubbed by his contemporaries the Russian Oscar Wilde'.[97] Many of his statements on art reveal an acknowledged intellectual and verbal indebtedness to Wilde, most notably in the remark that 'it's not so much that the stage has to borrow from life, rather life must borrow from the stage'.[98] His empathetic engagement with his material; his highly personal ideas of theatre combined with a reading of the play consonant with the author's; his willingness to explore the sexuality of the piece in both design and performance style, and the censorship first of the text and then of the whole production, all contributed to making this finally unstaged event 'a theatrical legend, a significant part of Russian artistic life'.[99]

Evreinov's theatrical ideas and achievements were rich and complex.[100] His work on *Salome* came quite early in his theatrical career, at a time when it is possible to define some of his qualities in contradistinction to those of others working in Russia at the same date. As noted, for example, he was opposed to Stanislavsky's psychological 'method' as it was being developed at the MAT, while he also repudiated both the literariness and the symbolism propagated by Meyerhold at this time.[101]

In 1907–8 Evreinov masterminded a season of plays by his Starinnyi (Ancient) Theatre at St Petersburg. At the Starinnyi Evreinov sought to recreate the theatrical style and spirit, as opposed to the archaeological detail, of former epochs in an endeavour to refocus attention on the actor, and on the imaginative understanding between actor and spectator. It was after this season that he succeeded Meyerhold as artistic director of Kommissarzhevskaya's theatre. From 1908 to 1909 he put more theoretical flesh on the bones of his ideas of 'theatricality', arguing for an expressionistic, anti-mimetic 'monodrama' whereby the audience perceived events through the consciousness of a central protagonist, this identification being established in part through changes in lighting and décor which corresponded to changes in the emotions of the protagonist (and spectator). In 1908, for instance, Evreinov's production of d'Annunzio's *Francesca da Rimini* 'featured the expressive use of pools of light to denote changing moods after the manner of Appia'.[102]

Later in the same year Evreinov attempted to stage *Salome*, which he retitled *Tsarevna* (The Tsar's Daughter) as part of a strategy of escaping the censor by eliminating biblical references. Kommissarzhevskaya's 1908 season had proved financially disappointing, and the decision to stage Wilde's play appears to have been rushed, leaving only a fortnight for all preparations before the dress-rehearsal on 27 October.[103] Evreinov himself revised the translation by N. I. Butkovskaya. For the title-role he selected N. Volkhova, the theatre's second leading lady after Kommissarzhevskaya herself, ahead of the much better known Ida Rubinstein, who attended the rehearsals and had offered to play the part.[104] As we shall see in the last chapter, Rubinstein was subsequently to perform the Dance of the Seven Veils on several occasions.

Evreinov began by explaining to the actors the basis on which he conceived of the play. He took from Nikolai Minsky's article, 'The Idea of Salome', the suggestion that Christ had two precursors, the saintly Iokanaan and the beautiful Salome, whose opposition indicated both a divided consciousness and the possibility of future harmony. This view of the play would soon surface again in the even more important Russian production of Alexander Tairov, considered below. Evreinov, however, was less interested in imposing theories upon the play than in theatrical experimentation. He aimed for 'a grotesquely harmonic mix of styles', of which the Beardsleyesque became predominant.[105]

This decision was arrived at by agreement between Evreinov and his designer, Nikolai Kalmakov, yet another artist for whom work on *Salome* was a formative theatrical experience. According to Spencer Golub, Evreinov and Kalmakov set the play 'inside a giant scenic vagina, stripping away all pretense of illusion and metaphor', a *mise en scène* which 'literally made a spectacle out of gender consumption (the vagina dentata) and artistic self-consumption'.[106]

Such a design would be consonant with the Beardsleyesque style of the production as a whole. It would also be the first attempt to signify visually the 'castrating woman' which many have detected in Wilde's Salome,[107] and would subtly gesture towards the homosexual subtext which productions elsewhere had so far carefully evaded.

Golub has placed Evreinov's daring approach to *Salome* within the context of the director's understanding of the 'grotesque', which he 'likened . . . to "gallows humor" or "black comedy"', and which logically was impelled to interrogate the taboo.[108] In particular, Evreinov was interested in the scandalous possibilities of nudity and eroticism in the theatre, writing a number of articles on the subject,[109] and Golub notes that he considered his production of Wilde's play 'the first example in Russia of an approach he called "the grotesque as such"', which 'implies exploring the very essence of the grotesque for its own sake rather than for any value it might possess as an element in various art forms'.[110] While the formal structure of the grotesque appears inapplicable to *Salome* – Golub instances the amazed laughter occasioned when a comic ending is substituted for the expected tragic one – its impulse is undoubtedly present in Wilde's play. *Salome*, its history riddled with charges of blasphemy, pornography and perversion, allowed Evreinov to explore, without gratuitousness, the possibilities of the naked human body on stage, while for many the play also teeters uncomfortably on the edge of comedy; in the opinion of Kerry Powell and others, deliberately so.

Whether Kalmakov's intended scenic effect impressed itself on the audience attending the dress-rehearsal is unclear. Golub's earlier research 'indicates that [the production] was not at all obscene',[111] while according to C. Moody '[i]t was apparently the opinion of nearly all present . . . that there was nothing blasphemous or porno-graphic about the play'.[112] As M. Vaikone's review in *Teatr i Isskustvo* makes clear, Evreinov had already acceded to censorial interference:

> The changes made by the censor are highly significant. The most dangerous scene from the point of view of our 'guardians' – that involving the prophet's severed head on the silver plate – has been completely cut; neither head nor body appears on the stage . . . The playwright is misrepresented and foreshortened and the director, inspired by his 'reciprocal madness', restricted and tied by the censor's text.[113]

Even these cuts proved insufficient to allow for public performance.[114] The Holy Synod, which had been tipped off some days
before what was evidently a well-attended dress-rehearsal on 27
October, pronounced on 28 October that it was an 'unheard-of
blasphemy', and the production was duly banned the following day.
While Moody records the presence in the audience of numerous
reactionary figures, but no Church representatives, there seems little
reason to doubt his conclusion that it was pressure from the Church
which finally enforced the prohibition. Evreinov, no stranger to
bouts of paranoia, suspected the involvement of the Tsar.

Knowing that the performance would probably be banned
altogether, Vaikone was careful to preserve a detailed account for
posterity, and it is possible to reconstruct aspects of the production
with some precision by considering his account alongside that of
one of the actors, A. A. Mgebrov, who played the Young Syrian.[115]
Vaikone sets the scene:

> This intense, dark and bloody tragedy, saturated with vice and
> sensuality, unfolds against a backdrop of deep blue sky with occa-
> sional, strangely formed stars and a huge crescent moon within which
> swims the hazy image of a naked woman. Then there is the palace
> portico and the nearby cistern, from whose depths the ringing, insis-
> tent voice of the prophet can from time to time be heard. The black
> executioner, Naaman, Narraboth the Syrian and the beautiful page-
> boy with his dazzling marble-white naked body are very picturesque
> figures, mingling harmoniously both with the deep blue of the sky
> and the sinister night-time light.

Mgebrov records that Evreinov wanted to establish a state of frenzied
ecstasy in this scene (very much in contrast to Lugné-Poe's evasive-
ness), and thought that this could be achieved by deliberately
strained and mannered postures. Specifically, he asked Mgebrov to
adopt the pose of a fencing thrust, with the Page, likewise ecstatically
immobile, standing behind him dressed in a white body stocking
with a grapevine tied around his waist. Mgebrov was resistant, feeling

that the passion of the Young Syrian would naturally force him into a myriad of different gestures, but he finally had to submit to the director's wishes. This minor dispute suggests that Evreinov was attuned to the kind of symbolist performance style appropriate to the play; as we have seen, all of the play's earlier directors had likewise recognised the necessity for stylised gestures and moments of stasis.

Mgebrov commented that each costume was a work of art in itself, and gave a detailed description of his own. He wore

> a huge, fanciful, baroque-style silver helmet in the shape of a silver mane; a silver sword of similarly huge proportions; a small yellow and black striped cross-belt round the waist; knee-high white satin boots, and silver rings around the arms and legs . . . My hair was a blue-black colour, falling on to my naked, entirely coffee-brown body. I was intoxicated by this costume.

Having established in the opening scene the expected air of strangeness, Evreinov's characteristic emphasis on the grotesque was introduced with Herod and his wife. Mgebrov thought these figures effective in their monstrosity, but for Vaikone they toppled over into a vulgarity which he (probably wrongly) thought must have been at odds with the director's intentions. Herod (A. Arkad'ev) wore Evreinov's trademark harlequin costume, and was physically repellent: in Vaikone's words 'short, fat and bestial, with his flabby neck, red lips, black beard, grey body and wheezy voice', while Herodias was 'a harsh figure with long, deep blue curls and sharp facial features'. Vaikone was more impressed by Iokanaan, who was played by A. Zakushnyak:

> The prophet, raised gently up to the surface of the cistern, with his pale-green body pale as a blade of grass, his purple hair, deeply hollowed eyes and hands raised to the skies, gives an indelible impression of spirituality, incorporeality and unworldliness, and if the actor had given to his character a more inspirational, 'prophetic' voice, it could have been said that the part of the prophet had been brilliantly realised by the director.

Ribs were drawn on to Iokanaan's green painted body, and according to Karina Dobrotvorskaya Evreinov thought this design would connote holiness.

The most striking discrepancies between these detailed accounts concern the role of Salome and the sexual charge of the performance as a whole. Mgebrov thought the 'exquisitely formed feminine figures', who were dressed similarly to the Page and scattered throughout the playing area, contributed to the production's 'refined erotica', while Vaikone thought they were there merely to add to the stage picture, and that when they spoke their voices shattered the impression of harmony.

We can form a reasonably clear picture of the stage action surrounding Salome's dance, if not of the dance itself. Salome had long red hair and was dressed in white muslin. The eyes of everyone on stage were turned upon her as she began the dance, during which a red light connoting sexual passion gradually flooded the stage. (Earlier, at the moment when the horrified Tetrarch hears the ominous beating of mighty wings, the lower part of the moon was tinged with red.) The dance, as described by Mgebrov,

> was accompanied by the whoops and passionate cries of Herod and all those present at the feast, rising to a crescendo which increased a hundredfold with the fading and blazing of the blood-red light, becoming a positive frenzy by the end of the scene. Then, it seemed, came the sound of a whiplash; human faces were transfigured into the snouts of beasts, teeth bared in passion and terrible hunger for the human body.

When the seventh veil was discarded there was a final, blinding flash of light and a magnesium flare, followed by darkness. The lights were slowly raised again to reveal Salome being dressed by her maids, who like many others in the production wore flesh-coloured body stockings. A modern critic considers that the production represented Salome as a 'perverse deviate',[116] and there is evidence for this in Mgebrov's enthusiasm for the 'frenzied zeal' of the dance; against this, Vaikone thought the dance 'sluggish, lacking fire and passion', and criticised the actress for being 'too subtle in her speech and gestures', which were 'inexpressive of sultriness and passion'.

Vaikone thought Herod became vulgar and prosaic in attempting to dissuade Salome from demanding the head. As Naaman descended into the cistern, a movement followed by the sound of a falling body, his hands and feet were seen to be red, as if already steeped in blood. This recurrent use of red, like the consistent appearance of flesh tones in the minor characters, recalls the ways in which previous directors, and Wilde himself, had orchestrated the piece in patterns of colour. Also familiar are Evreinov's difficulties with the scene in which Salome addresses the prophet's head. Earlier productions in Paris and London had encountered serious practical problems at this point, but Evreinov's solution of keeping the head unseen in the depths of the cistern was arrived at only in order to meet the demands of the censor, and Vaikone understandably felt it weakened the scene.

Although it was mangled by the censor and remained unseen by the public, Evreinov's conception of *Salome* was clearly an important event in its stage history. This is seen most evidently in its Beardsleyesque design and relative sexual frankness, as well as in Evreinov's more individual touches. Of these, Vaikone emphasises 'his use of colour, fabric, character groupings, poses and other methods', while according to Dobrotvorskaya

> *Tsarevna* turned out to be a splendid, fancifully decorative and dark production. Its ornamental, picturesque nature, its grotesque imbalance, stylisation, exotic elements and its spice all marked it as a modernist production. Evreinov staged the play for the sake of the cult of beauty and, like a true disciple, sacrificed much to his cult, including the complexities of the drama and of live actors.

But what these verdicts perhaps overlook is that in many ways the director was demonstrably following what had already become established methods of staging this difficult work. Vaikone records Evreinov's statement that the only 'correct and permissible style' for

Salome was a Wildean style, and the backdrop of sky and 'strangely formed stars' recalls the ideas Wilde outlined to Charles Ricketts, while the colour-scheme and arrangement of terrace and cistern seem largely to follow the familiar pattern. The account of the lighting certainly suggests the influence of Appia, and the director seems to have found that the play was not suitable for development as the kind of expressionist monodrama with which he had been experimenting, since changes in the lighting correspond to changes first in Herod's emotional state and then in Salome's. Again, this is in accordance with Wilde's use of symbol, whereby the moon signifies something different to each character who mentions it. It seems that the play was already sufficiently consonant with Evreinov's aesthetic concerns for the extravagant staging to appear as part of a unified theatrical experience rather than as a design imposed from without.

KAMERNY THEATRE, MOSCOW, OCTOBER 1917

In the spring of 1912 another Russian actress, Olga Grovskaya, escaped the Russian ban on *Salome* by performing the role at Prague's National Theatre.[117] Grovskaya was regarded as a highly talented actress, her particular strength in comedy being due to 'her clear pronunciation, her attention to detail and her gentle irony'. In *Salome* she was attempting to establish herself as an actress accomplished in tragedy as well. Her performance took its inspiration from suggestions of the heroine's virginity, but perhaps because of her inexperience in tragic roles Grovskaya's insistence upon Salome's purity made the character appear coquettish and lacking in passion or depth, closer to Flaubert's creation than Wilde's.

Grovskaya's interpretation was well received, however, and influenced Konstantin Balmont, a symbolist poet whose new translation was used when Grovskaya finally had the opportunity to perform the piece in Russia, after the ban on seditious drama was lifted following the revolution of February 1917. In August of that year she performed at Moscow's Maly Theatre in a production directed by Ivan Platon, with Konstantin Korovin as artistic director. While Grovskaya acted the role in the same manner as previously, this time critics thought her cold, prosaic and even somnambulistic, perhaps because her style did not suit a play which had now been turned into 'a sultry, burning, luxuriant romantic drama' (Dobrotvorskaya), in which Grovskaya's performance did not harmonise with the more spirited playing of M. Lenin as Herod and N. Smirnova as Herodias. While the set and the other costumes were colourful, Salome was dressed, as at Prague, solely in white throughout, the whole effect being to eliminate all eroticism even from the dance and the kissing of the head.

While according to Laurence Senelick the Maly's *Salome* was performed in August 1917,[118] more recently Karina Dobrotvorskaya has stated that the première did not take place until the final days of October. If the later date is correct, it would mean that two important and very different productions were running in Moscow more or less simultaneously. Certainly, the Kamerny (Chamber) Theatre's production, which is surely the most significant of the Russian *Salome*s and a fitting conclusion to a decade of experimentation on the play, took a very different approach from that of the Maly despite using the same translation by Balmont.

The Maly Theatre's production had only become possible after the February revolution, which made a range of previously banned material available for the first time. This process was accelerated after the nationalisation of the theatres following the October revolution;[119] but by a nice irony, the Kamerny's production seemed almost reactionary in its modernist aestheticism, and was staged in Moscow at the precise moment that the victorious revolution was unfolding in the streets outside.

Such political coincidences were not unknown to the company, which had been founded just as the First World War was impacting on Moscow in 1914, and went into liquidation in

February 1917, at the time of the first revolution, only to be re-launched at new premises with the first performance of *Salome* on 9 October, commencing the season which its director, Alexander Tairov, called 'the turning point in our work', and during which the Kamerny developed its '*theatre of emotionally-saturated form*'.[120]

The Kamerny, then, was actually championing a form of aestheticism at the very time that the Bolshevik revolution was creating the conditions for the politicisation of all art, which would bring Tairov into repeated conflict not only with fellow-directors such as Meyerhold, but with the political authorities. Tairov had no time, for example, for the kinds of participatory event which would soon come to be seen as a necessary part of artistic propaganda; he insisted on a separation between stage and auditorium, on the grounds that the spectator was an observer of an action which was at once dynamic and already completed, the real artistic work having been done in rehearsals and the performance being simply an enactment of that work.

Tairov worked in close collaboration with his wife, the actress Alisa Koonen, and their production of *Salome* tends to be considered in relation to the well-documented development of their aesthetic ideas, and especially as a precursor to their work on *Phèdre*. For the director himself, the production represented 'the first steps on the path to a solution of the *problems of dynamic transformation of scenic atmosphere*';[121] but as Dobrotvorskaya has recently remarked, it should also be seen as the culmination of a decade of Russian *Salome*s. Like Evreinov, Tairov had discovered in the play a central tension between Salome's 'earthly feeling' and Iokanaan's 'spiritual negation of the flesh', and another within Salome herself, who was at once 'searching for something pure and good' while unable to resist the impulses towards eroticism inherited from Herodias.[122] Unlike Evreinov, however, Tairov rejected Beardsleyesque decadence and the concomitant reading of Salome as perverse, and instead aimed to present her as what Dobrotvorskaya describes as 'the natural person . . . with her emotional openness, her ability to obey her own instincts, to submit to her biological nature and give herself over freely to passion'. This very clearly distinguished Koonen's interpretation of the role from Grovskaya's the same year at the Maly, which was characterised by coldness and self-denial. In this attempt to recuperate a harmonious and natural personality, and in the emphasis upon myth in place of a rootless aesthetic decadence, the production engaged some of the central concerns of modernism.

Like Evreinov again, Tairov developed his artistic ideas in conscious opposition to both the 'representational' naturalism of Stanislavsky on the one hand, and the 'presentational' stylisation of Meyerhold on the other. Naturalism, Tairov felt, banished art by attempting to imitate real life, while stylisation led to a hollow, mechanised, two-dimensional reduction of life. In contemporary theatre history naturalism was the thesis and stylisation its antithesis; in their place, Tairov wanted a theatre and an acting style which would offer a 'scenic synthesis' both of naturalism and stylisation, and of the various arts of drama, ballet, opera, pantomime and so forth, as well as of the different media available to any stage performance (costume, lighting, set design, music, colour, words, and so on).

The actor, whose centrality to the theatre Tairov championed, was to discover the basis for 'scenic emotion' not in life but in fantasy, and in working on his role the actor (and costume-designer) created a visible form for this emotion. The essence of Tairov's method was to capture this 'emotional form' by means of rhythm. This emphasis on rhythmic form was of course most obvious in *Salome* in his approach to language and music. The Kamerny used the translation Konstantin Balmont had written for the Maly Theatre's production, Balmont having previously translated *Shakuntala*, the Kamerny's first-ever production in 1914. Wilde's text is in any case replete with the kinds of poetic cadences Tairov found especially amenable to the stage. A Czech musician, Jules Gyutel, had written the 'exotic music, half barbarous, half over-civilised, composed principally for the horns',[123] while the Dance of the Seven Veils was placed under the direction of Mikhail Mordkin of the Moscow Ballet.

Tairov quite consistently described in orchestral terms the development of rhythm and interaction in *Salome*. He saw the need for performance to bring to life the 'rhythmic and contrapuntal pattern' of the language, and set himself the task of 'orchestrating the whole work (the contra-basses of the soldiers, the flute of the Young Syrian, the oboe of Salome, the sounding brass of Jochanaan, etc.)'.[124] It is possible, too, that rhythms of movement upon the stage were determined by Tairov's perception of forces of attraction and repulsion, for instance between Salome and Iokanaan. Of greater practical complexity was the question of how rhythmic form could manifest itself in stage design. Tairov discarded both the 'model' set of the naturalistic theatre and the stylised set of Meyerhold, which reduced the stage to a two-dimensional painterly sketch. He restored the three-dimensional stage, but now as a non-naturalistic 'neo-model'. The stage floor was to contain several horizontal and sloping levels, to allow for various appropriate rhythmic effects in movement. At the same time, experiments with vertical constructions allowed for the creation of different effects of scale, while the lighting, and the geometric shapes which formed the set, likewise contributed to the effect of a harmonious rhythmic structure.

Tairov's designer, Alexandra Exter, had begun her career in the theatre by working on the Kamerny's production of *Famira Kifared* the previous year. She was associated with cubism, although her work on this first production contributed to what Nick Worrall has claimed as 'the first authentically "constructivist" approach to the staging of a play'.[125] Tairov had been impressed by Exter's recognition of the dynamic element of theatre design, a dynamism evident not only in her creation of a multi-dimensional playing space but also in her attempt to create the feeling of movement in her use of colour and costume.

At the same time, that Exter was working with cubism helped

to distance the play from the Beardsleyesque designs favoured by Evreinov, and helped to resolve many of the practical difficulties confronting Tairov in realising his ideas. Cubism, as it had been developed in Paris since approximately 1907, especially by Picasso and Braque, had been associated with the attempt to resolve particular problems in two-dimensional art by presenting various perspectives on an object within a single painting. Never purely abstract, since it retained recognisable visual forms within the composition, the cubist painting nevertheless was not representational, since it prevented the viewer from organising its planes into a stable and coherent whole. This tension is particularly apparent in cubism's approach to space. Cubists exploited Cézanne's experiments with *passage* – 'the running together of planes otherwise separated in space' – so that the surface of a painting such as Picasso's *Portrait of Ambrose Vollard* (1909–10) consists of 'a series of small, intersecting planes, any one of which, because of *"passage"*, may be understood as being both behind *and* in front of other, adjoining planes'.[126]

These principles, when applied by Exter to the scenic design and particularly to the costumes of *Salome*, strikingly and satisfyingly resolved one of the major problems in staging the play. Symbolism, as we have seen, had encountered difficulties in reconciling the human form with its ideal theatre, which was essentially static; but as all directors of *Salome* had already recognised, the action of the play demands several moments of immobility and tableau. Exter's stylisation of the body and its clothing by such methods as *passage* allowed these static moments to be presented without destroying either the three-dimensionality or the effect of movement essential to effective stage performance. Her costume designs (plate 4) were angular and marked with dark shadows, the effect being increased by exaggerated folds in the costumes themselves, which consequently cast abnormally large shadows on the stage.

A greater difficulty was presented by the movement of the

Plate 4 Costume designs by Alexandra Exter for Alexander Tairov's 1917 production of *Salome*, Kamerny Theatre, Moscow.

actors, but in practice Oliver M. Sayler, who witnessed the production and has left a very detailed account, was led to comment on 'the endless possibilities revealed in the expression of emotion by this new and exaggerated school of gesture. True to the nature of cubism, it is angular and vividly picturesque in its static moments, –

moments which it seems constantly to be trying to attain, only to release them and work toward a new moment through intermediary movement.'[127] A good example of this style was provided by Koonen's movements after Iokanaan, having spurned her advances, descended into the cistern:

> Ever since Jokanaan has departed, Salome has clung infatuated to the cistern wall, holding her body strained against it. The white of her arms cuts an obtuse angle of yearning passion against the black of her robe and against the blue of the curtain behind her. And, increasing the passionate tension beyond power of word, her body bends far to one side along the line of one of the arms.[128]

While the cubist design facilitated the performance of scenes such as this, Tairov was nevertheless able successfully to interweave them with moments of more immediate dramatic excitement, as when the Young Syrian 'kills himself on the staircase and flings his body headlong between prophet and princess'.[129] More characteristic, however, were those 'intermediary movement[s]' between moments of stasis, movements which, like Salome's first entrance, were 'sinuous and graceful'.[130]

Tairov conceived of the play as a dynamic process, in which primal energies and passions erupted with the force of revelation, accompanied by a kind of biblical scenic transformation. He described how at the beginning of the play, 'in a melody pregnant with action, suddenly, like an ominous warning, like the first call of inevitable doom, in the strident brass of Jochanaan's frenzied rhythm, a dark silver curtain opens before the spectator, revealing the fatal cistern, just as the golden gates open in the temple when the voice of the Lord is heard'. Later, when Salome promises to dance, Herod's howl of joy 'tears the backdrop asunder and carries it aside with waves of reverberating ether, revealing in the blood-drunk rays of the moon the red curtain of the dance and of death'. Finally, at Salome's death, 'the black wings of the lowered banners vibrate in the air, a funereal canopy, abandoned by the moon, over the shield-tomb of Salome'.[131]

This emphasis on biblical prophecy and revelation could be seen as highly provocative, in view of the political events unfolding in Moscow at the time. On the other hand, as the response to Reinhardt's Berlin production had shown, the play had always been able to express powerfully the death-knell of an apparently corrupt civilisation, and indeed this had doubtless contributed to its popularity in the last years of pre-revolutionary Russia.

The effect of these ideas on the audience can be gauged by Sayler's account. The cubist influence was apparent even before the parting of the first curtain, which was 'a bold study in the grotesque':

> Black and gold are its dominant colors . . . Facing inwards at the
> centre are two monsters – a goat and a leopard, perhaps, standing on
> their hind feet. Facing outward are two equally eery demons – one a
> peacock and the other the swan's progenitor, it may be. The rest is
> a background of distinct post-impressionist or even cubist humors.
>
> This intriguing curtain parts to the strains of exotic music . . .
> Still another curtain is now disclosed . . . with a sharp pointed sun-
> like arc in white against a black background and above it to the right
> three flaming banners in red – military pennons set dead against the
> wind.[132]

The parting of this second curtain, which was painted in a strongly cubist fashion, revealed a set apparently not unlike that envisaged by Wilde, although it was characterised by angular pillars and planes. Exter divided the stage into two distinct areas. On the left, from the spectator's point of view, was a platform, painted a dark colour, with the cistern placed upstage. Beyond this was a dark curtain and a large green disc, representing the moon, projecting beams on to the stage. The right-hand side of the stage was light in colour and placed at a lower level. The foot of the staircase upstage was bathed in a red glow within which a group of soldiers was disclosed.[133]

After Iokanaan's first speech the red light spread over the terrace, portending Salome's arrival, while the curtain holding the moon was withdrawn to reveal 'two silver streamers of unequal length suspended from above and extending nearly to the ground'. Later, when Iokanaan descended into the cistern to escape Salome's advances, the streamers rose slowly out of sight. The lighting, then, seems to have been quite conventional: the red glow became deeper or more expansive at ominous moments, while to herald Herod's arrival '[t]he light grows redder and then blends into a portentous yellow'. But the peculiar and symbolic use of streamers to represent moonlight was highly stylised, and the idea was repeated at the end of the play: as Salome was crushed by the soldiers, black streamers fell from above, to be followed by the drawing of the curtains.

Sayler gives a detailed account of the dance:

> The first [red] veil descends gradually to the floor. The air underneath it buoys it up an instant and then the attendants stealthily draw it aside, as the second veil, red as well, falls from Salome's shoulders. Now the princess increases the tempo of the dance, pulls a green veil from about her breast, and sinks suddenly to the floor. Slowly, sinuously, she rises again and her whole body loses itself in the dance. Again and again she faces the well, rushing at it with a fury and a swiftness that lash the beads of her skirt against its sides, and then turning away from it as violently. She tears the fourth veil from her breast and the rhythm becomes quieter and more regular. A slow, free dance of ecstatic joy now carries Salome from one side of the terrace to the other, first toward Herod and then toward the well. The dance becomes wilder and faster, around and around, with the beads of the skirt lashing the well again in frenzy. Madly up and down she rushes, bending her body in an impassioned arc first at the well and then toward Herod. From her waist she pulls the fifth veil as if it were a part of her body. And then as she hurls herself at the well for the last time and wrenches the sixth from her body, the lights vanish except for a torch or two which throw the tense and ardent form of the princess into sharp silhouette. Even the torches now are smothered, as the music of the dance dies away. When the lights return, Salome is fastening about her a gold and black robe and her attendants are replacing her head-dress.

The prophet's head, which Naaman presented to Salome on a charger, was concealed beneath a red veil. At one point Salome held it over her head and blood appeared 'to drip from the charger on her face and into her mouth', although unfortunately it is not absolutely clear from Sayler's account whether this effect was realistic or stylised. Salome's address to the head was alternately passionate, revolted, fascinated and finally triumphant, until Herod gave the order for her death and she was crushed beneath the soldiers' shields.

Sayler was impressed with Koonen's lithely erotic performance, which was 'a masterpiece of impassioned action'. Interestingly, he compared the onstage dominance of this physically small actress with that of another Russian actress, Alla Nazimova, who five years later starred in a Hollywood film which remains the most daring cinematic interpretation of *Salome*. Sayler thought the rest of the cast suffered by comparison with Koonen. Nikolai Tseretelli's Iokanaan was 'a highly strung human being, sensitive to passion as are other men, but controlling his emotions and consciously turning them into the hard mold of the ascetic and the prophet', while Ivan Arkadin as Herod displayed 'a trenchant mastery of the grotesque', although neither actor was able to inject much variety into his delivery. The primary significance of the minor roles was that they were performed ensemble, in a manner which did not detract from the coherence of the overall design.

While the Kamerny's was not the final Russian production of this period (Konstantin Mardzhanov, for example, staged the play at Petrograd's Troitsky Theatre the following month, and was involved in further productions in Kiev in 1919 and Tbilisi in 1921), and although Tairov himself was finally dissatisfied with his *Salome*, feeling that technical difficulties prohibited the effective realisation of his ideas, there can be no doubt that the Kamerny Theatre's production is a landmark in the stage history of the play. *Salome* had begun its career in Russia, rather problematically, as a quasi-revolutionary document, yet at the precise moment of the revolution's success Tairov developed a style which appeared deliberately to emphasise the aesthetic in opposition to the political. In this modern style he found a coherent solution to what had seemed intractable difficulties in staging the play. For Sayler, the tragic force of the Kamerny's production came from its 'austere attitude toward the passions', creating a performance which was 'intensely impersonal and at the same time hotly and passionately intimate'.

CHAPTER THREE

SALOME ON THE ENGLISH STAGE,
1911–1990

The history of *Salome* on the English stage does not allow for a fully coherent narrative. Hampered at first by censorship and amateurish production and management in the early years of the century, culminating in a notorious trial in 1918, the play nevertheless came back into favour between 1929 and 1931, as the result of a more relaxed attitude exemplified in the lifting of the ban on public presentation. Perhaps it is not surprising that with the removal of the prohibition *Salome* seemed to lose its power to shock, so that in the middle decades of the century there was no production of lasting significance. It is only in more recent times that the play has gained new importance as a work enabling the stage presentation of complex attitudes towards sexuality, and as a vehicle for idiosyncratic talents to explore the limits of possibility within the theatre. In so doing, *Salome* is increasingly coming to be recognised as a neglected work of major importance.

Although it was to be nearly twenty-five years before a production of comparable importance to Ricketts's would be staged in London, and despite the disappointments which attended his efforts, the play did not disappear from view. For example, in May 1909 an entertainment called *Salome* was presented at London's Fulham Theatre with music for the Dance of the Seven Veils composed by Granville Bantock, which we may assume was similar if not identical to the music supplied by the same composer for J. T. Grein's production of Wilde's play in 1918.

In the interim, on 27 February 1911, Wilde's *Salome* was presented at the Royal Court, the venue George Alexander had unsuccessfully suggested to Ricketts in 1906. In the 1911 production Adeline Bourne played the title-role; Herbert Grimwood was Herod, with Edyth Oliver as Herodias and Arthur Wontner as Jokanaan. The play's producer, Harcourt Williams, took the part of the Young Syrian; the stage-manager was Leslie Crowther, and the production featured music by Easthope Martin and choreography by Louis Hervey d'Egville.

The production received an unfavourable review in *The Times*, whose commentator recognised that it misrepresented the play.[1] Noting 'the pedantic if praiseworthy effort to reproduce the atmosphere of Palestine in the year AD 30', the writer notes that '[t]he date of *Salome* is really the late eighties or early nineties of the last century'. Despite earlier boycotts the critic had evidently seen both the 1905 and 1906 productions, since he contrasted unfavourably the attempts at historical accuracy with Ricketts's designs, and considered Grimwood's Herod inferior to Farquharson's 'astonishing interpretation at the previous productions'. With few exceptions he found the acting weak, with Adeline Bourne singled out for particular dispraise. While the critic regarded the 'modernity' of the play as 'excessive', and commented, presumably adversely, on 'the tense dramatic opportunity it affords for exhibiting the phenomena of neurosis in different phases', there is nevertheless some truth in his presumption that these qualities caused the play to be more highly regarded and better performed in Europe. Certainly this production seems to have done nothing to reverse that trend.

ROYAL COURT, LONDON, APRIL 1918

The same was even more true of the next London performance, albeit for quite unique reasons. In 1904 the impresario and critic J. T. Grein, who had been impressed on seeing Reinhardt's production of *Salome* at Berlin's Neues Theater two years previously, had hoped to become the first to stage the play in London by mounting a production with *mise en scène* designed by Edward Gordon Craig,[2] who in 1905 was to publish his essay *The Art of the Theatre*, calling for a non-naturalistic theatre equivalent as an art form to poetry or music. Although this project was not eventually realised, Grein returned to the idea when, in 1918, he decided to revive his Independent Theatre. The performance was intended as a charitable contribution to the war effort, and a further incentive was supplied by the wish of the dancer Maud Allan to act as well as dance in a dramatic role.

Grein's employment of Maud Allan, and the patriotic impulse behind his project, were to cost him dear. The advertisement for the production came to the attention of Noel Pemberton-Billing, the Independent MP for Hertfordshire, who had been trying for some time to provoke any sort of libel action which would give him the opportunity to demonstrate publicly that Britain's ineffectual prosecution of the war effort was due to hidden German influence.[3] An article in the 26 January 1918 issue of Billing's privately circulated newspaper, the *Imperialist*, had alleged that the Germans had compiled a dossier containing the names of 47,000 men and women in Britain who had been corrupted by German agents. Billing had heard about this dossier, the 'Black Book', from a Captain Harold Spencer, who on 17 September 1917 had been discharged from the British Army suffering from 'delusional insanity', and who became the assistant editor of Billing's newspaper, which from 9 February 1918 was renamed the *Vigilante*.

On 10 February Marie Corelli, a Billing supporter, sent the *Sunday Times*'s announcement of the forthcoming production of *Salome* to the *Vigilante*'s offices, along with a note suggesting that 'it would be well to secure a list of subscribers to this new "upholding" of the Wilde "cult" among the 47,000'.[4] Spencer saw that this news might offer the opportunity to expose the conspiracy of corruption: Wilde had been convicted of sodomy, and *Salome* was banned on grounds of blasphemy; Grein was a foreigner, having been born a Dutchman; Allan was a reputed lesbian, whose relationship with

Margot Asquith, wife of the former Prime Minister, had long been a subject of gossip (as indeed had her relationship with Asquith himself); and it was rumoured that the play was to be performed abroad as a morale-boosting propaganda exercise sponsored by the Ministry of Information, which was headed by Lord Beaverbrook, another *Vigilante* hate-object.

Since Maud Allan's was the only name to appear in the *Sunday Times* advertisement, Spencer needed to find a means of attributing vice to her. Under medical guidance from a local doctor Spencer invented 'The Cult of the Clitoris', under which title the following announcement appeared on 16 February: 'To be a member of Maud Allan's private performances in Oscar Wilde's *Salome* one has to apply to a Miss Valetta, of 9, Duke Street, Adelphi, W.C. If Scotland Yard were to seize the list of these members I have no doubt they would secure the names of several thousand of the first 47,000.'[5] On 5 March Grein saw the article and showed it to Maud Allan. After they had consulted their solicitors, a libel writ was issued, followed by another when they discovered what 'the first 47,000' meant.

Billing's hearing took place on 6 April and 13 April, and the attendant publicity undoubtedly influenced reviews of the performance on 12 April, which was received with hostility in the press. After the hearing Billing was committed for trial, but nevertheless the Ministry of Information withdrew its support for Grein. Billing's trial finally began on 29 May and lasted for six days, concluding on 4 June.

In the course of this farcical trial Billing and Spencer were permitted to make endless unsubstantiated allegations concerning the morals and judgement of the most senior members of the political establishment, including the Asquiths, and purported to find in Wilde's play a whole range of erotic obsessions, a reading which in retrospect seems rather less outrageous than it did to many of Grein's supporters at the time.

They attempted to discredit Maud Allan as a 'hereditary degenerate'[6] by dragging in a family tragedy, the execution in 1898 of her brother Theo for the murder and subsequent 'outraging' of two girls in a church in San Francisco; and later in the trial Billing's expert medical witness and sympathiser, Dr Serrell Cooke, was actually led by Mr Justice Darling to the conclusion that anyone who played the title-role in such a play must be a sadist. Earlier Cooke had inferred from Grein's description of *Salome* that Grein was a homosexual, and should therefore be locked up. As for the audience, Spencer contended that any non-medical person who understood the meaning of the title 'The Cult of the Clitoris' must be a pervert and member of the cult, while the judge accepted Cooke's argument that the play was a sadistic piece which would induce orgasms in the 'lunatics' in the audience. Cooke chose the word carefully, claiming Wilde had deliberately exploited the image of the moon to excite any 'female erotomaniacs' watching. It was even suggested that the full effect would only be achieved if the play were performed 'on certain days of the month, during which the moon is passing through certain phases', since 'that is the time when these erotomaniacs usually are most susceptible'.[7] In addition to sadism and this quasi-lycanthropy, Cooke identified the presence of fetishism, masochism and incest. Billing denied that his remarks about Maud Allan were to be taken as impugning the dancer's character, and was acquitted.

The verdict caused near-despondency in artistic circles. Grein's wife Alix ('Michael Orme'), who produced the play and took the part of Herodias, later wrote (and it was generally agreed) that this verdict could only mean the jury had concluded that the play itself was 'unfit for presentation'.[8] In a letter to Robert Ross in June, Charles Ricketts accounted for the verdict by referring to the 'musical comedy optimism of the period which resists tragedy', and to a 'non urban' streak in the English character:

> *Salomé* in which the very moon is coloured by the idée fixe of the persons, in which the psychology is at once elaborate and naif, the circumstances fantastic, the *fond* deeply coloured by the strangeness of absolute standards now remote; the form, wilfully modified by its

baserelief [*sic*] like conditions, all this is so foreign and new to us that its novelty, its foreigneering tendencies arouses [*sic*] . . . hysteria.[9]

It is perhaps significant that Ricketts mentions receiving a letter from a Russian friend on the front who was 'astonished and, I fear, amused' by the upshot of the trial,[10] for as we have seen, Russian theatres had already staged a number of experimental interpretations of the play, while London remained hampered by a censorship and conservatism intensified by the experience of war.

There was in Ricketts's reaction, it seems, a certain myopia unsurprising in someone who confessed to an 'entire lack of contact with public opinion' at this time.[11] The English were 'intoxicated into failure', as Ross put it in his reply of 13 June, and 'enjoyed tearing Maud Allan to pieces, simply because she had given them pleasure, and kicking Oscar's corpse to make up for the failure of the Fifth Army'. Ross, who had predicted Billing's acquittal for these reasons, now found as Wilde's literary executor that '[e]very American and provincial theatre company cabled or wired cancelling their contracts. The cinemas [*sic*] of the plays and stories were withdrawn; the booksellers cancelled their orders to Methuen.'[12]

Orme's biography of her husband contains a detailed account of the troubles surrounding the production. The imminent trial, and later the trial itself, left Grein's nerves shattered, although pre-publicity for the play was anything but hysterical. Prior to news of the libel case, for instance, *The Globe* had commented that *Salome* would 'in itself save the year from the charge of artistic sterility'.[13] As the performance date grew nearer, however, Grein's troubles increased, and he encountered crises which demonstrate that nothing had been learned from Ricketts's experiences in 1906. Orme's co-producer departed; the scenery had been designed for a larger stage, and was being adjusted at the eleventh hour; in consequence the dress-rehearsal was shambolic and incomplete, getting no further than Maud Allan's dance; and the actor playing the Cappadocian had disappeared so late that fifteen minutes before the curtain went up Orme was still at a loss, until the manager–agent Herbert Woodward stated that he would memorise the part, a feat he apparently accomplished with aplomb.

Despite the troubles, Orme felt there was some cause for satisfaction. The music – Granville Bantock's 'Dance of the Seven Veils' and a prelude by Howard Carr, who also conducted the orchestra and who was later to achieve acclaim for his *Three Heroes* – strengthened the production, Maud Allan's performance 'testified to her very real artistry as a dancer', 'George Relph as "Herod" gave a superb performance, rising to tragic heights, and Ernest Milton's "Jokanaan" was poignant and arresting'. The play was well received by an audience which, *pace* Billing, 'differed not at all from any matinée gathering'.[14]

It is not surprising that a scandal which at times kept even the prosecution of the war effort off the front pages should have eclipsed the performance itself as the focus of interest, and inevitable that Orme's account as well as the few reviews which appeared give little indication of the production style. The effect of Billing's onslaught is evident in the tone adopted by the reviewer for *The Stage* on 18 April.[15] Grein had given a brief speech after the performance in which he stated that *Salome* was 'not an impure work'. *The Stage* directly contradicted him, regarding it as 'very repellent to a healthy taste' and drawing attention to 'the explicit carnal desire of the daughter of Herodias for Jokanaan', the 'sickly voluptuousness' of the atmosphere, 'the gaudy harlotry of words', the 'effeminacy' of the 'constant use of the adjective', the dialogue 'rouged and painted like a courtesan's face', 'vitiated by a propensity that may perhaps be called – not unentirely in the Greek meaning – cosmetical'. Formally, the play was essentially a melodrama, with 'here and there attempts at realism, which often revolt because they have no measure of reticence'.

Having completed its hatchet job on the play, *The Stage* then went on to give a surprisingly favourable account of the production:

The performance on Friday was as a whole artistically done, with scenery on impressionist lines by Mr Guy de Gerald and Mr H. W. Owen, set in murky half lights, and with appropriate music, semi-barbaric in colour, by Mr Howard Carr, who composed the prelude, and by Mr Granville Bantock, whose music for the dance was full of pulsating rhythms. In the dance Miss Maud Allan was naturally in her element, for she is a mistress of expressive poses and graceful movements. In her acting as Salome she seemed to feel more than she could express, and her elocution was very faulty. To the suggestion that Salome is only a child influenced by the first stirrings of puberty, Miss Allan did not lend any support. Her Salome, on the contrary, suggested a passionate woman, and this reading is of course the only one consistent with the text.

These closing remarks were clearly aimed at Grein, and are not easy to disagree with. *The Era's* review, on the other hand, was a brief but generally positive response to an 'impressive performance' of a play which 'contains passages of much poetic beauty', and curiously did not in any way allude to the current controversy.[16]

Despite the distress caused to all concerned, the production had a run of performances and interest was high; in a letter of June 1918 Ricketts complained to Ross that he had tried to obtain a box but could only get seats in the stalls, because 'the house was almost sold out'.[17] He continued: 'You will doubtless have heard that the Censor has insisted upon the head of Iokanaan being replaced by a sword owing to Miss Maud Allan being unable to impersonate Salomé.' According to Margery Ross in a footnote to this letter, Allan 'was prevented from performing this dance after the result of her libel action', and it would appear that the censor's objection was not to the dance itself but to the fact that Salome addressed the decapitated head.

The trial, of course, was a travesty; but in an important sense Billing had done justice to the play. Both Maud Allan at the Old Bailey, and the magistrate at the preceding hearing at Bow Street, had asserted that the indecency might have been in the mind of Billing himself; and to judge by the hysterical outbursts of Billing and Spencer, and the extraordinary testimony of Serrell Cooke, this was probably true. Equally, however, it is difficult to accept that neither Grein nor Allan saw *any* form of sexuality in the play which might at the time have been considered deviant. Although the verdict was undoubtedly occasioned in part by a moral conservatism framed by feelings of national peril and betrayal, nevertheless the trial sufficiently clearly indicates the persistence of a phenomenon Michel Foucault was to observe in the Victorian age: that a repressive policing of sexuality actually produced more and more varied ways of perceiving and talking about it.[18] Billing may have been deranged, his version of the sexualities explored in the play may have been chaotic and bizarre; but he had succeeded in exposing something in the play of which many others must have been aware, and no future production could be staged in innocence.

The repressive atmosphere did not last. With the ending of the war came a rejection of the 'Victorian' attitudes of seriousness and moral responsibility which many felt had produced it, and in the new climate of the 1920s Wilde became the focus of a cult which looked to the 1890s for alternative modes of expression.[19] Nevertheless, it was not until the decade was nearly over that a trickle of productions and the lifting of the ban signalled that the play could finally be approached in a more relaxed and creative fashion.

RISE AND FALL, 1929–1954

Possibly the most important British production yet staged, and certainly the most important since Ricketts's effort in 1906, was given at the Festival Theatre in Cambridge on 9 June 1929. The Festival itself ran from 1926 to 1933, producing plays during term-time for a largely undergraduate audience, often at the rate of eight or more plays a term. The Festival's producer, Terence Gray, was almost violently opposed to realism, and had succeeded in creating a theatrical architecture and a style of performance which eliminated the illusion of the real.[20] He had virtually removed the distinction between stage and auditorium by eliminating the proscenium, creating a broad sweep of steps which connected the forestage with the audience, and multiplying the entrances and exits so that the actors frequently found themselves in the midst of the spectators. The stage itself consisted of multiple levels, allowing for novel grouping and blocking, and facilitating continuous performance which had particular advantages in stagings of Shakespeare. Scenery was non-realistic and had to be strictly relevant to the meaning of the play. Gray's partner at the Festival, Harold Ridge, was formerly a metallurgist, which may explain a fondness for aluminium, or aluminium-painted, sets. Ridge was also a brilliant lighting technician, having previously published a book on the subject, and as the fluid lights continually played upon the metallic sets some extraordinary effects could be achieved.

Gray, as Norman Marshall pointed out, is an example of that trend in the modern theatre which sees the text as merely one element in a synaesthetic art form composed also of sound, movement, light, colour, and so on, and which is given shape not by the playwright but by the producer or director. Consequently Gray was interested less in discovering new writers than in doing new things with old writers. This, however, does not do full justice to the selection of material; Marshall concedes that in his interest in Shakespeare and the Greek drama Gray more or less reinvented their plays in a theatre able to do them justice, and the same is true of *Salome.*

Although a public theatre, and therefore subject to censorship, the Festival nevertheless occasionally mounted private performances before invited audiences. It was in this context that Gray staged *Salome,* first as a single performance on 9 June 1929, and then for a series of performances from 23 to 28 November 1931. In 1929 his

Salome was Vivienne Bennett, with George Coulouris as Herod and Doria Paston as Herodias, Noel Iliff as Jokanaan, and Hedley Briggs as the Young Syrian. In the 1931 production Bennett was replaced by Beatrix Lehmann and Coulouris by Robert Morley. Both productions employed Constant Lambert's music and Ninette de Valois's choreography of the dance.

In purely artistic terms it was a breakthrough, the most challenging and sympathetic treatment of the play yet mounted in Britain. The Festival's programmes were justly famed for the critical perspectives they offered on all aspects of theatre, and Gray's 'note on production' in the *Salome* programme helps to situate this production in the context of his ideas about theatre in general:

> In producing Oscar Wilde's *Salome* the producer is beset by a great temptation. For many generations playgoers have been used to visiting theatres in order to see life by proxy. Whatever the type of play, it has always been performed Realistically or Romantically, which for the purposes of this exposition are in the same category because in both cases each member of the audience seeks to identify himself with the life presented to him on the stage and to enter into the trick of illusionism . . .
>
> Modern art has cast away this idea. Modern art seeks to be abstract, pure, it spurns sentiment and naturalism as poison and the antithesis of art . . . Oscar Wilde was modern when he wrote *Salome*, but his modernity belongs to an earlier phase than ours. Starting from a basis of Ibsenian naturalism, he was influenced predominantly by Maeterlinck in his early period, and this type of work is Romantic in an artificial and stylised way that is well interpreted by the illustrations of Aubrey Beardsley.
>
> The producer of *Salome* must be sorely tempted to produce the play romantically even if with a stylised romanticism, with a setting fundamentally naturalistic, a mysterious night-sky strewn with stars, great dome terraces and moonlit colonnades, a visual illusion so easy to attempt in this theatre . . . [But although] *Salome* was reared on a foundation of naturalism . . . it is not naturalistic in any respect by which it can lay claim to greatness and dramatic value. Its dramatic

value lies in its success along lines that lead it away from its naturalistic foundation and into stylisation, artifice, rhythmic structure, musical repetition and 'expressionist' methods allied to Shakespearean soliloquy and Greek chorus which belong to the early period when drama was pure art unsullied by Realism or Romanticism. To give it naturalistically merely because it sprang from the naturalist method of the time would be purblind. Romantic to some extent it remains and this should not be obscured, but the duty of the modern theatre-artist in producing *Salome* is to present it in its full artificiality as an abstract work of art, which is its essential character and the source of its real value and permanence as a work of the theatre.[21]

The scenic design shows how Gray attempted to create this 'full artificiality'. Upstage was a massive, stylised construction, a gigantic staircase whose upper reaches represent three thrones of unequal height. The effect superficially recalls the architecture of an Aztec temple, perhaps subliminally creating the anticipation of human sacrifice. The huge cylindrical columns which dominate the stage-right area contrast sharply with this angular structure, immediately removing all sense of architectural or historical consistency and dividing the stage into clearly defined worlds, with the columns separating the onstage world of displayed political power from the offstage banquet. The sense of threat, of an abstract power lacking in human sympathy, is heightened by the metallic paint with which, characteristically, the entire set is coated. The remainder of the stage is largely empty save for a small diamond-shaped podium just upstage of the sunken cistern downstage centre, within which a masked Jokanaan will later be revealed. As noted, the Festival's forestage extended well into the auditorium, somewhat in the manner of the Olivier Theatre today, which may have stimulated an empathetic relationship between the audience and the action focused on the cistern. But the artificiality for which Gray strove is accentuated by the way in which the set towers over this downstage area, so that when Salome addresses Jokanaan, Jokanaan curses Herodias, or Salome dances for Herod, the effect is consistently metatheatrical, of a performance observed both by those seated in the auditorium and by the distant but visible onstage spectators.

Developments in mood were achieved by an innovative approach to lighting. Initially purple, the light was in keeping with the sombre set; but the 'vast red moon' which rose over Herod's throne, and the 'garish lights' thrown by Herod's feast through the columns, developed a mood of 'lurid decadence'. When Jokanaan emerged from the cistern a green light, projected from within on to Salome's face, extended upstage to illuminate Herodias.[22] The danger of unintentional comedy, never far from the surface in *Salome*, is perhaps particularly acute here; but this use of lighting overcomes practical difficulties in situating Jokanaan in relation to both Salome and Herodias, and is in keeping with a design concept akin to the calculated non-realism of science fiction.

The huge staircase ascending to Herod's throne also enabled Gray to overcome an obvious difficulty any director of the play must address. The Tetrarch's lengthy speeches, in which he implores Salome against demanding the head of Jokanaan, are both inherently undramatic and tend to focus attention too exclusively on himself. In 1906 Farquharson had simply spoken very fast, which rather impressed Max Beerbohm.[23] The staircase in Gray's production, however, created a practical obstacle between Herod and Salome. The obvious solution would have been for Herod to descend imploringly towards Salome. Gray, however, did the reverse: Salome turned her back on the cistern and climbed the steps to the throne, creating a powerful tension between Herod's excessive language and Salome's largely silent but relentless advance.

It was a good example of how Gray's innovatory approach could solve problems in the staging of *Salome*, and must have helped to convince others that Wilde's play could be produced in both a challenging and an artistically satisfying way. The new experimental approach to *Salome* in England was continued by Peter Godfrey, who in May 1931 mounted a production at the Gate Theatre Studio in London's Villiers Street. Godfrey, in fact, was closely associated with Gray, whose Festival Theatre company had once stepped in to perform at the Gate when a medical emergency closed down one of Godfrey's productions. Indeed, the season after that in which *Salome* was performed saw an amalgamation between the two theatres, although ultimately this was to the detriment of both. These close ties are evident in Godfrey's *Salome*, for which Ninette de Valois and Constant Lambert repeated from the Festival's 1929 production their respective roles as choreographer and composer.

As a venue, however, the Gate could hardly have been more different from the Festival. Whereas Gray had been fortunate in being able to occupy a custom-built theatre, Godfrey's premises in Villiers Street had previously been a restaurant, and then a skittle alley.[24] Of a total floor space measuring just fifty-five by thirty feet, over a third was occupied by the stage. Because the ceiling was low the stage was raised just eighteen inches above floor level, and the seats were raked quite steeply to ensure visibility from all parts of the auditorium. Dressing-rooms were just a few feet away. Consequently the relationship between actor and audience was exceptionally intimate, with even offstage actors being constantly aware of the play. On the stage the actor's smallest gesture or sound was discernible throughout the auditorium, which discouraged over-acting, although among the 'emotional actresses in the grand manner' who were nevertheless successful at the Gate by 'acting with absolute sincerity and never overstraining' Marshall cites Margaret Rawlings (who played Salome), Flora Robson (Herodias in the same production), and Beatrix Lehmann (who did not appear in Godfrey's production but subsequently took the title-role in Gray's revival of *Salome* at the Festival in 1931). Also in the cast at the Gate were Robert Speaight (Herod), John Clements (Jokanaan) and Esmond Knight (the Young Syrian).

The twenty-four-year-old Rawlings was the daughter of a clergyman, but had few misgivings about playing Salome, regarding what she described as the 'nakedness' to be essential, and revealing that 'although I have never danced before, the dance completes my idea of Salome, and the music which has been written for it I find tremendously inspiring'.[25]

Godfrey's conception of the Dance of the Seven Veils was daringly innovative. In the earlier parts of the play Salome was dressed in stylised Eastern costume, wearing a dark, teddy-style corset with shoulder straps over a white, ruffled, full-sleeved top and ruffled white trousers extending to the ankle; in fact, since the corset covers the waist, it is possible that Rawlings was wearing a single-piece suit beneath it. On her head she wore a hat resembling a fez.[26] The transformation from this outfit to the bejewelled bra and pants dressed in which she seduces Herod was achieved by a remarkable *coup de théâtre*, helpfully described by the reporter from the *Express*:

> Margaret Rawlings, black-haired and white-skinned, made the audience gasp when she first appeared behind the seven veils. The veils in this production are not draped round the dancer, but are hung across the stage, and withdrawn one by one to discover the rhythmically-moving limbs of Salome, dressed in little more than a handful of pearls.
>
> She dances with an increasing wildness to obtain the head of John the Baptist; until the last veil is torn aside, and she sinks triumphantly exhausted, to be covered by slaves with a white shift and crowned with scarlet flowers.

Clearly, Godfrey used the dance not to draw attention to the actress's body but to draw the audience into a critical relationship to the whole stage scene.

The performance style was adapted to suit the theatre. The reviewer for *The Times* described it as 'suppressed', but perhaps missed the significance of the Gate's acoustics in complaining that Godfrey was 'mistaken in lowering as far as he does the tone of the actors' speech. This prose is almost to be chanted; it must rise and swing; it must be capable of dreadful lulls like the lulls in the mounting rhythm of a storm.'[27] This is over-prescriptive, and seems to demand an outmoded style like that of Bernhardt, better suited to a larger venue; at the least, it overlooks the linguistic variety of the play, although this is easily done. The twin productions of Gray and Godfrey had opened up the play to radical interpretation in two very different venues and styles, and seemed to herald a renaissance in its fortunes consolidated by the lifting of the censor's ban on public performance in 1931. The first company to take advantage of this new freedom was Nancy Price's People's National Theatre, which gave the first-ever public performance of *Salome* in England at the Savoy in October of that year.

The cast was intriguing, for a number of reasons. Robert Farquharson, who had first played Herod in 1905, reprised the role yet again, while Robert Donat, soon to be a major star of the cinema, played the Young Syrian. The producer, Nancy Price, who played Herodias, was married to Charles Maude, and her twenty-two-year-old daughter, Joan Maude, was the surprise choice to play the title-role when Mlle Nikitina resigned from the production. In some ways the casting of Maude was a brave decision, but in practice it reinforced a conservatism in production style which was in direct contrast to the experiments of Gray and Godfrey and recalled instead the rather staid attempts of the first decade of the century.

Eyes rendered exaggeratedly large by expression and make-up, hair swept stiffly upwards and back, Joan Maude is striking but forbidding in the publicity stills. In performance, however, she nevertheless struck some rather protective reviewers as a well-groomed young Englishwoman, responses which recall objections to the performances of the leading ladies in the first London productions some twenty-five years previously.[28] A. E. Wilson felt that 'she remained, I am afraid, not the creature of evil perversity, but obviously a nice English girl in Eastern undress', and several others also thought her manner resembled that of a schoolgirl.

J. T. Grein's review went some way towards explaining the disparity between the reviews and the production stills, and gives some

insight into how he may have intended Maud Allan to portray the
role in 1918:

> Miss Joan Maude was, in effigy, an ideal Salome, quivering with
> youthful ardour, with the fervour of her passionate blood, with relent-
> less vengefulness for her frustrated advances. But she was too much
> given to strange and ill-placed posturing, and her dance – a dance of
> serpentine wriggles and alluring attitudes – was (as we saw it) a vain
> and immature effort. Yet in the death-scene she was affecting; her
> fear, her cry, her woeful collapse, were the one really pathetic
> moment of the play.

This apparent contradiction between make-up and performance
may simply reveal the inability of an inexperienced actress fully to
assume the identity of the character. But an interview given to the
Evening Standard suggests instead a more radical confusion in the
production concept itself. In response to a suggestion that she was
'not wicked enough to play such a wicked woman', Maude told the
Standard's reporter:

> I think Salome has been generally misjudged. She was not altogether
> bad. She was an inexperienced girl, but liable, through being a daugh-
> ter of that perverted family, to evil impulses of the blood. There is
> nothing more dreadful than the sight of a girl who is naturally good,
> in the grip of an evil passion which she cannot control. That was the
> character I tried to play. It would have been easy to make Salome
> a common vamp – but how crude, and how untrue!

Given that the actress was under the direction of her own mother, it
is likely that this was the kind of response Nancy Price was hoping to
elicit from the audience. Evil impulses, evil passions, blood, perversion: this is the language of Pemberton-Billing and Serrell Cooke,
now used in the service of the familiar concept of *hamartia*, the
tragic flaw. The Billing trial had exposed the sexuality of the play.
Terence Gray had seen the dangers of emotive responses to the
undoubted presence of this theme, and broke new ground by
deliberately alienating the audience from the passions it depicted.

The Savoy production, by contrast, was trapped. Directing the first production since the lifting of the ban, at a highly respectable venue, Price was either unaware of the experiments of Gray and Godfrey (unlikely), or failed to recognise the importance of stylisation. It is highly possible that she felt that anything other than what Gray had termed realistic and romantic modes of production would make the play seem perverse in artistic as well as moral terms. The only alternative was a rather genteel style of production and a defence of the play's morality; but Billing had exposed the weakness of that strategy thirteen years previously in his treatment of Grein.

Perhaps it was the generally indifferent critical response to Nancy Price's tame production that deterred other companies from staging the play in the years immediately succeeding the relaxing of the ban, although that critical response also contained within it a residual moral disapprobation. For example, on 7 October 1933 the Vice-Chancellor of Oxford University refused permission for a production by the Oxford Repertory Company at the Playhouse. A few productions were staged in the years following the Second World War, but once again by minor companies in small venues, signalling a continuing regression in the fortunes of the play since the hopeful days of 1931.

The marginalisation of the play at this time should also be related to the conservatism of the theatre in the post-war years. The scene was dominated by star actors and actresses such as Laurence Olivier, John Gielgud and Edith Evans, but the drama itself was generally unchallenging, and little changed until John Osborne's *Look Back in Anger* famously erupted in 1956. In this context the Centaur Theatre Company, which staged *Salome* in a double bill with T. S. Eliot's *Sweeney Agonistes* at London's Rudolph Steiner Theatre in 1947, can be seen at least to be attempting something comparatively radical, eschewing star names in favour of an ensemble company of players, and seeking to present 'serious drama' and 'certain stylisations of movements, incidental music only if essential, and ballet or singing if indicated in the play'.[29] Such aims are in themselves disappointingly tame, although the double bill did give the public an opportunity to see two rarely produced pieces by famous dramatists, Wilde's play not having been produced professionally in London for sixteen years, and Eliot's never having been seriously intended for the stage.

The director of both plays, Peter Zadek, was only twenty; his Herod was Michael Yannis, René Goddard played Herodias, and Neville Bewley played Iokanaan. The title-role was taken by one of the few non-professional members of the cast, twenty-three-year-old Bernice Rubens, who, like Margaret Rawlings and Joan Maude, was a comparatively inexperienced actress with little formal training in dance.

A photo-feature published in a pictorial magazine shows how the Dance of the Seven Veils was presented.[30] Dancing before Herod, Salome first removed a white veil, worn on the head and denoting purity, to a slow and appealing musical accompaniment. The music changed as a second, green veil, indicating flirtation and coquettishness, was cast aside, Salome now adopting a more open stance and exposing her legs which had been hidden beneath the remaining veils, the third of which, of blue, was now thrown angrily and disdainfully into Herod's face. The dance became whirling and tempestuous before the mood changed again to one of love and passion, denoted by the fourth, red veil, which was removed from the left arm and lowered to Herod's feet. The fifth veil, gold for seduction, was tauntingly tossed around Salome's head as she swayed to and fro before the king. The symbolism of the sixth veil (pale blue) and the seventh (yellow) is not fully explained in the article, but the effect of their removal is obvious: the sixth was wrapped around the upper body and the seventh around the lower, so that as the music became wilder and more passionate in approaching a crescendo Salome was first topless and finally naked save for shiny briefs and cups covering the nipples.

Two further productions were staged in the early 1950s, before the play went into a long period of total eclipse. The first was another minor effort, by the New Torch Theatre Club, based at 50 Wilton Place, which gave a run of performances between 20 May and 8 June 1952 in a double bill with R. H. Ward's *The Soldier and the Whore*, while another double bill directed by Frederick Farley featured Wilde's play alongside Jean-Paul Sartre's *The Respectable Prostitute* at the 'Q' Theatre at Kew Bridge on 15 June 1954, before transferring to the St Martin's in the West End.

Although *Salome* had once more fallen almost out of sight, it was no longer routinely dismissed by the critics. A. E. Wilson, who had been bored by Nancy Price's Savoy production in 1931, now thought the play 'combines the morbid horrors of Grand Guignol with a suggestion of the Folies Bergère in its celebrated Dance of the Seven Veils and with an almost indigestible richness of phrase with which Wilde bedecks this legend of lust and cruelty'.[31] As before, Wilson's review was typical, but whereas in 1931 he had found the play boring, in 1954 he captured most critics' more judicious impression of the play as a fable, macabre and visually spectacular, but difficult to act due to the peculiar cadences of the language. Some remained unconvinced ('really no more than a series of florid speeches reminiscent at times of religious fanatics steaming up in Hyde Park, and its poetry consists mainly of repeating one line many times', according to Cecil Wilson), but only the language of the *Standard*'s Milton Shulman, barely distinguishable in its moral fervour from that of the play's detractors at the turn of the century, now appeared idiosyncratic. He thought *Salome* 'managed the not inconsiderable feat of being both repulsive and boring in about equal measure' and was 'heavy with the stench of decadence and lust', while the kissing of the head 'stimulates in us nothing but disgust'. Shulman's absurd remark that 'I could never, for example, believe that a well-spoken young woman like Miss Agnes Bernelle could be guilty of such bad taste' recalls the response of many to Joan Maude's Salome, but with an intolerance largely lacking even in 1931.

Bernelle's performance was generally well received. Joan Maude,

Margaret Rawlings and Bernice Rubens had been young and inexperienced actresses, and Maude and Rawlings in particular appear pale and thin in publicity stills, which perhaps accounts in part for what reviewers consistently perceived as their 'Englishness'. The signification of the publicity stills for Frederick Farley's production is quite different. Lipstick has made the lips full and round, and while there is heavy make-up around the eyes and eyelashes the effect is to make the eyes longer and narrower, signifying sensuality and sexual passion. The long black hair is braided and swept back over one shoulder, and the figure is fuller and the complexion darker than Maude's. The clothing, and in particular the jewellery pinned in the hair and suspended from the ears and around the neck, again carry connotations of Eastern luxury. This is a human, sensual and seductive figure.

For all the efforts of these companies, however, none of the productions since 1931 could be considered a major event in the history of the play. It had become once more the province of minor companies which generally lacked the resources or expertise to challenge received ideas concerning an oddity which now lacked even the *frisson* of prohibition. After Farley's staging it would be decades before *Salome* appeared again in London; and when it finally arose from the ashes it had been transformed into something drastically different from the tame productions of the past.

ROUNDHOUSE, LONDON, FEBRUARY 1977

The first professional production of *Salome* in London for over twenty years was staged by the Lindsay Kemp Company at the Roundhouse in February 1977. Two aspects of this performance demand particular emphasis: its style, which was a kind of postmodernist 'total theatre', and its foregrounding of the homosexuality which previously had almost invariably been treated with extreme caution.

Kemp returned with a vengeance to the kind of synaesthetic experience which Reinhardt and Strauss had made of the play in Berlin at the start of the century, but which had fallen by the wayside in the rather genteel and amateurish styles which had characterised most previous work on the play in London. His production was an assault on the senses, with deafening drumming, green and blood-red lighting, joss sticks in the hair of the slaves, incense burning in braziers, a live snake and a live dove, smoke, feathers, snatches of Wagner and Mozart, and more besides.

Since childhood Kemp had been fascinated by the Russian dancer Ida Rubinstein, who performed Salome routines several times in the early decades of the century; but he was best known as a mime artist, having trained with Marcel Marceau, while he also had extensive experience as a choreographer in a wide range of genres. In the 1970s his cult status was maintained partly as a result of his association with the rock-and-roll star David Bowie, who was to make homosexuality, bisexuality and cross-dressing fashionable, and who constantly reinvented himself by drawing on eclectic influences in creating new musical styles and new personae.

It was this same kind of plundering of the past to engender new forms which characterised Kemp's work. He aimed to 'restore to the theatre the glamour of the Folies Bergères, the danger of the circus, the sexuality of rock 'n' roll and the ritual of Death'.[32] The great experimental productions of *Salome* earlier in the century, such as those of Reinhardt, Tairov or Gray, had all sought to bring together the various elements of the theatre to create unified and coherent mythic interpretations of the play, and there was something of this same desire to build a performance around a single idea or style in Kemp's reading.

Nevertheless, the very eclecticism of the production challenged any simple interpretation. Drawing on elements of both the French and English versions, and drastically cutting the dialogue so that barely a third of the lines were retained, David Haughton's scenario not only refused to privilege one version over another but denied the written text any authority as the basis of production, so much so that the first words were not spoken until half an hour had elapsed and the audience had already been subjected to a sustained assault from the drums. The immediate effect, and one the audience would naturally expect from a mime troupe, was to render the text subordinate but complementary to the plastic display of dance, movement, lighting and colour.

Inserting elements of the French text into an English production might also encourage us to recall certain aspects of the play's history, and in particular the problematic role of Sarah Bernhardt in its origins. Since Wilde had been especially keen for the celebrated actress to take the title-role, he must at some stage have intended Salome to have the kind of prominence which, in practice, is almost invariably gained instead by Herod. Kemp's radical cutting of Wilde's text created this prominence for Salome, as did the choreographing of a number of dance movements additional to the Dance of the Seven Veils. Kemp, then, was the first since Bernhardt – and Wilde – to give the dancer the fully central role which Herod usually occupies, and he did so in a manner which is likely to recall Bernhardt to mind.

In this and several ways Kemp's production drew on diverse influences in a manner which was oblique rather than fully coherent, dispersive rather than integrative. Another example was the presentation of Jokanaan, played by David Haughton. Following the non-verbal prologue, a snake and a dove issued from under Herodias's skirt, providing visual emblems of the tension in the play between sexual licence and moral law, before Haughton entered to give a quite extraordinary re-interpretation of the prophet's signification. Previous productions had usually emphasised his asceticism, but few had attempted to provide a visual correlative to account for Salome's attraction to him. In this interpretation, however, in which Salome was quite obviously a man in drag, a specifically homosexual iconography was created for Jokanaan, although the usual thin white body, long black hair and red lips

Plate 5 Salome (Lindsay Kemp) confronts Jokanaan (David Haughton) in Kemp's Roundhouse production, 1977.

were retained (plate 5). An imprisoned prophet of doom in Wilde's text, at the Roundhouse a white-feathered Jokanaan descended from the skies, 'pictured as an angel brought down by Herod's archers'.[33]

This creates all sorts of conflicting interpretive possibilities. The ominous sound of mighty wings which so disturbs Herod in Wilde's version could now be associated even more obviously with the prophecies of Jokanaan. On the other hand, the dove-like descent inevitably suggests the descent of the Holy Spirit, as if Jokanaan were a presiding angel of love. As the performance continued, these associations became more complex: first, the wings were stripped away by '[n]ear-naked attendants in Herod's palace tread[ing] solemnly through the auditorium in various shades of body paint, scattering the feathers as they go',[34] an action which caused one critic to recall the dismemberment of Dionysus;[35] and then Jokanaan was killed in a manner very different from that in Wilde's version. There, Jokanaan's death is hidden from the audience, but in Kemp's production it became an iconographic tableau as the prophet died in a flurry of arrows, an image which calls to mind the death not of John the Baptist but of Saint Sebastian. Sebastian, renowned for his physical beauty, carries a particular significance for gay men; Wilde, indeed, had used the name in France as an alias, and Guido Reni's *San Sebastian* was one of the author's favourite paintings.[36] From ascetic harbinger of doom to prophet of sexual liberation, from Dionysian Master of the Revels to sacrificial victim, Jokanaan projected multiple selves and multiple interpretive possibilities, although all cohered in a gay reading of the play.

The entrance of Kemp's Salome was redolent of sophisticated cabaret. A typical complaint, indeed, was that the production fell too easily into 'Folies Bergère cliché – sequinned nipples and powdered rumps, plumes and mirrors and silver paint'.[37] This, of course, was precisely the point: in aping the conventions of heterosexual role-play, Kemp's all-male cast was challenging its assumptions. Salome first appeared at the head of a tall staircase wearing a cape of green plumage, head 'covered in a riot of painted green feathers', and descended to the strains of 'La Paloma'.[38] This exotic creation carried a double signification, for the audience would anticipate the removal of the veils of drag during the dance, which finally revealed, in a sequinned body stocking, what was known from the beginning: that beneath the layers of adornment was a middle-aged man making no pretence at conventional sexual attractiveness, a rather muscular, stocky figure with 'close-cropped ginger hair, mask-like face' and 'toothless grin'.[39] The implication is that this was an unveiling of the self, an honest exposure of the actor's essential being. The five-minute dance contributed to this effect. Lacking all conventional signs of artistic excellence, seemingly unchoreographed, Kemp 'twirls flat-footedly on the spot, registering his usual facial expressions of hope, despair, panic and vulnerability'.[40] While several reviewers discovered a kind of paradoxical grace in the dance, they seemed unable to explain how this happened, and the first response of most was in keeping with the production's rather straightforward theme of unmasking.

This theme in itself, however, creates complications. If it is possible to see the shock of the play as lying in the expression of an unfettered female desire, equally that desire can be condemned as mere vampishness, Salome as archetypal whore. All the more devastating if that desire is now transformed into a mere effect of camp, a desire sanctioned and ultimately possessed by the male. Some feminist critics have, indeed, argued against the play on similar grounds.[41] The shock dénouement, which anticipates Ken Russell's 1987 film *Salome's Last Dance*, both celebrates the validity of male homoeroticism and appropriates female sexuality for its own uses.

The green head-dress, and other touches of green throughout the production, were probably deployed to heighten the homosexual emphasis, although the significance may not have been apparent to many in the audience. Kemp perhaps took his cue from Salome's promise to the Young Syrian: if he lets her see the prophet, 'I will let fall for you a little flower, a little green flower.' Evidence that Wilde wished the colour to have greater prominence in performance comes from Charles Ricketts. Although his discussions with Wilde left unresolved the question of whether the turquoise of the sky was to be blue or green, Ricketts is quite specific in attributing to the author various additional touches of green in their initial scheme: the soldiers in 'bronze green', Salome 'green like a curious poisonous lizard'.[42]

Several commentators have pointed to the homosexual connotations of this colour. Wilde had commented on 'that curious love of green, which in individuals is always the sign of a subtle artistic temperament, and in nations is said to denote a laxity, if not a decadence, of morals'.[43] According to Neil Bartlett, Wilde may have imported the fashion for green carnations from Paris, where they

were reputedly worn by homosexual men as a sign of sexual orientation. Wilde and his supporters sported these flowers on the opening
night of *Lady Windermere's Fan* on 20 February 1892, and in so doing
the author 'declared himself to be one of an anonymous group of
men for whom the wearing of the green carnation meant homosexuality'.[44] The flower was artificial, the product of a white carnation
placed in a solution of green dye, and Bartlett argues that its
appropriateness as a homosexual sign arose from its being an 'artist's
flower', unnatural, sterile, luxurious, existing only for pleasure. In
offering the green flower to the Young Syrian, therefore, Salome
reveals 'that she is part of an elaborate imagery and system of beliefs
associated with homosexuality'.[45]

The production's flirtatious approach to gender was encapsu-
lated equally in the casting of The Incredible Orlando as Herodias.
His name suggesting affinities with the hermaphroditic, eponymous
hero/ine of Virginia Woolf's novel, The Incredible Orlando paro-
died the domineering Herodias which Wilde's version of the story
had already subtly undermined in diminishing her motivating role
in the tragedy. In Kemp's production Herodias was a black-lipped,
bald-headed monster, contemptuous of Herod's sexual attraction to
her daughter; but her crude, tyrannical appearance and cruel laughter were ironised by the huge plastic breasts projecting from the
chest of a man in drag. Again, this creates a double response: evidently playful and celebratory, the figure could nevertheless be taken
as a parody not of Herodias but of her sex.

The only character who did not seem fully integrated into the
production was Vladek Sheybal's Herod. Sheybal was the one
member of the cast whose background was predominantly in
spoken drama as opposed to mime and dance, and his comparatively
conventional performance was at odds with the riotous happenings
around him. His make-up differed little from that of previous
Herods, with long, thin, drooping moustache and heavy, dark
shadows around the slanting eyes. Where his playing differed from
tradition was in its comparative understatement, which diminished

the credibility of his passion for Salome. However, the intention may have been to belittle the conventions of heterosexual performance: as the one 'straight' role in the production, Herod became cannon-fodder for the taunts of Herodias and her daughter.

While visually the production was characterised by display and excess, there were nevertheless more subtle effects which gestured towards the legacy of symbolism. The programme for the production stated that the company aimed to 'explore the limits of experience, and through discipline present that experience in theatrical terms as a gift to the audience and as an invitation for them to go beyond themselves, even momentarily'.[46] The production was clearly aiming for the effect of a dream, or at least of an altered state of consciousness. The action was played almost in slow motion, with lengthy entrances, exits and parades contributing to a playing time of an hour and three-quarters. Climactic moments were frozen, as when 'Jokanaan slides by imperceptible degrees under Salome's silver cloak up to the moment of her blood-drinking kiss', while comparable dream-like states were also induced 'by changing to ghastly floor-level lighting whenever the prophet's voice interrupts the festivities'.[47] Kemp believed that it was possible to create a sense of enchantment through 'the art of hypnosis, which is an essential part of the artist's technique'.[48] That this was a powerful and influential strategy with regard to *Salome* is confirmed by the fact that the next London production, the last we shall consider in detail, exploited similar techniques of hypnotic motion and lighting in a performance which was nevertheless unconcerned to follow the homosexual emphases of Kemp's work.

STEVEN BERKOFF PRODUCTIONS, 1988–1990

Steven Berkoff's *Salome* generated a great deal of mostly positive critical attention. In many ways this work encompasses *two* productions, with the same scenic design and similar performance styles, but wholly different casts; and each of these productions played at two different venues. The play was first staged at Dublin's Gate Theatre in April 1988, in a highly successful experiment which was again well received when it was revived for the Edinburgh Festival in August 1989. In November of that year *Salome* played with a new cast at the National's Lyttelton Theatre, initially to fill a gap in the schedules occasioned by the postponement of another play, but interest was sufficiently strong for the production to transfer to the Phoenix Theatre the following January.

The most significant of the wholesale cast changes at the National was that Berkoff himself took on the role of Herod, who had been played by Alan Stanford. The production became indisputably identified with Berkoff as actor–director, which, as we shall see, had an importance far beyond the direct consequences for the staging of the play, which themselves were visually obvious and far-reaching. Stanford played Herod as a corpulent figure, 'fleshy, petulant, oddly dignified, unmistakably Wildean',[49] a 'carmine-lipped heavyweight',[50] a portrayal which followed in the footsteps of Beardsley in associating Herod with the author. Berkoff could hardly have cut a more different figure: thinner, rather gaunt, with very close-cropped hair, his Herod seemed to gesture not towards Wilde as author, but towards himself as director: an inevitable comparison given his dual role, but one apparently insisted upon in Berkoff's visual and aural semiology. Bullet-headed, his general appearance redolent of the cartoon malevolence he had recently displayed in the enormous commercial successes of Hollywood's *Beverley Hills Cop* and *Rambo: First Blood II*, Berkoff's pre-eminence was magnified by his brightly patterned waistcoat and red lips, overtly colourful touches in a largely chiaroscuro design, and by what came out of that mouth: strangled vowels, elongated and mannered enunciation, everything played to excess in a manner which in this respect at least compelled comparison with his previous work.

There was the usual divided response to Berkoff's performance: either he was a superlatively theatrical talent, or a ranting egomaniac devoid of subtlety in thought or expression. But if many felt that Stanford's was the better individual performance, nevertheless the substitution of Berkoff produced a more coherent production, as can be seen in the way the other changes preserved the original, radical conception. As Michael Billington remarked when the play transferred to the National, '[t]he production overturns everything we prize in the British theatre: the autonomy of the individual actor, representational accuracy, swift, light speaking'.[51]

The most common view was that Berkoff had set the play in the 1920s, although he himself stated less specifically that it was set 'in a period close to Oscar's own time'.[52] The action unfolded at an affluent dinner party, with music provided by an onstage pianist (Roger Doyle, who also composed the music, deliberately minimalist in contrast to Strauss; he was replaced in the London cast by Eleanor Alberga, but Doyle's music was retained). The device of designating the minor characters – Jews, Syrians, Romans – as dinner guests created a uniform visual style made still more homogeneous by the favourite Berkoff technique of replacing set and props by a choreographed and ever-moving human chorus acting in unison. Berkoff was developing an idea he had encountered in the work of the French mime artist Jacques le Coq, according to which the chorus was 'able to be and reflect whatsoever you wished', conveying 'atmosphere and emotion . . . The body is the unconscious mind at work, while the talking head may be more likened to the engine that sets it in motion.'[53] This technique undoubtedly contributed to the dreamlike effect which was such an important feature of the production.

Whereas Max Reinhardt had long ago represented the excessive luxury of Herod's court iconically, by filling the stage with extravagant drapes and props, Berkoff and his set-designer Robert Ballagh imaginatively took the opposite course and left the stage almost entirely bare. In place of the lavish harmonies of colour conceived by Wilde and executed by many designers, Ballagh's set and David Blight's costumes recalled Beardsley's black and white illustrations, the monochrome picture fractured only occasionally, for example by Herod's red lips and brightly coloured waistcoat, while a cold white moonlight shone throughout, with only occasional variations, as when a pink spotlight illuminated the Dance of the Seven Veils. There were no props: when, for instance, Berkoff as Herod lit a cigarette, the action was pure mime, as if the character literally embodied the materialist world he inhabited.

This consistent use of mime also correlated startlingly with the remark of the First Soldier (in Wilde's text) early in the play that the Jews 'only believe in things that one cannot see', the stage becoming slowly more populated by unseen presences which gained greater credence in comparison to the monochrome world on stage. That Salome (Olwen Fouere, then Katharine Schlesinger in London) remained fully clothed while miming both the dropping of the veils and the kissing of Jokanaan's invisible head reinforced the impression she gave of being a rather petulant, wilful adolescent. The effect of Salome's 'Englishness', which had been created, deliberately or otherwise, in such London productions as those at the Bijou in 1905, the King's Hall in 1906, and the Savoy in 1931, had previously seemed rather incongruous; here, it was in keeping with Berkoff's conception of the play.

Berkoff had earlier experimented with many similar motifs of theme, style and performance in such pieces as *Decadence*, one of his own plays, and setting *Salome* in the 1920s clearly invited the audience – particularly, perhaps, the London audience – to think of the fabled indulgence not only of that decade but of the present time. As we have seen, the most imaginative productions of the play had rejected historical realism, which creates a sterile theatrical experience, and almost invariably sought to suggest an equivalence between the biblical period and Wilde's. Berkoff, of course, was far from being the first to suggest a more contemporary significance, while as we shall see in the next chapter Alla Nazimova's extraordinary film version of 1922 suggested parallels with the same decade in which Berkoff apparently set his production. The Gate/National *Salome* gained much of its suggestiveness by indicating these overt or subliminal equivalences between no fewer than four historical periods.

Berkoff argued in an interview that the play had been presented so infrequently on the English stage because 'our theatre prefers plays about concepts – class war, for example – to those about feelings. The British can't cope with emotions; but what Oscar Wilde dealt with was pure feeling – sensuality, love, desire, passion.'[54] He states a similar case in his introduction to the Faber edition of the play. Curiously, however, the production itself consistently flattened feeling into stylisation. Comparing this *Salome* to the plays of Noel Coward, one reviewer at Edinburgh commented that 'passion is here deemed bad manners, a reduction of Wilde's purpose'.[55] The comparison is significant, and far from damaging. In Coward's plays, as in the society comedies of Wilde, the sexual tensions are often negotiated through etiquette, an approach which can create powerful conflict between wit and sexual emotion, or indeed expose sexuality as a matter of style. The reading of the works of both dramatists as homosexual has often depended on this observation. If anything, those who have responded with hostility to *Salome* have tended to do so on the grounds of emotional and aesthetic excess, and in drawing the play back into the context of Wilde's major achievements in society comedy Berkoff suggested a far more subtle interplay of forces.

Unlike Kemp, Berkoff made few alterations to Wilde's text, although several sequences of dialogue were transposed and many archaisms and awkwardnesses eliminated, particularly in the first half: for example, 'one might' was consistently changed to 'you would', 'aspect' to 'look'; 'You are making me wait upon your pleasure' was changed to 'You keep me waiting!', while 'I have ever been kind towards thee' became 'I have always been kind to you.' However, very few cuts were made, and only two of any significance, both of which were theological debates. Berkoff omitted the discussion between the five Jews concerning the invisibility of God, as well as the lines immediately following in which Herod asks if Jokanaan is Elias the prophet; and the discussion of Jesus' miracles shortly afterwards was also cut. These debates were, perhaps, of only implicit significance to the play as it was performed in Berkoff's productions, but more obviously the textual editing did something to shorten an interpretation of the play which, astonishingly, took well over two hours to perform.

The reason for this lies in the production's extremely stylised and unnaturally slow methods of enunciation and movement. The actors moved throughout as if under water, or on a lunar landscape, creating a dream-like and metronomic effect heightened by the piano accompaniment. Similarly, most of the lines were delivered excessively slowly, projecting, in the words of one reviewer, 'a consistent vision of an exaggerated norm',[56] suggesting again that the decadence of this play has nothing to do with deviation and everything to do with conformity. In defamiliarising the enunciation of everyday words Berkoff risked unwanted comic effects, but the overall impression was of an Ionesco-like paradox: a cast which spoke 'as if they had only just learnt the use of their tongues'[57] thereby focused attention on the words themselves. In consequence the language came across variously as pure aestheticism, a trance-like manner of speaking for sound rather than sense, or on the contrary as heightening the moral stakes by giving the audience time to reflect on the implications of what was being said. For one critic, at least, 'Berkoff allows [the] litany of incantations to take wing and show us, possibly for the first time, the dark morality beneath its seeming decadence.'[58] Berkoff himself argued that such an approach treated the language delicately, as if it were something fragile and easily broken;[59] and certainly this was a sympathetic manner of treating dialogue which had so often been ridiculed as unspeakable, and it worked harmoniously with the choric movement.

Many suggested, unfairly, that in London Berkoff created a normative style of speaking so that he could create a more distinctive role for himself. It is true that the effect of downplaying the erotic was to diminish Salome's role and to emphasise Herod's; but the real and logical exception to the dominant style was not Herod but Jokanaan, played by Joe Savino in Dublin and Edinburgh, and by Rory Edwards in London. Isolated in the cistern (a dark square which kept him permanently in view) and caught in a spotlight, unmoving while the dinner guests were constantly choreographed into different friezes and patterns, this Jokanaan once again appeared the opposite to his counterpart in previous productions. Usually Jokanaan's prophecies are delivered as if from a dimension beyond our own, his prophetic judgements contrasted to the earthly sensuality of Herod's court. In this production, however, it was the court which appeared as if trapped in a dream-state, detached from the processes and obligations of the world, while Jokanaan, literally earth-bound, spoke in a booming voice as if attempting to recall them to wakefulness. Jokanaan was of course further distinguished from the rest of the cast by his appearance, bearded and bare-chested.

All things considered, this was perhaps the most startling and effective treatment of the play since Tairov's production at Moscow's Kamerny Theatre in 1917. All the more unfortunate, then, that at Edinburgh Berkoff, his cast, and the Irish press became embroiled in public rancour which detracted from the artistic achievement. The most obvious focus of disagreement concerned remarks Berkoff made in a BBC interview: in a stage Irish accent, he said he had had difficulty in getting his cast out of the pub, and that the only way he could get them to visualise dramatic values was by asking them to imagine drinking a pint of Guinness slowly.[60] Not surprisingly, this generated hostility in the Irish press and unhappiness in the company, musician Roger Doyle stating that the cast felt 'hurt and humiliated'.[61] Berkoff publicly apologised in a letter to Irish newspapers, claiming the remarks were meant humorously and affectionately, as an attempt 'to debunk the clichés so fondly held by the Brits regarding the Irish'; and although he accepted that 'as an Englishman, I have probably no right to the privilege', he assumed with a Wildean flourish that 'most people will know that I am not serious; let those of modest works talk "seriously"'.[62]

Behind the particular misunderstanding, however, lay a more general and serious problem of cultural appropriation which was immediately perceived by Irish commentators in the response of English critics to the Edinburgh performances in August 1989. Without exception, English reviewers seemed to regard the production as 'Berkoff's *Salome*', and all the men and women on the stage as merely players. In a piece headed 'Licence under Discipline', for instance, the critic of *The Times* argued for Berkoff as *auteur*, commenting on his stage 'vocabulary', and stating that in Berkoff '[t]he indulgent Wilde meets a master of stage discipline';[63] the *Observer*'s review was typical in thinking that 'Berkoff is very well served by his actors, the Gate Company from Dublin'.[64] The use of the possessive makes the assumed power relationship all too clear, and disregarded what Irish critics saw as the – at least – strongly collaborative nature of the project.

That this argument should have erupted at this particular moment is, perhaps, peculiarly appropriate. At the very time when post-structuralist debate about sexuality and the self was beginning to find that its arguments had been prefigured in Wilde's life and works, Berkoff staged a production of *Salome* during which that debate came to be grafted on to equally contested notions of national identity and cultural imperialism. Along with a recent American production which placed the play's imagery of disease in the context of the contemporary AIDS crisis, Berkoff's adventure provides further evidence that *Salome* will continue to command potent and exciting re-interpretation well past the turning of our own *fin de siècle*.

CHAPTER FOUR

TRANSFORMATIONS

That a *Gesamtkunstwerk* by a major dramatist should have generated many transformations in other media is hardly surprising. What is remarkable is that several of these transformations became more prominent than Wilde's *Salome* itself. The illustrations by Aubrey Beardsley, the opera by Richard Strauss, one or two dance routines and several films all testify to the capacity of the play to fire the creative imagination of major artists in spheres related to but distinct from the stage for which the play was written.

AUBREY BEARDSLEY, 1894

The first and in some ways the most radical transformation of Wilde's piece took place early. It cannot be established categorically that Wilde was personally responsible for selecting Aubrey Beardsley as the illustrator of the English version of *Salome* published on 9 February 1894, though it seems inconceivable that it was arranged without the dramatist's consent. Undoubtedly the assignment had a certain appropriateness: not only were the two men acquainted, having first encountered each other at the home of the artist's mentor Sir Edward Burne-Jones on 12 July 1891,[1] but their aesthetic tastes and opinions had been fashioned by much the same forces, with James McNeill Whistler a key influence on them both. Even had this not been the case, Beardsley's growing reputation as an innovative and exciting black and white draughtsman of unusual facility and fecund invention would have made him a natural choice as illustrator for *Salome*; but in the event the indelible association of

Beardsley's name with that of *Salome* was to prove of equivocal value to Wilde, if not invariably detrimental to his image.

Beardsley's artistic genius and brief fame closely mirrored the *Zeitgeist*. As Holbrook Jackson wrote (not without some personal animus), '[t]emporally he was so appropriate that an earlier appearance would have been as premature as a later would have been tardy'.[2] Only twenty-five when he died of tuberculosis at Menton in March 1898, Beardsley conveyed in his art an air of the sickroom – all limpid finesse and fervid luxuriance – which appealed to the mood of the times. Rumour claimed that he was incapable of working unless the room was in total darkness save for the light from 'two tall ormulu Empire candlesticks',[3] and this reputation as a nocturnal fantasist added to the pallid glamour of his personality.

His first major commission offered him the opportunity to illustrate a two-volume edition of Malory's *Morte Darthur*, which appeared in monthly parts beginning in June 1893, and aroused much interest. Meanwhile, the first issue of *The Studio* in April 1893 featured a Beardsley design on its cover, and contained an appreciative article by the prominent American Quaker etcher Joseph Pennell, accompanied by several studies executed by the talented newcomer. Of these the outstanding example was a pen, ink and green-watercolour wash drawing inspired by Wilde's piece, showing Salome with the severed head of the Baptist, and embellished with a quotation from the play: *J'ai Baisé Ta Bouche Iokanaan, J'ai Baisé Ta Bouche*.[4] This picture, which had also been put on view at the Spring Exhibition of the New English Art Club, seems to have led John Lane to commission Beardsley to execute the illustrations for the English version of *Salome*, to be published by The Bodley Head, founded by Lane and his partner Charles Elkin Matthews.[5]

Beardsley would appear to have begun work for the English translation of *Salome* during the summer of 1893. The designs, for which he received a fee of fifty guineas,[6] included the front cover, title-page, contents-page, tailpiece, and a signature for the back cover, along with eleven full-page black and white illustrations.[7] In visual terms Beardsley's *Salome* represents one of the finest books of the century, but its admirers divide into those who believe that in several ways the artist wilfully bypassed or misrepresented the poet's self-consciously crafted atmosphere in order both to satirise Wilde's aims and indulge personal imaginative preoccupations without being over-concerned to match them to those of his author, and those who consider that Beardsley subtly captured the true flavour of the work. At all events Lane (and quite possibly Wilde too) was unhappy with several of the original batch submitted, and Beardsley reluctantly introduced changes which perhaps satisfied neither party.

In recent years it has become almost orthodox to justify Beardsley's apparent selfishness or insensitivity towards Wilde's words by claiming that text and pictures are so closely related that they constitute the outcome of 'one of the most successful collaborations of poet and illustrator in history'.[8] Advocates of such an approach suggest that the apparent impudence, irrelevance and independence of Beardsley's drawings in fact mirror the spirit of the play relatively faithfully. The artist's alleged parodic mockery finds an echo in the work's own comic exaggerations, while the self-reflexive element which has been much commented on is again replicated in Beardsley's seemingly textually unresponsive imagings: 'Beardsley offers, in support of Wilde's daring exploration of the possibilities and limits of a self-reflexive life, an equally startling visualisation of that life.'[9] Critics also suggest the sexual power-struggle in the text finds its graphic counterpart in the potent illustrative matter. For example, in a series of perceptive analyses Linda Gertner Zatlin has demonstrated just how explicitly Beardsley mirrored Wilde's assessment of the nature of Salome's rebellion against the spirit of patriarchy she confronts:

> Salome is a woman who clearly understands the reliance of male sexuality on female sexuality for its definition. She is angered by the refusal of John the Baptist to accept the lure of her sexuality, for when she desires most to be vindicated as a woman by the conventions of

the patriarchy, she is rebuked. To restore her sense of her sexuality and as a rebuke to the patriarchy, she defies the social conventions which confine her. Like her mother Herodias, Salome uses the only power she has in male society, her body, to bargain with Herod for John's head. In arousing Herod through her dance, Salome succeeds in reconciling him to her ends, manipulating the patriarchal authority into achieving what she as a female could not.[10]

Beardsley's work has also come under scrutiny from Ewa Kuryluk, who traces the anthropological and mythological strands in the Salome story with particular relation to the grotesque in artworks down the centuries. For Kuryluk Salome's 'strange figure and story . . . symbolised the obscure paradoxes of conscious desires and fears', and in her view Beardsley's illustrations to *Salome*

> provide the European tradition with a formidably epigonistic [derivative] epilogue, tying together remembrances of an archaic earth-and-moon goddess with the caricatures of a fin-de-siècle femme fatale oscillating between the universal and the local, the obscene and the sacrilegious. Beardsley mixes together distinct times and cultures in a unique pursuit of grotesque heterogeneity. His illustrations transcend the territory delineated by Wilde's apocalyptic drama.[11]

One of Beardsley's agreed choices of subject, Salome's climactic encounter with St John's head, was redrawn from that exhibited at the New English Art Club and reproduced in *The Studio*. Beardsley dispensed with the original's elaborate curlicues and fronds around and behind the kneeling figure of the princess in order to focus on a white-robed Salome who glares at her ghastly trophy, by setting them against a white cloud-like background featuring a mass of stylised perihelions equally evocative of storm, thick foliage, the night-sky, or even clusters of blood-cells. The overornateness of the first Salome's snaky locks is toned down, though the Baptist still retains *his* Medusaesque appearance which mirrors that of his murderess. The firm regular ellipse suggestive of the rim of the cistern has been replaced with an irregular lozenge with a broken edge, although the watery area (with its proud lotus and its flaccid reed) into which John's blood flows in an artistic stream is scarcely altered from the first version. The Whistlerian peacocks' feathers are abandoned, though their loss is compensated for at other points during the sequence and form the dominant feature of Beardsley's original sketch for the front cover.[12] The title is now 'The Climax'.

Associated with 'The Climax', and in some respects duplicating it, is a new drawing entitled 'The Dancer's Reward'. Once again the facts of decapitation are treated decoratively, even wittily, with the bare black sinewy arm of the Executioner thrusting up from the bottom frame of the picture to present the trophy on its rimless salver to Salome, who bends predator-like over it with one finger touching the spilled blood. Here extraneous background embellishment is dispensed with: the princess and the head from which the oozing blood hangs suspended like strips of ragged black cloth constitute virtually the entire scene. If 'The Climax' is a celebration of line, 'The Dancer's Reward' is a triumph of mass, though tiny delicate details – the roses on the inside of Salome's cloak, her tiny discarded slippers, the fine hairs on the Executioner's upraised arm – attest to Beardsley's flair for minutiae which induce subtle responses through extreme economy of means.

In such scenes the necrophiliac undertones of Salome's action may have stimulated the artist's pen, and the lurid subject-matter derives directly from the play. These illustrations, if macabre, possess direct relevance to the textual matter, as does 'The Eyes of Herod' with its assemblage of diverse elements – towering twin cypresses; magnificent stylised rose-trellis; single peacock with clouds of plumage; Gothic candelabra borne by two naked putti – united under the gaze of a peacock-plumed Salome who is scrutinised in turn through narrowed eyes by a bloated Herod. Equally pertinent are the exuberant swirls which create 'The Peacock Skirt' in which Salome, in half-profile, is crowned with another more lavish peacock head-dress echoed by the floral crescents and moon-marks of the eponymous skirt, which might equally be taken as depicting the dark night-sky of the action. The second figure whom the princess almost encircles is surely to be taken as that of the Young Syrian dominated into granting Salome's whim to have the Prophet brought forth, unless it is meant for Iokanaan who certainly finds a place in 'John and Salome', a curiously static confrontation between two elongated androgynous protagonists which has complete textual relevance but which was inexplicably excluded from the 1894 publication.

In an inscribed copy of *Salome* Wilde was to claim that only Beardsley apart from himself knew the true nature of the Dance of the Seven Veils 'and can see that invisible dance'.[13] Its graphic equivalent may therefore be thought to be the illustration provided under the title of 'The Stomach Dance' (plate 6), another superlative example of Beardsley's innovative approach to illustration. The print is split horizontally into black earth and white sky, against which is superimposed the dancer's form, while lower down a strange grotesque crouches at her right foot accompanying the *danse du ventre* on a long-necked stringed instrument. The gleeful minstrel's undisguised erection testifies to the erotic impact made by the sinuous, bare-breasted, rose-nippled Salome, but a major distinction between this routine and that often presented on stage is that the dancer's features in no way portray seductive allure but are set in a mask-like stare which emphasises her adoption of the role of avenger rather than temptress. Her accoutrements too are more those of some contemporary courtesan *en déshabille*. The same applies to the more conventional view of Salome supplied in 'The Black Cape', which resembles nothing so much as a slightly hyperbolised contemporary fashion-plate, though the protective cape in Zatlin's view represents a Beardsleyesque warning to women to keep their predatory designs on male prerogatives well under wraps.

The element of homoeroticism present in several of the pictures is notable, and is not only inoffensive, but has some textual justification: the intimately linked male figures depicted in the frontispiece entitled 'The Woman in the Moon' observing the moon

Plate 6 'The Stomach Dance' by Aubrey Beardsley (an
illustration from the English translation of *Salome*, 1894).

among the clouds of the night-sky are the Page and the Young Syrian of the play's opening. But for a drape over one shoulder, the Syrian is totally naked, with genitals exposed; the Page's is a more androgynous presence, long-haired, in a long robe fastened with a tassel, reminding us that in several productions the role of the Page has been assigned to a woman. Perhaps the second figure is intended for Salome, but the lack of elaboration in costume or coiffure would seem to contradict this, and both figures are almost certainly masculine.

So far it might appear that Beardsley had not unduly flouted the traditional principle of *rapport* between text and pictures. This stance is less easily maintained in the case of other offerings, where it has been argued that the wayward artist interpreted his mandate far more freely than he had warrant for.

Indefensible to some in terms of Beardsley's brief is the frontispiece's caricature of Wilde which adorns the moon's face. Beside this is placed what many have identified as the notorious green carnation much favoured as a badge of identification by homosexuals of the period, though it may be nothing more sinister than a rose. Wilde's fleshly features also crop up on at least two further occasions, once in those of the showman-character in 'Enter Herodias' who presents the queen to an unseen audience, and again in the face of the Tetrarch who gazes at Salome in 'The Eyes of Herod'. While such devices strike some observers as witty private jokes or as indicative of Wilde's presence as the play's principal spectator, others query their fitness in work undertaken to complement and enhance the vision of a fellow-artist.

John Lane does not appear to have objected to the nude Syrian of the frontispiece, or to the male comradeship latent in the naked Page (bisected by a drape) mourning the dead Syrian in 'A Platonic Lament', but other nakednesses invoked his censure. While he missed or ignored the aroused lutanist in 'The Stomach Dance', he ordained that penises be expunged on both a horned hermaphrodite and a naked love-god adorning the draft title-page, and that the nude male attendant on Salome's mother in 'Enter Herodias' be fitted with the obligatory if exiguously attached fig-leaf which seems actually designed to draw maximum attention to itself. In the case of the first version of 'The Toilette of Salome' the masturbatory pre-occupation of the central figure herself and at least one of her male servants, and the nudity of both the princess and another attendant led to the substitution of a completely fresh drawing, magnificent and entirely uncontroversial but for the presence of Zola's *Nana*, *The Golden Ass* and the work of the Marquis de Sade among the works of literature on the shelves of an attenuated dressing-table. Here, where Salome sports a marvellous picture-hat and a Pierrot plays the ingra-tiating beautician, there is no attempt to echo the oriental timbre of the text: the picture gives us the spirit of Beardsley's milieu rather than Wilde's. Apologists argue that this is a perfectly legitimate pro-cedure to give added resonance to Wilde's prose-poem; detractors see a brash attempt to outshine the sun.

Whatever the truth, Beardsley's open depiction of male or female bodily parts is unlikely to offend today, but some may feel that in introducing coyness and prurient references into a work of frank rather than covert sexuality, Beardsley helped to create an ambience in which Wilde's play could hardly be assessed fairly. His best evocations of Wilde's principal figures capture something of their quality, but sometimes the connotations of the accessories with which the artist surrounds his protagonists may divert readers from what Wilde strove to achieve. The fey, narcissistic, slily priapic, lisping figures with their powder-puffs and black dominoes, dainty slippers and secretive reptilian joys, the Thumbelina-style Salome of the tailpiece, buried in a powder-pot by a satyr and a major-domo, may be considered to reduce Wilde's disturbing fable to no more than a fanciful piece of pretty nonsense, although here again Zatlin argues that the final drawing depicts the patriarchy's efforts to trivi-alise and prettify what feminists interpret as a heroic struggle against masculinity.[14]

However, Wilde either did not object too strenuously to his

young protégé's decorations or was simply too generous-hearted (or vain) to express his disappointment. In the month of publication he could tell Mrs Patrick Campbell that Beardsley's drawings were 'quite wonderful',[15] and when Leonard Smithers published *Volpone* with Beardsley's illustrations after the artist's death, Wilde told the publisher that the quality of the *Salome* work far outshone that expended on the Jonson.[16] On this point, opinions may differ, but at all events the Beardsley legacy to *Salome* proved to be an enduring one, not least in the field of the performing arts. From the dancer Loie Fuller's peacock costume of 1907, through Evreinov's experimental stage production the following year, to Karsavina's ballet costume of 1913 and Nazimova's film of 1922, Beardsley and *Salome* seemed inseparably linked. In 1989 both set and costumes for Steven Berkoff's presentation demonstrated that the artist's influence remained as potent as ever.

RICHARD STRAUSS, 1905

The success Wilde's play enjoyed in Germany when first presented in Hedwig Lachmann's translation at Breslau during 1901 formed the prelude to probably its most exciting and enduring artistic transformation. Although Frederick Delius had previously negotiated with Wilde's literary executors for the libretto rights, he had hesitated before embarking on an opera,[17] and as a result of the enthusiasm of Anton Lindner, a Viennese poet, *Salome* was brought to the attention of Richard Strauss. 'The bold bad man of music at the turn of the century',[18] Strauss was at the time not merely Germany's leading composer, but also conductor to the Berlin Court Opera and the Berlin Philharmonic Orchestra.[19] Lindner, who had already supplied the words for Strauss's *Hochzeitlich Lied* (1897–98), now ventured to send him a copy of Lachmann's German translation of Wilde's French original, accompanied by an offer to create a libretto for a putative opera from it. The composer himself was one of those who witnessed the play privately presented at Reinhardt's Kleines Theater in Berlin on 15 November 1902 with Gertrud Eysoldt in the title-role, and indicated to an acquaintance on that occasion that he was already engaged in creating a music-drama on the Salome theme. Lindner had indeed provided him with 'a few cleverly versified opening scenes', but inspiration only flared when Strauss returned to Lachmann's text and set the opening words of her translation: 'Wie schön ist die Prinzessin Salome heute Nacht.' The realisation that the German prose version, suitably purged of its more digressive and exotic passages, would prove a more conducive point of departure than Lindner's verse resulted in Strauss setting Wilde's own phrases, even if in an attenuated adaptation. In Lachmann's faithful if unflamboyant prose rendering of Wilde, suitably pared down to what Strauss believed to be its essential core, he found his route to a new manner of handling words for music which led on to some of the finest achievements in twentieth-century opera.

Strauss wrote two separate versions of the vocal parts, one geared to Lachmann's translation, the other to suit Wilde's French original.[20] In both instances, however, changes there naturally had to be if a leaner, tauter text for musical setting was to result. Several of Wilde's characters were deleted, including the young Roman Tigellinus and the Nubian of the exposition, while Herodias's Page, the Soldiers, and the Cappadocian retained few of their original lines. Information deemed irrelevant to the central plot was also eradicated: the fate of Herodias's first husband in the same cistern-prison that the Baptist is to die in; the familial background of Narraboth and also his friendship with the Page (a role which Strauss was always to insist be played by a woman); the discussions of rival brands of religion; the political context supplied by allusions to Caesar and the King of Cappadocia, all disappeared. Verbal elaborations and repetitions which contributed to *Salome*'s characteristic verbal texture were often given short shrift at the composer's hands, so that the discussion of Herod's favourite wines, the accretive images of peacocks, the cumulative listing of precious stones with which the Tetrarch attempts to divert his step-daughter from her gruesome quarry, were all suppressed. Certain of the Irishman's more decorative and extravagant comparisons were excised by the more prosaic German, as in the case of the likening of the Baptist's eyes to 'black holes burned by torches in a Tyrian tapestry', or the picture of a naked moon refusing to permit the clouds to cover her nudity. Nor did Strauss always capitalise on much of Wilde's recurrent imagery: he refused to assign a leitmotif to the moon, which not only plays an indispensable role in the total impact of the play (Wilde playfully told Bernhardt it was the leading performer), but might well be regarded as the arbitress of the piece's overall action.

Critics have often objected to certain aspects of Strauss's textual tamperings, such as the scaling down of the part of the Cappadocian, which precludes the provision of several pieces of information which enrich the play's exposition. If the identification of the offstage Herodias or of the Tetrarch's taste in wines is dispensable, the omission of any reference to the (unhistorical) murder of Herodias's first husband in the cistern deprives that location of its sinister associations, veils the Second Soldier's emphasis on the Executioner's unquestioning loyalty in obeying orders, and reduces the extra *frisson* which might accompany Herodias's later action in withdrawing the ring of death from Herod's finger once the order for Jokanaan's dispatch has been reluctantly given.

Finally, one might wish for rather less ambiguity in the presentation of the heroine. Despite Strauss's omission of any verbal clues as to Salome's chaste condition, the sensuous quality of the music does very little to confirm it, and occasionally might be felt to contradict it. Through the textual lacunae Strauss may have hoped to convince the censor that his princess was a stranger to sexual desire, but the music is hardly in keeping with the composer's vision of Salome as an uncorrupted sixteen-year-old and not 'a cheap seductress'. While his omissions may be held to increase the significance of Salome's sexual awakening by the Baptist, in some respects they may be said to reduce the impact of that achievement, although this factor is less obvious in performance, where few singers have been able (and others have not tried) to convey the presumed degree of physical inexperience that Strauss apparently had in mind.

The alterations affecting linguistic register offer less cause for concern, in that readers doubtless accept that Wilde's poetic prose is intended to exude its own verbal melody, and that for Strauss to have set the entire text of the play would have constituted a gross instance of gilding the lily. Faithful to the spirit and mood of his original, the composer very wisely saw that many of Wilde's intended effects could be more effectively transposed into their musical equivalents rather than retained in textual form. However, while many of the Maeterlinckian repetitions which form such a feature of the original were excised, where the patterned nature of the original offered him precedents for a sensitive musical response, Strauss did not scorn to introduce some of his own additions into the libretto, as when he rearranged the word-order in the translation before him, or when he rephrased Jokanaan's lines relating to the coming of the Messiah which begin in German 'Wenn er kommt, werden die verodeten Staaten frohloken' ('When he comes, then shall all the desolate places be joyful') to enable him to introduce the words 'Wenn er kommt' three times rather than once.

Work on the score began in earnest in August 1903, Strauss starting operations in a tiny room at the home of his parents-in-law in Upper Bavaria. Some have argued that he 'worked backwards', beginning with the celebrated Dance of the Seven Veils and Salome's lengthy final monologue, but the manuscript evidence shows that the Dance was not actually completed until August 1905, at least two months after the rest of the score which the composer inscribed with the date 20 June 1905.

By that time Strauss had been able to play most of the score to Gustav Mahler, then Director of the Vienna Court Opera, who hoped to give *Salome* its world première in the Austrian capital; but given the strict censorship prevailing in Vienna, particularly where the depiction of biblical figures was concerned, the opportunity passed to the Royal Opera House, Dresden, where Strauss's *Feuersnot* had been first staged four years previously, and whose chief conductor, Ernst von Schuh, was a man for whose work the composer had much respect. However, at Dresden he found himself sandwiched between a director, Willi Wirk, determined to realise the potential for 'perversity and outrage' in the piece, and a company in which both vocalists and instrumentalists protested that the music made impossible demands upon their professional competence. Richard Aldrich, the New York music critic, was later to observe: 'The score of *Salome* is unquestionably the most stupendously difficult that has ever been written, the most complex, the most exacting upon the skill of the individual players.'[21] Marie Wittich, to whom Salome was assigned, also protested on moral grounds. She allegedly insisted that she would reject the role: 'I won't do it, I'm a decent woman.'

On 9 December 1905 the world première of *Salome* met with considerable acclaim, the Dresden audience according the cast thirty-eight curtain-calls. But despite the general approbation of his peers and several favourable notices – Gerhard Schultz claimed that 'Never until now has a sound like this been heard in the opera house' – Strauss found critical controversy quick to kindle. In Vienna Mahler had already been informed by the censor that 'the representation of events which belong to the realm of sexual pathology is not suitable for our Court stage', and now a first-night reviewer for a Berlin newspaper reported: 'this poem is not lacking in more strongly artistic qualities; but the scene in which Salome kisses the severed head of John is for me the most nauseating that has been brought to the stage so far'.[22] Before long Adam Roder was to draw more general and possibly more damaging inferences from the presentation: 'if sadists, masochists, lesbians and homosexuals come and presume to tell us that their crazy world of spirit and feeling is to be interpreted as manifestations of art, then steps must be taken in the interests of *health*. Art has no interest in sanctifying bestialities which arise from sexual perversity. Only this cry matters: out with them!'[23] Such comments of course reflected, to some degree at least, distaste for Wilde's original play, which many believed did not merit the musical artistry Strauss had bestowed upon it. One of the composer's French advisers, Romain Rolland, very quickly let Strauss know his own opinion of the matter:

> Oscar Wilde's *Salome* was not worthy of you . . . In spite of the pretentious affectations of the style, there is an undeniable power in Wilde's poem; but it has a nauseous and sickly atmosphere about it: it exudes vice and literature . . . Wilde's Salome, and all those who surround her, except that poor creature Jokanaan, are unwholesome, unclean, hysterical or alcoholic beings, stinking of sophisticated and perfumed corruption. – In vain do you transfigure your subject, increase its vigour a hundredfold, and envelop it in a Shakespearean atmosphere – in vain do you ascribe moving accents to your Salome: you transcend your subject, but you can't make one forget it.[24]

Such strictures, whether voiced publicly or privately, did not deter the average opera-goer from sampling Strauss's latest offering in person, for by the end of 1907 the piece had been presented in more than fifty cities in Germany and abroad, and on fifty separate occasions in Berlin itself, where the vulnerable religious sensibilities of Kaiser Wilhelm II and his consort were mollified by the ingenious if incongruous device of concluding the action with the sudden appearance in the sky of the Star of Bethlehem. As *Salome* began to make its way in the opera-houses of the world, so the bastions of convention and polite taste gradually caved in. Banned from the boards of the Vienna Court Opera until 1918, a decision which in part led to Gustav Mahler's resignation as principal conductor, *Salome* still surfaced at the Volkstheater there, performed by a touring company from Breslau, and in May 1906 Graz undertook what the capital shied away from, the presentation attracting such enthusiasts as Mahler, Puccini, and Adolf Hitler.[25] Arturo Toscanini premièred the piece (very badly) in Milan in 1906 and in December Strauss himself conducted the work in Turin; initial performances in the French and Belgian capitals followed during 1907.

But it was from the more prudish English-speaking world that the fiercest opposition was to be expected, and in the case of America the fears of the pessimists were confirmed by the reception accorded a single benefit performance of *Salome* at New York's Metropolitan Opera on 22 January 1907 under the baton of Alfred Hertz. The Herod was the same Karl Burian who had created the role at the Dresden première, while here, as in Dresden, for the Dance of the Seven Veils a heavyweight Salome (Olive Fremstad) was metamorphosed into a lithe ballerina (Bianca Froehlich).

But the transformation was not permitted to be repeated: the puritan lobby protested vociferously, among them the powerful financier J. Pierpont Morgan. A cartoon depicting a more acceptable dance where the seven veils bore advertisements for prominent products – Morgan's Trusts, Rockefeller Oil, Vanderbilt's Railroads, and Pears' Soap among them – shrewdly linked commercial aspiration and aesthetic conservatism. With press opinion, too, crackling in 'righteous fury', the management was compelled to withdraw *Salome* after only one presentation, and a similar ban was enforced in Chicago. A spirited defence of the aborted production in the *Musical Standard* brought forth the following riposte from E. A. Baughan, dramatic and music critic of the *London Daily News*:

> You speak of fighting for liberty in art. If such exhibitions of degraded passion are included in what you call 'liberty', then you will be fighting for the representation on stage of satyriasis and nymphomania, set forth with every imaginable circumstance of literary and musical skill. I can conceive of no greater degradation of Richard Strauss's genius than the illustration of this play by music.[26]

Such a response augured badly for the British opening, and the often-told tale of those circumstances surrounding the first London presentation on 8 December 1910 is worth rehearsing, if only for the surprising culmination. During his second season as conductor and impresario at Covent Garden the ebullient Thomas Beecham resolved to introduce *Salome* into the repertoire, following the production of Strauss's equally controversial *Elektra* earlier in the year. For the title-role a Finnish soprano, Ainö Ackté, was recruited, 'a slim and beautiful creature' who proposed to perform the dance herself, and not rely on a professional dancer to do it for her. Moreover, her costume, in which snakes played a prominent part, was announced in the press as being designed by Worth of Paris. Advance bookings were impressive, and certain reassuring modifications to the text, carried out by Beecham and the Lord Chamberlain's representatives, and supported by Herbert Asquith, the Liberal Prime Minister of the day, allowed the embargo on live performance to be rescinded. Jokanaan was to be referred to as simply 'Mattaniah the Prophet'; Salome's vibrant sexual longings were transmuted into expressions of spiritual devotion or requests for heavenly enlightenment; the line 'If you had looked upon me you would have loved me' was transmogrified into 'If you had looked upon me you would have blessed me'; all phrases of biblical derivation were expunged, and an empty platter covered with a cloth was to be substituted for the blood-stained head. With these somewhat farcical changes agreed to, the performance in its native German attire was permitted to go ahead. However, as Beecham revealed in his autobiography, the performers gradually lapsed into 'the viciousness of the lawful text' after about half an hour, and British officialdom, in the shape of a delighted deputation from the Lord Chamberlain's box, either turned a deaf ear to the deviations from the approved version or else remained blissfully ignorant of the substitution.[27] One cannot help but be reminded of Lady Bracknell's immortal dictum in *The Importance of Being Earnest*: 'German sounds a thoroughly respectable language, and I believe, is so.'

As the twentieth century has run its course, it has become more and more common for the female lead to be expected to follow

Ackté's example, and perform the dance in person, and today this usually includes the removal of the final veil. It is certainly a feature of at least two performances available on videotape, those of Teresa Stratas in 1974 and Catherine Malfitano in 1990. As Sir Peter Hall wrote in connection with his then wife Maria Ewing, who not only sang, but danced, herself into a state of complete nakedness at the Covent Garden presentation of the opera in 1988:

> We've tried to do the 'Dance'. It's completely danced, completely acted, it's completely done. It's very rough on Maria Ewing, because she has to do that after having been on stage for an hour singing, and she's still got another twenty minutes of singing to do after it. But I don't think there's any escape. I've seen *Salome*s where somebody else comes on to do the 'Dance'. I've also seen *Salome*s where the ladies do an approximate shiver and shimmy and leave it to the imagination. But you *cannot* leave the 'Dance' to the imagination.[28]

With this viewpoint many would agree, although Peter Brook, arguing in favour of stylisation in 1949, remarked that 'no singer is supposed to be a dancer; the more the dance could be carried by the orchestra and indicated by the singer, the less the embarrassment and the greater the illusion'.[29] Strauss himself composed a scenario for the dance at some point in the 1920s,[30] though sadly it is incomplete, most signally with regard to the removal of the seventh veil and its aftermath. But there is surely a key to the general effect Strauss desired the dance to create, in the composer's advice to the director Erich Engel in 1930:

> I would rather not have any dramatics in the dance at all. No flirting with Herod, no playing to Jochanaan's cistern, only a moment's pause beside the cistern on the final trill. The dance should be purely oriental, as serious and measured as possible, and thoroughly decent, as if it was being done on a prayer-mat . . . I have only once seen the dance done really aristocratically and stylishly.[31]

Not that the conclusion of the dance has been the only point of controversy in stagings of this opera. In 1949 Peter Brook, then

Plate 7 Salvador Dali's design for Peter Brook's
production of Strauss's opera, Covent Garden, 1949.

Director of Productions at London's Covent Garden, invited the
eminent surrealist Salvador Dali to design setting (plate 7), costumes and special effects for his November production starring
Ljuba Welitsch. Tradition was flouted at every turn, and so furiously
flew the expressions of indignant outrage and scornful mockery, not
merely from more philistine critics but from those of the so-called
'quality press', that Brook resigned. One contention was that had
Dali been able to supervise or even witness the production in
rehearsal, he could have curbed its 'excesses'; Welitsch herself maintained that the Spaniard misconceived the opera as a piece set in
northern darkness rather than southern light. A third view was that
the extravagant costumes were not merely distracting in their extravagance but extremely impractical when worn, handicapping rather
than enabling the singers. Compounding the problems of *mise en*

scène was the fact that the three main soloists were non-English yet sang in that tongue, and the overwhelming imbalance between orchestra and singers helped to complete a recipe for disaster.[32]

Brook defended himself vigorously in the *Observer* for 4 December 1949, citing as his artistic precedent the commissioning as Wilde's illustrator of Aubrey Beardsley who for Brook 'catches the flavour of Wilde by fantasy and distortion':

> What determines the style of a production of *Salome*? The music and the libretto. What are their most striking features? They are strange, poetic, unrealistic . . . So why Salvador Dali? Because he is the only artist I know in the world whose natural style has both what one might call the erotic degeneracy of Strauss and the imagery of Wilde.[33]

After going on to justify the aesthetic aspects of Dali's set, Brook emphasised its practicality which enabled its protagonists to project their voices 'over the impossibly loud orchestra' (though not all auditors were equally satisfied with this aspect of the production), and to adopt the stylised postures their 'built-up' costumes demanded. Brook also makes a general point, more contentious in the more naturalistic climate of 1949 than today:

> Why should we be afraid of fantasy and imagination, even in an opera-house? When the curtain rises, strange vulture-like wings beat slowly under the moon; a giant peacock's tail, opening with the opening of the dance, suggests the decadent luxury of Herod's kingdom. A handful of such visual touches over the ninety-six minutes of the opera are designed to lift the audience into the strange Wilde–Strauss world.

Forty years on from Brook, Nikolaus Lehnhoff achieved comparable notoriety, even in a world grown accustomed to artistic novelty. Siting his February 1989 New York Metropolitan Opera presentation within a 'harsh post-modernist set', Lehnhoff enforced attention on the correspondences he perceived between one *fin de siècle* and another, striving to convey a sense of impending disaster by having 'limp male corpses' being lowered into a pit early in the action, implying that some kind of cataclysmic plague had engulfed Herod's kingdom. The steeply raked stage too suggested a world about to implode under threats which the director identified as stemming from 'creeping noiseless catastrophes of nature and civilisation: the dying of the forests, the AIDS epidemic, Chernobyl'.[34]

At its inception, mercifully, the opera's capacity to shock went far beyond such capacity to *épater les bourgeois*. The 'exotic harmonies and disturbing cadences' of the music with their modernistic novelties of dissonance and atonality were heard with extreme suspicion by the musical conservatives of the day. Even thirty-five years later, Edward J. Dent could still remark that 'the voice parts are angular and unmelodious, based on a violent and exaggerated declamation'.[35] While unfamiliar in technique to all but *cognoscenti*, much of the strange orchestration was acknowledged at the time to be dazzling and evocative – Mahler, Fauré and Dukas praised its originality, colour, and atmospheric sonorities, as did Schoenberg, Berg and Webern later. But no doubt even the lay public could respond to the mysterious, evocative opening unsupported by the dubious benefits of an overture; the pair of orchestral interludes which introduce respectively the prophet's emergence from the cistern and the formulation of Salome's bid for vengeance; the multiple moods of the Dance of the Seven Veils. All of these have been extolled as examples of Strauss's finest writing, notwithstanding some strictures on the 'vulgarity' of the Dance music itself. Above all, many people have been subconsciously aware of the score's capacity to act as 'a running commentary' on the characters' shifting emotions, even if the personages are unable to recognise what they feel with any great precision. This is particularly so in the case of Salome herself, a young woman apparently surprised by the primal strength of newly aroused passions of desire, hatred and revenge.

However, there have always been those who criticise what they feel to be the inconsistent quality of the writing, arguing particularly against the 'banality' of the music assigned to the prophet himself.

In this instance it is indeed the case that Strauss himself might, in other circumstances, have scored the opera differently. He once made the revealing comment that he had originally planned the Baptist's part with comedic effect in mind. Writing in May 1935 he told Stefan Zweig:

> I tried to compose the good Jochanaan more or less as a clown; a preacher in the desert, especially one who feeds on grasshoppers, seems infinitely comical to me. Only because I have already caricatured the five Jews and also poked fun at Father Herodes did I feel that I had to follow the law of contrast and write a pedantic-Philistine motif for four horns to characterise Jochanaan.[36]

Since December 1905 many individual singers have brought differing qualities to the interpretation of *Salome*'s leading roles. Outstanding Salomes have included Maria Jeritza, the Austrian soprano who created many of Strauss's heroines (though not this); Christel Goltz; Inge Borkh; Ljuba Welitsch of the Vienna State Opera and Helga Pilarczyk of the Hamburg Opera in the years following the Second World War. In more recent years Grace Bumbry, Josephine Barstow, and Hildegard Behrens are only three among a number of superb singers who have brought passion, conviction and considerable physical energy to the part. Among notable Jokanaans mention might be made of Dietrich Fischer-Dieskau, Marko Rothmüller, Otakar Kraus, Hans Hotter and José van Dam, all of whom have made their mark since the Second World War.

An overview suggests that within the role of Salome singers have discovered not only the unsophisticated yet disturbed child, first a victim of her stepfather's lecherous advances, then overwhelmed by the onset of sexual feelings of her own, but also the feral predator whose destructive and anti-masculine instincts are on the alert from the first. Imposing sopranos of dominant presence (such as Birgit Nilsson) have achieved most success in the latter guise; singers of more athletic build (such as Teresa Stratas) have been more convincing in the more childlike spiteful mode. But perhaps the best performers have been those who have realised most fully the unstable mutability of the character; Ainö Ackté, for example, in Beecham's British première, was extolled in *The Nation* as 'an imperious princess, a spoilt child, and a woman intoxicated with sensuousness',[37] and in a similar manner *The Times* commended the voice of Ljuba Welitsch in her Covent Garden début as Salome in September 1949 as 'hard for imperiousness, soft for seduction, and susceptible of every intermediate modulation'.[38] For a recording made some thirty years later Hildegard Behrens won praise as 'a singer who in the early scenes has one actively sympathising with the girlish princess, and who keeps that sympathy and understanding to a point where most sopranos have been transformed into raging harpies'.[39] In the same way Cheryl Studer has won applause for building her interpretation 'so that the final scene conveys total evil while keeping a semblance of girlishness'.[40]

The role of Jokanaan is quite clearly less capable of being explored for conflicting nuances and contradictions in its interpretation. Here again, physical presence has had a large part to play in what critics have deemed to be an adequate rendition of the part: in 1924 *The Times* criticised Emil Schipper in a Vienna State Opera production at Covent Garden for the fact that the figure which emerged from the cistern was less impressive than the voice which had preceded it. In 1949 some critics complained of Kenneth Schon's operatic girth and weight which scarcely reflected Salome's tribute to 'a thin ivory statue'. Nobility and dignity are clearly prerequisites in this role, but in 1959 the *Financial Times* complained that Otakar Kraus was insufficiently romantic to inflame the desire of the princess. There is also a temptation (as with Salome herself) to make Jokanaan sound and look too old, which again has the same type of negative effect: vocally and physically he must command respect if not credibility, although the problem of projecting the voice from the cistern is not always successfully overcome, while some still regret the quality of music that Strauss gives his prophet to sing.

While there have certainly been those who deplore the presence of 'kitsch' in the score of *Salome*,[41] an unprejudiced spectator or listener must surely reject the majority of the aspersions cast upon the work since its creation almost a hundred years ago. Its subject-matter is indeed violent and harrowing, its characters fiercely uncompromising, its treatment original, powerful and disturbing; but, while some critics have argued that Wilde's material is unworthy of the composer's talent and that Strauss demeaned himself by selecting it for musical attention, many more have seen in the vibrant and scintillating score the perfect complement to Wilde's poetically charged, stylised prose and the densely concentrated, fluctuating, passion-filled nature of the action it articulates. As a play *Salome* is full of intense moments, but the remorseless pressure exerted by the score allows one even less respite from the absorbing battles of wills being fought out on stage, while the highlights of the drama are given that degree of emotional enhancement which, out of all the creative arts, music is best qualified to supply. Not everyone will be able to endorse Gustav Mahler's 1907 verdict that 'it is one of the greatest masterpieces of our time', but if Christopher Nassaar (echoing Pater) is correct in observing that *Salome* 'is a play that aspires towards the condition of music',[42] then Strauss must be agreed to be the man who more than any other made the greatest contribution to allowing Wilde's piece to fulfil that aspiration.

THE SALOME DANCER, 1895–1919

Given that a dance constitutes the major highlight in the Salome legend, it is perhaps surprising that we find it taking dance form so rarely in the theatre until the closing decade of the nineteenth century. One inhibiting factor until then may well have been directorial diffidence in confronting the scriptural inspiration for such performances; but, whatever the cause, it was apparently not until 1895 that Salome routines began to emerge.[43] When they did, it is most probable that Wilde's play served as an animating intertextual reference for dancers and choreographers who took the Judean princess as their subject. The accredited pioneer in this regard is the American-born speciality-dancer, Loie Fuller (1862–1928), whose influence on the development of modern dance is only now receiving proper recognition.[44] Fuller, though apparently self-taught as a dancer, received sufficient training as a singer and actress to enable her for some years to make a satisfactory living in the theatre on both sides of the Atlantic. In New York in 1890 she invented what became known as her celebrated 'Serpentine Dance'; in 1892 she became the latest toast of the Folies Bergères; for the Paris Exposition Universelle of 1900 she performed before rapt audiences in a specially erected theatre. As her repertoire evolved, it is perhaps not surprising that Loie should have incorporated a 'Salome Dance' into her programme. According to Richard Bizot, she first essayed the role in a 'pantomime lyrique' presented at the Comédie-Parisienne, Paris, around 19 March 1895. The piece involved the dancer presenting four tableaux preceded by a prologue, Armand Silvestre and C.-H. Meltzer being responsible for the scenario, and the music was undertaken by Gabriel Pierné.

The piece opened with Salome as a child carrying an armful of flowers; the four dances which followed were intended to convey contradictory moods – chaste purity; fearfulness; horrified terror; mute acquiescence in the role her mother had allotted her, even while attempting to move Herod to spare the Baptist. As Bizot expresses it:

> The changing character of her dances reflects her growing awareness of her mother's dastardly design, of which at the outset she has no inkling. In the course of the performance she becomes devoted to John the Baptist and looks to him for protection; she balks at dancing and has to be thrown on stage by her mother; she dances for Herod, hoping to soften his heart, but only succeeds in stoking the fires of his lust; and she resists Herod's advances until at last, desperate to save John's life, she submits. But by then, hélas! it is too late: the executioner

enters with the Baptist's bloody head and Salome collapses, her still form illuminated by the radiance emanating from the head.[45]

As Bizot points out, while no details of the mechanisms employed have survived, the final effect may have owed something to Gustave Moreau's painting of *L'Apparition*, where incandescent light irradiates from the Baptist's disembodied head. Certainly this appears to have been only one of a range of special effects achieved by Fuller and her technical assistants: they apparently included impressions of racing clouds, a storm, moonlit waves, and a sea of blood.[46]

Critical response to the Salome routine was predictably mixed. Roger Marx was much taken with the performance,[47] but Jean Lorrain savaged it: 'the unfortunate acrobat is neither a mime nor a dancer: heavy, awkward, sweating, and with her make-up gone after ten minutes of little exercises, she plies her veils and her heap of material like a washerwoman running amok with her paddle'.[48] However, Loie was clearly undaunted by her detractors' sniping, and in November 1907 she ventured once more, this time in a series of dances grouped under the title of *La Tragédie de Salomé*, presented at the Paris Théâtre des Arts. The music was no longer that of Pierné, but a score written by Florent Schmitt, a young Belgian composer, and the story line was based on a poem by Robert d'Humières. As Schmitt's biographer, Pierre-Octave Ferroud, points out, the piece suggests a conflict between Christianity and Judaic values.[49] As a ballet it was to be performed later by Karsavina in 1913 and Ida Rubinstein in 1919, both considerably younger at the time of performance than Fuller in 1907. Loie at forty-five no longer attempted to portray youthful innocence, but presented the image of the *femme fatale* which had attracted the attention of so many artists and thinkers of the past three decades. Her most exotic costume was that worn by her in the so-called 'Peacock Dance', no doubt inspired by 'The Peacock Skirt', Beardsley's striking illustration to the 1894 edition of *Salome*. For this sequence the dancer apparently wore a costume made up of 4,500 peacock feathers. In another number, entitled 'The Snake Dance', she appeared in the guise of 'a witch in green shining scales, playing with two snakes six feet long'. Perhaps fortunately for the star, the snakes were artificial, but they presumably created the desired *frisson*: 'She sets them down and as they writhe on the floor darting out their heads horribly, she capers round them with hideous glee.'[50] The artistic freedom Fuller claimed makes her in many respects a worthy precursor of such other explorers as her fellow-countrywomen Isadora Duncan (1878–1927) and Ruth St-Denis (1879–1968). The former seems never to have considered Salome a suitable case for balletic treatment, but St-Denis, her slightly younger contemporary, who saw Fuller perform at the Paris Exposition in 1900, did embark on a dance-project with the Jewish princess at its centre, which might well have proved one of her most remarkable successes.[51]

The initial impetus appears to have come in the autumn of 1906 from Max Reinhardt, seeking to revive his production of Wilde's play as part of his 1907/8 season, with the American dancer in the title-role. However, St-Denis clearly preferred the notion of a full-scale original presentation, in which Salome's dance would form the decisive feature, rather than a single striking episode in a play dedicated to other purposes. St-Denis's reaction to Wilde's version is found in two long letters dated 24 November 1906, written to Strauss's Austrian collaborator Hugo von Hofmannsthal by Count Harry Kessler, who was clearly eager to recruit the writer's services as author of the proposed new treatment. Kessler told his friend:

> St Denis is utterly opposed to [Wilde's] *Salome* – a whole crowd of objections, two of which are deep-rooted. She says that in any case it's a *purely literary* work (people can think differently if they wish to) in which the *dance can only be an incidental feature*, however people arrange things. And secondly, *she herself* has already conceived a *completely different Salome* (or Herodias), one in which the dance and the production correspond . . . She's basing it on an old woodcut that she's seen in a Bible . . . Salome's dance is now the vital feature. Successively she dances different routines, making Herod wilder and wilder until he finally utters the oath in a perfect frenzy.[52]

However popular the St-Denis–Hofmannsthal routine might have proved (Kessler's account suggests that it was conceived partly in terms of technical effects), it constituted a direct challenge to Wilde, but was abandoned within a short period. It would certainly never have achieved the fame or notoriety which came to be attached to *The Vision of Salome* as performed by the Canadian dancer Maud Allan (1873–1956), who was later to win notoriety in the ill-starred J. T. Grein presentation of 1918.[53]

A musical education of a high-class order was the basis of Allan's dance-programme, and her musicality contrasted markedly with that of a number of her rivals. Physically, too, she may be said to have come much closer to the average person's conception of Salome than Isadora Duncan would ever have done. Under the influence of the Italian composer, conductor and piano virtuoso Ferruccio Busoni, and another of the maestro's circle, Marcel Rémy, in 1901–2 Allan dedicated herself to the creation of a programme of dances to express the moods conjured up by a selection of pieces from the light classical repertoire. Like Duncan, Allan evolved a form of dance requiring no formal training, executed in bare feet and clothed either in a fluttering cloud of diaphanous draperies or an attenuated Grecian-style tunic, and consisting of mimed sequences of flowing movements in which improvisation was a marked feature.

What is certain is that Maud Allan was 'made' by the Salome routine she evolved without any hints from Duncan's or St-Denis's repertoire, and which she launched on 26 December 1906. It seems likely that a large part of the artistic inspiration for *The Vision of Salome* derived directly from Reinhardt's production of Wilde's play (although the costume was strongly reminiscent of Ricketts's design); certainly both Allan and her composer Marcel Rémy had attended performances in Berlin several years earlier. There appear to have been two phases to the new dance, which Allan herself entitled 'The Dance of Salome' and 'The Vision of Salome' (plate 8).[54] Visualising Salome as an innocent girl of fourteen, Allan imagined

Plate 8 Maud Allan in *The Vision of Salome*, c. 1908
(from a contemporary postcard).

the princess as being summoned to dance at the Tetrarch's whim and, overawed by the occasion, seeking advice from Herodias as to what she should ask as reward of her stepfather. After relaying her mother's vindictive answer, she flees in remorse to her own apartments, where

> [s]he stands panting, aghast, her hands pressed to her young breasts; she raises them, and, bowing her head to meet them, sees upon her naked flesh, upon the hands that seek her smarting eyes, the purple, sticky stain that she has not been able to avoid – it is the blood of the Baptist, John.
> The sight turns her for a moment to stone. Then it brings the whole ghastly scene back, as in a vision.

There is no indication as to whether or not there was any kind of pause between the Dance and the Vision, but the likelihood is that the work was performed as a continuous whole. In a dream Salome is forced to re-enact the 'awful moments of joy and horror which she has just passed through'. In the gloom of the palace garden she is torn between regret at obeying her mother and delight at her own evident potency as a performer:

> Salome, child as she is, realises a power within her and exults. She sees again her triumph approach, her swaying limbs are in readiness to give way, when suddenly from out of the sombre death-still hall the wail of muffled distress – and a pale, sublime face with its mass of long black hair arises before her – the head of John the Baptist!

Having taken the head and danced around it, Salome is moved by the presence of a superior power to her own. She swiftly perceives that her need is for spiritual help and comfort, but the grisly trophy is mute:

> Crazed by the rigid stillness, Salome, seeking an understanding, and knowing not how to obtain it, presses her warm, vibrating lips to the cold lifeless ones of the Baptist! In this instant the curtain of darkness that had enveloped her soul falls, the strange grandeur of a power higher than Salome has ever dreamed of beholding becomes visible to her, and her anguish becomes vibrant.

There is nothing of the *femme fatale* of the Decadents in Allan's apparent notion of the role: Salome's childish ingenuousness owes something to Flaubert's heedless, incurious daughter, and the vision of the head owes a good deal to Moreau and *L'Apparition*. But the sexual awakening and its manifestation in the fatal kiss seems pure Wilde, and the image of youthful innocence may be felt to be at odds with the principal impression conveyed by Maud's appearance and demeanour in performance. Whatever the assumed age of the character she sought to adopt, Allan was not a fourteen-year-old adolescent, but a mature and shapely woman in her early thirties, and she exposed a good deal of herself to the public gaze. The exotic details of her costume brought her closer than anyone before to Wilde's early vision of his heroine totally naked but for a profusion of precious stones. Whatever her declared intentions, her performance depended on creating sexual arousal and was no doubt designed to do so.

But her critics were generally inclined to give her the benefit of the doubt. Sir Frederick Ponsonby, no aesthete or admirer of exotica but the somewhat prosaic Equerry and Assistant Personal Secretary to King Edward VII, before whom Allan danced at Marienbad in September 1907, wrote of the performance: 'The dance was very exceptional, and I must say Miss Allan was really wonderful. Her dance of Salome with the head of John the Baptist was really most dramatic, and although I cannot say that she wore many clothes, there was nothing the least indecent about her performance.'[55]

When Maud danced in London in 1908 *The Times* (10 March) was judicious but generally approbatory:

> [E]very movement was beautiful. There is no extravagance or sensationalism about Miss Allan's dancing; even when crouching over the head of her victim, caressing it or shrinking from it in horror, she subordinated every gesture and attitude to the conditions of her art. It will, perhaps, be fair to the public to say that her dress as Salome is daring; it would be very unfair to Miss Allan not to add that, like her performance, it is absolutely free of offence.

On 26 March 1908, the same organ's *Literary Supplement* devoted a feature article to 'The New Dancer', remarking on the 'Eastern' spirit of the dancing, and noting that Allan 'achieves the distinction . . . between the lascivious and the voluptuous'.[56] Not everyone shared such enthusiasm. In addition to such journals as *The Academy* which disapproved on moral and aesthetic grounds – 'In our opinion it is a repulsive performance, and one which we should not consent on any account to witness a second time'[57] – there were those who found free dancing in itself unduly dependent on the performer's appearance and personality.

The same reservations may have been entertained regarding another female dancer who gained widespread notoriety.[58] Mata Hari (1876–1917), born Margaretha Geertruida Zelle in Leeuwerden, Northern Holland, had made her first appearance as an exotic pseudo-Eastern dancer at the Guimet Oriental Museum in Paris on 13 March 1905. Billing herself originally as 'Lady MacLeod', a piece of self-ennoblement rarely called in question, she soon adopted the more colourful appellation of Mata Hari, a Malayan expression for the sun (or less prosaically, 'The Eye of the Day'). Her pastiches of East Indian dance-routines rapidly acquired the status of collectors' items, and like Maud Allan, she became the fashionable cynosure, not only for such genuine artists as the operatic composer Puccini but also for a slightly raffish set of voyeurs, idlers and hangers-on.

Not without more creditable ambitions, when Strauss's operatic version of *Salome* was announced for production in Paris in 1907 Mata Hari apparently expressed a desire to substitute herself for Mme Kousnetzova who was to sing the title-role, and to perform the Dance of the Seven Veils in her stead, in much the same way that Olive Fremstad had been magically replaced by Bianca Froehlich in the New York première some months before. The dancing was eventually assigned to Natalie Trouhanova, who was to appear as Salome rather less impressively in Paris some five years later. However, in 1912 (the same year in which Diaghilev cast her in his aborted *Le*

Dieu Bleu) Mata Hari achieved her ambition in the sense that she was able to perform the Dance of the Seven Veils at a private party given in Rome by the Prince di San Faustino. A painting of the period shows her reclining on her stomach stripped to well below the navel, looking up from the salver which bears the Baptist's head, and smiling, content to wear considerably fewer jewels than even Maud Allan's costume boasted.

It is doubtless inevitable that down the years the role of Salome should attract such unconventional exotic talents. Hard on the heels of Mata Hari came Ida Rubinstein (1885–1960), a Russian of Jewish extraction in her early twenties, who was to enjoy an amazing if equivocally successful career on the ballet stage, amazing in that she never underwent the full rigours of a conventional dancer's training. Strikingly tall, boyishly slim, even angular, an admirer of Isadora Duncan and an associate of Leon Bakst, Rubinstein's personal fortune enabled her to secure Mikhail Fokine's services as her private tutor in ballet. With him she began to study in St Petersburg during the Maryinsky company's 1907/8 season, going on to work with Fokine in Switzerland during the summer of 1908.

While Evreinov was rehearsing *Tsarevna* in the autumn of 1908, Rubinstein sat daily in the auditorium, willing to undertake the leading role eventually assigned to Volkhova. Eager to play Salome, not least because it would necessitate a performance of the Dance of the Seven Veils, Rubinstein had Wilde's play translated into Russian, got Bakst to design sets and costumes, and worked tirelessly daily with Fokine to bring her dancing skills up to the required level. He in his turn choreographed a sequence for her to perform to music by Alexander Glazunov, while aware that he faced special problems: 'The work on the Salome dance was unique in my life. I had to teach Rubinstein simultaneously the art of the dance and to create for her the Dance of Salome . . . I felt that it would be possible to do something unusual with her in the style of Botticelli.'[59]

The culmination of such dedication was merely a sadly brief

St Petersburg début for Rubinstein in the hall of the Conservatoire on 20 December 1908, and only in the dance which Fokine had contrived for her. The Tsarist authorities, backed by the Holy Synod, forbade her to utter a word of the text on stage, confiscated the 'graven image' of the Baptist's head, and only allowed Wilde's piece to be represented in mime. There is some contradictory testimony as to whether officialdom stepped in to ban the production following the dress-rehearsal,[60] or whether it was stopped after a single staging. Certainly the volatile state of Russian politics played a part in its decision, but other reasons have been held to include Wilde's biblical source, the impious connotations of the fabricated head, and the fact that Rubinstein was rumoured to conclude the dance in a state of total nudity.[61] Stanislavsky apparently commented that he had never seen such nakedness, though the critic Svetlov felt the dance was 'full of the languor and chastity of animal passion'.[62] Elaine Showalter attributes the ban to contemporary anti-Semitism and misogyny,[63] but either way, baulked by the censor of her wish to present the entire play as Wilde had written it, the charismatic performer had to be content to have danced to a score specially written by one of Russia's leading composers, and with wearing a costume and performing within a setting created by Bakst, one of the greatest stage-designers of all time. Bakst's surviving costume sketch, now in the Tretiakov Collection in Moscow's National Museum, shows his protégée striding forth amid swirls of filmy silks, dressed in a strapless Allanesque top and a tight attenuated patterned skirt fastened with an elaborate belt. Jewelled armlets, bracelets, rings and ropes of pearl complete an outfit alluring enough, if not notable for its originality in the context of its period. Yet as de Cossart writes: 'Never before had the St Petersburg public been treated to the spectacle of a young society woman dancing voluptuously to insinuating oriental music, discarding brilliantly coloured veils until only a whisp of green chiffon remained knotted round her loins.'[64]

Despite the extravagances, through her performance Rubinstein established herself as a serious professional artist and her début as Salome certainly led on to even greater triumphs. When, in the spring of 1909, Diaghilev, Fokine, Gregoriev, Benois and Bakst began to plan the combined assault on the French capital which led to the formation of the Ballets Russes, Ida was put forward as someone able to mime the title-role in Fokine's *Cléopâtre*, and make the required visual impact in the part.

The triumph as Cleopatra of this relative newcomer, adorned with a stylised turquoise-blue wig and short gold braids framing her face, clearly owed something to the image of Salome established on the stage by this time. The generally acceptable exoticism of the costume; the blue wig which Bernhardt would have worn for the 1892 production; the gradual titillating unveiling of the androgynously slender figure; the abandonment of the player to what Benois interpreted as 'the ecstasy of love'; the farrago of races, colours and creeds that made up the *corps de ballet* – all may be said to have drawn on the spirit of Wilde's one-act drama.

With Edouard de Max as Herod, Rubinstein finally gave six performances of Wilde's piece from 12 to 19 June 1912 under the direction of Alexandre Sanine at the Théâtre du Châtelet in Paris. Few records of Ida's performance as pure actress seem to exist, but one doubts if her voice with its 'exotic accent' and tendency towards a dull monotone can really have done justice to Wilde's lines. However, freed from the deadening hand of the censor, her dance, that choreographed by Fokine to Glazunov's music in 1908, was much admired, although Jean Cocteau regretted that Rubinstein, while suggesting 'many wonderful things, from an arrow to an antelope', had not danced on her hands in the way Flaubert had envisaged and Wilde had certainly toyed with.[65] Certainly Ida's personality if not her performance overall must have come close to one of Wilde's early visions of his heroine's appearance. According to Karina Dobrotvorskaya,

> [Her] plastic portrayal of the role surprised by its unusual beauty:
> the long lines of her narrow body, her snakelike movements and slow
> leonine grace were emphasised by Bakst's costume made of iridescent

silver brocade trimmed with red, which fully revealed the legs, and a winding green scarf (as in Serov's portrait). Trained by Fokine, Rubinstein played upon the length of her body, lay sprawled on the stage, fell lightly in exhaustion and pressed herself up close to the cistern. In her Salome, however, there was no movement from cold virginity to one possessed with passion: she played on one note which was found in the very first scene, making her portrayal rather dry and monotone. As one critic [E. Pann] recognised, only in the finale could 'the ear of the audience detect in her performance slight indications of unfeigned passion, solemnity and despair'.[66]

Without doubt the highest praise went to Bakst for his splendid *mise en scène*. For Cocteau,

> The scenery is, to my mind, among the most appropriate we owe to the genius of Monsieur Bakst. The courtyard is surrounded by tortuous paths, worn unevenly by unsteady feet; the excessive size of the moon explains the exaggerated importance attached to it by all these moon-struck people; the exceptionally deep crimson ramblers cling helplessly to the walls, and the awning recalls a thundercloud streaked with lightning. From their sordid debauch the guests stagger on to a terrace which overlooks the gutter, redolent of rotting rose-leaves, and registering, presumably, a far higher temperature than the reeking scene of revel they have left. Can one wonder, then, at the peculiar character of the post-prandial entertainment provided?[67]

It was possibly as a riposte to Rubinstein, in Diaghilev's eyes a defector who had enticed both Bakst and Fokine away from their true benefactor, that a ballet featuring Salome was introduced into the repertoire of the Ballets Russes for their 1913 Paris season. Presented at the Théâtre des Champs Elysées, on 6 June, following hard on the heels of the controversial Nijinsky–Stravinsky *Sacre du Printemps*, *La Tragédie de Salomé*, first danced in 1907 by Loie Fuller, saw the début of two impressive young artists, whose contributions to the development of the Salome theme had distinctly Wildean affinities. The choreography was in the hands of a twenty-two-year-old pupil of Fokine's, Boris Romanov, while the décor was entrusted for the first time to Sergei Soudeikine, whose work clearly took Beardsley's illustrations as its inspiration, albeit eschewing his black and white colour scheme.

The ballet had been included principally to display the outstanding talents of Tamara Karsavina, whose recent roles had left her less and less 'to bite on'[68] as the charismatic Nijinsky claimed an increasing share of the limelight, both as dancer and choreographer. But though Karsavina seems to have believed that Schmitt's music had been commissioned especially for her, it had of course been composed originally to accompany Fuller's routines at the Théâtre des Arts in 1907. Moreover, in the spring of 1912 the same score had been employed by Natalie Trouhanova, during her Paris season at the Châtelet,[69] albeit rearranged and converted into an orchestral suite. All Diaghilev seems to have been responsible for was to request Florent Schmitt to adapt his original to fit a larger musical ensemble.

The ballet did not feature the Wildean quartet of Tetrarch, Baptist, Herodias and dancing princess; instead, it was conceived as taking place in some extra-terrestrial domain where Salome was compelled to dance out her expiation, accompanied only by four executioners and eight slaves, all of whom wore blackface. Against a richly decorated background of 'giant vegetation' in purple and gold, the slaves who began the ballet were adorned with white ostrich plumes and wore wigs or turbans of white wool with gloves and anklets to match; the white-gaitered executioners carried scimitars. After these figures had cavorted a while at the foot of a column bearing what was perhaps intended to represent the severed head (although in London The Times saw it as 'a vague mess'), Karsavina made her entry. As leaf-patterned curtains parted, the dancer was revealed standing motionless at the head of a flight of stairs which she descended as a long, Beardsleyesque, elaborately patterned train of gold and black unwound behind her, completely covering the steps by the time she reached stage level. Once she had discarded the robe, she stood before the audience in a tunic which fell above the knee and whose gauze bodice gave the impression that her breasts were bare,[70] with a tightly fitting beehive-style head-dress, and bare arms, legs and feet. To one side of her right knee-cap Soudeikine had himself painted a single stylised red rose (though Karsavina was later to recall in conversation with Richard Buckle that it was the work of an associate and admirer, Baron Dmitri Gunsbourg).[71] The picture was completed by white facial make-up, the pallor so produced contrasting with 'her mop of raven hair', and long artificial eyelashes. In this guise she performed a frenetic solo around the head-bearing pillar. The dance itself was a frenzied affair which left the dancer panting at the foot of the edifice bearing the head, at which she stared up as the curtain fell.

Sadly for the company and for Karsavina, the ballet was not adjudged a success. Of the dancing the admittedly hostile critic André Levinson was carpingly dismissive, detecting a retreat from the Ballets' revolutionary beginnings.[72] Others were guarded in their views. When the piece transferred to Drury Lane, in the *Daily Mail* the following day Richard Capell clearly felt Karsavina to be miscast, though he praised the production: 'The piece bears no relation to any other stage *Salomes* of recent years. Eyeing the extravagant production with delicate approval, the spirit of Aubrey Beardsley was, one felt assured, haunting the house last night.'[73] The *Pall Mall Magazine* believed that only the première danseuse redeemed *Salome* from being a fiasco: 'the thing is preposterously absurd, childish, without any redeeming feature, save the exhibition of Mme Karsavina's extraordinarily graceful movements'.

It is worth recording, by way of a coda, that on 1 April 1919 a gala performance took place at the Paris Opéra to raise funds to assist those French *départements* which had suffered from German occupation during the First World War.[74] On the bill with Sarah Bernhardt, who might have played Wilde's heroine in 1892, was Ida Rubinstein dancing *La Tragédie de Salomé* to Florent Schmitt's music, but with new choreography by the Italian Nicola Guerra, until recently ballet-master of the Budapest Opera. Rubinstein again scored a great personal success, amazing spectators by dancing on her points throughout the performance, and as a result the piece was incorporated into the Opéra's regular programme until almost the end of the season. Thereafter Rubinstein never essayed the part again, but her several successful impersonations of Salome, along with those of her illustrious contemporaries featured here, had ensured that generations of aspiring successors eager to dance the role would never be lacking during decades to come.

SALOME ON FILM

The British Film Institute's catalogue lists twenty versions of the Salome story, several of which are renditions of the opera, while many others finally have little to do with Wilde. All, however, of course post-date not only Wilde's play but Strauss's opera (although by only a very few years in some cases), and even on the often frag-mentary evidence available it seems that Wilde's text must generally have been prominent in whatever ur-scenario predated the shooting. It is, of course, unusual for any screenplay to escape the innumer-able, often fundamental, changes customarily demanded by direc-tors, producers, actors, distributors and censors, while early, silent transformations in particular tended to draw on and add to the most sensational aspects of the many versions available to heighten the visual spectacle, maximise the sensational aspects of the story, and place greatest emphasis on the star performers. The most prominent exception to this rule in the silent period is a 1922 film which closely follows Wilde's play and makes prominent use of Beardsley's illustra-tions in the scenic design.

The most significant failure of almost all filmed versions is their uninterest in capturing the symbolic structures of Wilde's play. The repetitions, refrains and cadences of the language, the peculiar offstage sounds, and the visual emphasis on organised masses of colour and light, all conform to symbolism's attempt to approximate the condition of music, and to suggest the presence of unseen forces. Film, although a predominantly visual medium, is capable of analogous approximations, most obviously by means of lighting and sound-track, but most subtly and effectively by means of montage. The cut from image A to image B is capable of suggesting to the audience an image or idea C which need never be seen or spoken. But it was not until the 1920s, in the work of Eisenstein (and arguably of Buñuel and Dali), that the possibilities of montage were fully realised and theorised. Early silents tended to place greater emphasis instead on sensational story lines and on single shots which presented either a huge and impressive visual spectacle, or, in lengthy close-ups, the emotion on the face of the star-protagonist, and this is as true of films of *Salome* as of any others. Even Nazimova's experimental treatment in 1922 was not immune to these temptations, and displayed a similar emphasis on the purely visual in the attention lavished on the Beardsleyesque costumes and sets. From the available evidence, then, it seems that in all of these early films the plenitude of the single shot takes precedence; montage is subordinated to spectacle, and symbolism to narrative.

The first screen version of *Salome* was directed for Vitagraph by J. Stuart Blackton in 1908. Casting details are a little hazy: Ralph Ince played John the Baptist; Herod was probably played by Maurice Costello, but it is unclear whether Salome was played by Florence Turner or by Florence Lawrence, the original 'Biograph Girl'. The screenplay, by 'Liebler', was derived from Wilde, and a synopsis published at the time of the film's release suggests that Wilde's story line was followed unusually closely:

> Scene 1: The Capture of John the Baptist. John the Baptist is observed with his followers trudging over the hilly country when he is set upon by the soldiers of the times, who bind him, and lead him before the King.
>
> Scene 2: Banquet of Herod. A long table is richly laden with golden goblets, fruits and delicacies. Herod, his wife, his step-daughter, Salome, a young man in love with the latter and others are drinking

and laughing as John the Baptist is brought before them. The captive upbraids the King and his associates for their revelry, and for this presumption he is condemned to prison. Salome has fallen in love with the prisoner, and as he is led away she glides out after him.

Scene 3: John the Baptist Condemned to Prison. A large cistern serves as the place of confinement, and into this the soldiers drag their prisoner and compel him to descend. Salome, who has followed, pleads with the soldiers to let her see the prophet, but the request is refused.

Scene 4: Salome begs the love of John the Baptist. Outside the cistern Salome again implores the soldiers to bring the captive out. They finally consent and the prophet is brought before her. She kneels to him, kisses his hands and garments. He repulses her and reproaches her for her manner of living and her disregard for the Almighty. Salome is wild with anger at being thus spurned.

Scene 5: Herod asks Salome to Dance. Herod and his Queen are seated on their throne. Salome approaches and the King asks her to dance. She consents, calls to the slaves to remove her sandals and she dances the dance of the seven veils, throwing each veil at the feet of Herod.

Scene 6: Salome finishes the dance, approaches the King, kneels before him and indicates that he command the soldiers to bring her reward, the head of the prophet.

Scene 7: John the Baptist Taken out of Prison. The soldiers repair to the cistern and, after much resistance, remove the prisoner.

Scene 8: John the Baptist is Beheaded. The prophet is brought before King Herod and his court. A black slave stands by with a huge axe. The King hesitates in giving the command, and Salome approaches with a silver tray and again demands her reward. The slaves depart to carry out the order.

Scene 9: Salome Receives her Reward. The slave enters with the head of John the Baptist, kneels before the King, who commands him to give the reward to Salome.[75]

This bald summary suggests a surprisingly close adherence to the principal source. Some introductory material has been added to explain the presence of the prophet at the court, and the nature of Salome's attraction to him has been simplified, but no significant character has been added to or omitted from Wilde's version, and events follow the same sequence. The principal changes, in fact, are the surprising omissions of the deaths of both the Young Syrian and Salome herself. The sole publicity still in the British Film Institute's library suggests that the costumes and make-up were much as one might expect, with Herod, Salome and Herodias dressed a little unimaginatively in robes and veils; Herod wears a disappointing stage crown, while a youngish John the Baptist is naked to the waist save for a leopardskin sash. Vitagraph placed a white dove over his head for the photograph. More peculiarly, it would appear that the principal set was an incongruous Egyptian temple, adorned with hieroglyphics. The obvious conclusion is that Vitagraph reduced Wilde's play to its principal scenic events, and to save money shot more than one film on the same set (a commonplace occurrence).

Two *Salome* films appeared in 1910, one made by the British company Brockliss, the other by Pathé in France. The brief synopses published in *Bioscope* suggest there may have been some indebtedness to Wilde: both, for example, close with the incident, seemingly omitted from Blackton's version, in which Herod's soldiers crush Salome beneath their shields.[76] An Italian film of *Salome*, made by one Dr Garriazzo for Savoia-Film in 1913 and starring Signorinas De Labroy and Costamegno as Salome and Herodias respectively, was stated in a favourable review to have been based on Wilde's text, although this version too added some introductory material, this time the strangling of Herodias's first husband Philip, an incident which was also to feature in a much later version in 1986.[77]

Hollywood's next attempt at a *Salome* picture came ten years after its first. Directed for William Fox in 1918 by J. Gordon Edwards, it featured G. Raymond Nye as Herod, Albert Roscoe as John the Baptist, hundreds of extras, and vast exteriors; but what really matters is that this production was unequivocally a 'vamp' film. The iconography of the vamp is rooted firmly in the 1890s, and culminates by way of a surprisingly direct line in Theda Bara's

Salome of 1918.[78] In 1897 Philip Burne-Jones exhibited at the New Gallery, London, *The Vampire*, which depicts a pale-faced, dark-eyed, hypnotically malevolent woman, dressed in white but bathed in green light, brooding over a prostrate male figure apparently drained of blood. It was hardly an original idea; as Bram Dijkstra has shown, the economically depressed later Victorian period is saturated with the iconography of woman as semen-draining carnivorous competitor, while the pale skin and dark eyes suggest the physical symptoms of the habitual masturbator, no longer requiring men for the satisfaction of her sexual needs.[79] The image of the female vampire conflates these fears, projecting on to woman the voracious sexual appetite encoded in the eponymous male anti-hero of Bram Stoker's *Dracula*, which appeared in the same year as Burne-Jones's painting. When it was exhibited *The Vampire* was accompanied in the catalogue by his cousin Rudyard Kipling's six-stanza poem of the same title. The first line of this poem, 'A fool there was', became the title of a play (and subsequently a novel) written by Porter Emerson Browne in 1906, which owed its popular success to the figure of the home-wrecking, sexually aggressive anti-heroine; and it was this role which launched Theda Bara's career when the play was filmed. In the following years she played variations on the vamp in films with give-away titles like *Eternal Sin*, *The Forbidden Path*, *The Serpent* and *She-Devil*; *Salome* came towards the end of the sequence, the public soon becoming so tired of the figure that her career was effectively over by 1920.

Theda Bara is perhaps the first example of the manufactured Hollywood star, her films selling on the appeal of a wholly spurious personality cult. Supposedly born in the shadow of the Sphinx, the offspring of a sheik and a princess, she was in fact Theodosia Goodman, daughter of a Cincinnati tailor. The creation of the cult depended to a large extent on an iconography drawn from stereotypical representations of the oriental temptress, grafted on to the Victorian female vampire. The former strain is apparent in Bara's bejewelled but minimalist costumes, with twin asps serving for a bra, the whole design strikingly reminiscent of Maud Allan's costumes for her *Vision of Salome* dance, which reappear with little modification in some of the outfits of Bara's Salome. Equally, the vampire is suggested in the long dark hair (sometimes stretching below the knee), the bare, slender white arms, and the make-up which offsets the general pallor against the huge black circles around the eyes. A famous publicity still shows the crouched actress full-face, staring into the camera, a human skeleton at her feet.

The full-length feature film having become properly established by 1914, it is not surprising that at 7,500 feet, Fox's film was more than ten times longer than Vitagraph's. Whereas the earlier film reduced the story to a logical sequence of scenes, J. Gordon Edwards seems to have assumed that the audience was less interested in narrative coherence than in a series of sequences which progressively intensify already established emotions centring on the star performer. In consequence, the story line is almost too ludicrous to bear repetition. The *American Film Institute Catalog* cites Flavius Josephus's *The Jewish Antiquities* as a source, but *Bioscope's* reviewer let a host of people off the hook by remarking that

> [t]he story is to a large extent a purely original drama, written around the personality of the Princess Salome, in whom are revealed fresh and terrible depths of depravity. The play bears a closer relationship with Oscar Wilde's drama than with the brief Biblical narrative, but it is greatly different from both in numerous respects. Herodias disappears altogether, and the entire responsibility for John's death is placed upon the shoulders of the outrageous Salome . . . Salome is, in fact, pictured as an inhuman fiend, with an insatiable passion for wickedness for its own sake . . . [E]ven Oscar Wilde's conception of the Princess does not achieve quite the complete heartlessness and abandoned devilry of the heroine of this film. Theda Bara succeeds, however, in making the character convincing, and her performance is a thoroughly effective piece of work, despite her inclination for rather prolonged poses.[80]

The 'pure originality' is of course illusory. Edwards's Salome none too subtly blends a hyperbolic representation of the most sensational aspects of several versions of the tale with numerous additional acts of stereotypical villainy: even before we get to the

Plate 9 Theda Bara in the 1918 film version of *Salome*.

episodes resembling those in Wilde's play, for example, Salome has arranged for the drowning of David the High Priest, attempted to poison Herod's wife Mariamne, and tricked Herod into having his wife executed.

All of this is, perhaps, peripheral to Wilde; but although *Bioscope* found the picture unobjectionable, it is clear that Salome as vamp represents in pure form the misogyny which many have detected as unconscious motivation behind Wilde's fascination with the figure. More problematically, however, the emphasis is shifted more than usually away from Salome's erotic fascination with the prophet and towards the audience's erotic fascination with the actress playing Salome. Theda Bara dances on a huge empty terrace before the entire court (plate 9); or recoils, apparently in horror, as a leering Herod, the stereotypical Eastern potentate, makes a grab for her shoulder. Most of the publicity stills are close-ups of the characteristic vampish face. Having said that this face encodes an evident misogyny, it should nevertheless be remarked that there is something in the huge baleful eyes and the situations of isolated peril which resists quite such a simple reading. The combination signifies not so much pure malevolence as that extremely familiar trope of a kind of corrupted (and corrupting) innocence, as if her entrapment within the audience's gaze, the audience's desire, were somehow her fault, and she were both virgin and whore at the same time; all manoeuvres which lie at the heart of pornography. Moreover, there is a contradiction, both in surviving film of Theda Bara and between the story line and the stills of her *Salome*, a contradiction between the active force for evil which the sequence of events supposes her to be, and the passive figure, the observed object, into which she is turned by repetitive and predictable actions and by huge and inordinately lengthy close-ups.

On the other hand, feminist critics have found in Theda Bara a figure of more active resistance. While in many films now forgotten she portrayed a genuinely innocent figure, and while at times publicists attempted to make her less threatening, the 'misunderstood vampire', the actress herself found something transgressive in the vamp: 'The vampire that I play is the vengeance of my sex upon its exploiters. You see . . . I have the face of a vampire, perhaps, but the heart of a "feministe".'[81]

By 1918 the vamp was coming to the end of her life, shortly to be impaled by a host of more credible figures. Audiences had become more sophisticated, and the assertiveness of the flapper, the 'It Girl' and the *femme fatale*, all of which remained 'types' representing a threat to male security, was nevertheless more clearly anchored in a post-war social context in which women were more evidently beginning to compete with men for work, in which desires amounted to more than the capture of a man at the expense of his wife and children, and in which those desires could less easily be projected on to Other-figures of unregenerate evil.

Many commentators have therefore found it a little curious that in a highly sophisticated film of Wilde's play in 1922, directed by Charles Bryant, the director's then wife Alla Nazimova, a famous star of the silent era, should have played the title-role in a way which conformed so readily to a number of already outmoded stereotypes. But if Theda Bara was able to discover an affirmative resistance in the vamp, it is still more likely that Nazimova, reputedly a lesbian and surely familiar with the Billing case, would have found in Wilde's play a transgressive sexuality all the more powerful for its inscription within roles all too easily reduced to heterosexual stereotypes. A recent commentator may be going too far in asserting that Nazimova was responding to the omission in several earlier productions of the Page's love-lament for the Young Syrian by 'ruthlessly purging every taint of heterosexuality from the Princess';[82] instead, as in the 1918 film, although to a far greater extent, the significance of the central performance arises from a coded tension between conformity and transgression.

Born in Yalta in 1879, and initially trained as a musician, Nazimova later studied with Nemirovich-Danchenko and Stanislavsky at the Moscow Art Theatre. She emigrated to New York in 1906, and became known for her performances in plays by Ibsen and Chekhov, but this training in realism and in the Stanislavsky 'method' seems to have had little influence on her performances in Hollywood, where she began working about ten years after first arriving in the States.

There was nothing particularly surprising about this flamboyant actress's decision to play Salome. What was unusual was the decision to make an art film out of a story which Hollywood had previously exploited for its sensationalism. It has been remarked that, '[f]ollowing on the success of the "artistic" European films and the experimental avant-garde productions . . . Salome was the boldest, and most expensive American attempt in stylisation'.[83] Paradoxically, the cinematic experimentalism of Nazimova's version was to some extent to be found in its gestures towards an archaeological reconstruction and synthesis of the most prominent

Plate 10 Alla Nazimova in her own 1922 film of *Salome*.

versions of the tale in different media: Wilde's text, Strauss's score, and Beardsley's designs. Not only was the scenario, written by Nazimova under the name Peter M. Winters, a reasonably faithful adaptation of Wilde's play, but the designs and costumes – 'probably the strangest ever to appear in an American feature'[84] – by Rudolph Valentino's second wife Natasha Rambova, were an attempt to capture both the spirit and the detail of Beardsley's illustrations. These designs, and Charles Van Enger's photography, make no attempt at illusionism: it is clear throughout that we are watching a drama acted on a studio stage with a minimalist, and pointedly stylised, set (plate 10). Strauss's music was rendered in the auditorium on a Wurlitzer organ.[85]

This bold approach produced an extraordinary film, albeit one perhaps happier in conception (and in the frequently reproduced stills) than in execution. Nazimova conceived of *Salome* as 'a kind of dream or fantasmagoria [*sic*]'.[86] Much of this quality is an effect of the creative use of Beardsley's designs, which are followed seldom slavishly and often somewhat obscurely. In general, the effect is to offset visual references to Beardsley against conventional, contemporary cinematic tropes, so that each comments obliquely upon the other. Perhaps the most effective examples of this technique are the various costumes worn by Nazimova as she enacts 'successive styles of movie glamour' throughout the film.[87] On her first appearance she wears an extraordinary pearl-studded black wig which bears some resemblance to the stylised curls in Beardsley's illustration of 'The Dancer's Reward'; but the resemblance is far from exact, and the wig equally recalls the clusters of white and dark circles which embroider illustrations such as 'The Climax'. With the pearl wig she wears a dark, thin gym slip which invites comparison to a 'Mack Sennett bathing beauty'.[88] But crucially, and in contradiction, it also emphasises Nazimova's very slim, almost boyish figure, combining effectively with the Beardsleyesque wig and stage design to undermine the heterosexual signification; and it is while she is dressed in this outfit that the Young Syrian kills himself to conquer his unrequited love for her. During the dance she appears very differently, now sporting a shocking bleached blonde wig, and dressed to match in a veil of white chiffon, beneath which she wears, incongruously, what appears to be a pair of white tennis shorts. The change of appearance may be an attempt to capture some of the apparent contradictions and inconsistencies in Beardsley's designs – perhaps the white Salome acknowledges the blonde (unfinished?) figure in 'The Toilette of Salome II' – but if so it is nothing more than a vague approximation, and more importantly the blonde wig and contemporary shorts recall the audience of 1922 to its own period, whose conventional notions of femininity it again seems to question, especially given the erotic associations of the Dance of the Seven Veils. After the dance Nazimova appears finally in oriental garb, with heavy black eyeshadow and lipstick, wearing a Japanese robe and a turban, in which guise she kisses the head of Jokanaan and is killed; the robe aside (a gesture to Beardsley), we are clearly invited to recall Theda Bara's vamp.

It was not only the costume change which made the dance stand out. In part this was achieved by contrast of rhythm, the remainder of the action being very slow-moving; but also by contrast of style, the 'stylised pantomime technique' of the remainder of Nazimova's performance offsetting the 'bewitching grace' with which she 'creat[ed] her own variations upon Duncan and St Denis styles of interpretive dance'.[89] Like many actresses before, including Theda Bara, Nazimova performed the dance in a white veil, but quite striking effects of contrast were achieved in this instance by the device common in operatic productions, that of having Salome assisted in the unveiling by a group of helpers, in this case 'weirdly garbed dwarfs who jumped up and down, copied from the Indonesian lute player in Beardsley's drawing'.[90] The *New York Times* thought the dance cheated the audience, which was shown 'an exceedingly tame and not very graceful' performance, which did not match up to the reception it received at Herod's court, although in the paper's view *any* performance of the dance would necessarily fail to match the expectations created of it.[91] When the film was re-shown in 1966, however, critical response was more favourable.

Further examples of an inventive and synthetic imagination are found in the set design. Most of the action unfolds on a single, circular, rather bare stage, but peripheral areas establish clearly demarcated zones of influence, all of which are however fully visible in wide-angle shots. The most significant area is the cistern: the sunken prison within which the clean-shaven, excessively thin Jokanaan (Nigel de Brulier) is confined occupies a slightly raised area enclosed within a large, locked cage. Nearby is an elaborate, stylised trellis-work design, adorned with flowers, which has the function of repeatedly placing the action inside a frame or against a background which pointedly recalls Beardsley's creeping rose bushes, redolent of forbidden passion and homosexual love. This scenic minimalism is in itself strikingly effective, achieving the quality of strangeness Nazimova desired, while throwing still greater emphasis upon the other elements in the overall design.

The significance of the film does not lie solely in such ambitious synthesising constructions, however, but in the tension between its visual reference to the 1890s, on the one hand, and the time and place in which it was made on the other. Nazimova's *Salome* establishes itself as modern, contemporary, by its insistence on designs and motifs familiar in other media but radically new in American film. And this naturally encourages us to look for parallels between the film's ostensible subject and its contemporary world. As noted, for all its novelty, there does appear to be a certain aping of the cinematic conventions of the 1920s and slightly earlier. Other than in the dance, Nazimova, despite the revolutionary nature of the film and her familiarity with a sophisticated acting method still relatively unknown in the Hollywood of this period, made no attempt to escape the conventional modes of silent-film acting; indeed, she displayed 'the exaggerated petulance of any vamp of the Twenties',[92] a view supported by a contemporary columnist who thought her Salome 'a petulant little princess with a Freudian complex', while 'Herod and his queen . . . savor a bit of Sennett rather than of old Judea'.[93] That most commentators draw attention to the fact that Nazimova was forty-three years old at the time, however, perhaps suggests a subliminal awareness that these roles are being destabilised in their very performance.

Much of the characterisation does, indeed, seem surprisingly stereotypical for what is in many ways an extremely sophisticated film. The leering Herod (Mitchell Lewis), for example, is exaggeratedly ugly, with heavy greasepaint around the eyes and lips, huge misshapen ears, a flat hat rather suggesting baldness, and an inelegant costume exposing unflatteringly hairy legs; while Earl Schenek's Young Syrian is rather a parody of the fey lover, with stylised curly wig and huge bead necklace, and a tendency to stare dreamily or obsessively either at Salome or into the distance. In isolation, of course, none of these elements is incompatible with Wilde's text; cumulatively, however, they suggest a mildly exaggerated reading of the play, a faint distortion of emotion and response to the point at which they become affected and almost break the frame, in a fashion consonant with the stylised designs.

It is therefore not easy to agree with the perception by many critics of an inconsistency between scenic design and acting style, of sophisticated visual constructions undermined by crude and incongruous performances. It is tempting to suggest instead an equation between theme, design and performance style. The action and theme of the biblical story, Wilde's self-fashioning as decadent aesthete in the 1890s, and the social and cinematic conventions of 1920s Hollywood could all be characterised as performances of indulgence and excess, and Nazimova's film, therefore, as an oblique commentary upon a fantasy world in which, by 1922, her own star was fading. In the play, Herod and Salome both display a narcissistic self-regard, a determination to indulge their sexual desires regardless of consequences; similar charges, of course, were brought against Wilde and his play; while from the beginning Hollywood had aroused the wrath of Righteous America, for whom the crumbling Babylonian sets of D. W. Griffith's *Intolerance* offered a powerful symbol of moral decay.

Still more suggestive, however, is the manner in which this film engages the question of sexuality. Nazimova's lesbianism had long been rumoured; so, too, had that of her protégée, Natasha Rambova, whose marriage to Valentino was never consummated. Indeed Kenneth Anger, chronicler of Hollywood decadence, among many others, states categorically that for *Salome* Nazimova 'employed only homosexual actors as "homage" to Wilde'.[94] It is surely significant, then, that Nazimova adopted and adapted the role of vamp for this performance. Invading the space reserved for the aggressive – but heterosexual – woman in Hollywood, Nazimova's Salome turns that convention against itself by the simple expedient of parodying its mannerisms, in a style analogous to the kind of camp performance of the male homosexual enacting a female role. The parodic exaggerations in the presentation of heterosexuality in Herod and the Young Syrian are wholly compatible with this strategy.

Nazimova's all-gay cast anticipated by more than fifty years Lindsay Kemp's in 1977, a production in which the sexual dynamics were focused upon Kemp's own portrayal of the title-role. The return to Wilde and Beardsley in Nazimova's film signifies more than just a desire for reconstruction; it represents instead the first attempt fully to integrate a common reading of the play's sexual subtext with a design concept and performance style fully informed by that subtext. That it attempts this covertly, and in Hollywood, makes it possible to see Nazimova's *Salome* as a coded act of resistance to perhaps the most influential contemporary medium in the regulation of sexual behaviour.

In a way which rather anticipated the first 'legitimate' stage production in 1931, Nazimova's attempt to film a relatively faithful version of the play did not generate further ideas; while all agreed the picture was striking, one reviewer praising it as 'the most extraordinarily beautiful picture that has ever been produced',[95] several were extremely hostile, audiences disliked it, and it was in any case too much of a curiosity to stimulate further experimentation. Aside from a little-remarked production by Malcolm Strauss the following year, in 1923, with Diana Allen in the title-role, no new *Salome* film appeared until 1945, and nothing resembling Wilde's version was filmed until 1970. But a more obvious reason why no interesting work on *Salome* should have been attempted in Hollywood after 1922 is that in the same year the industry, in response to increasingly embarrassing scandals (notably that involving Fatty Arbuckle), set up the Motion Picture Producers and Distributors of America (the 'Hays Office') to sanitise publicity; the first code of practice was issued in 1930, and was strictly enforced after Joseph Breen joined the office in 1934, the year in which the Catholic Legion of Decency was founded.[96]

A Wildean version of *Salome* could never have survived the code, and for nearly fifty years nothing on the theme was attempted, with the exception of two films, both of which make very free use of the story, and at least one of which demonstrates very clearly how closely film-making conventions were bound up with the effects of moral policing. The 1945 production was Charles Lamont's *Salome Where She Danced*, a bizarre western which perhaps conflates elements of the Mata Hari and Maud Allan myths in its story of the spy-dancer (played by Yvonne de Carlo) who escapes from the Austro-Prussian war and winds up in Arizona. This was followed in 1953 by William Dieterle's *Salome*, a film which exposes as well as any the pressures to conformity in story line and characterisation which typified much of Hollywood's product during this period. The screenplay, by Harry Kleiner, was adapted from Dieterle's own novel, *The Good Tidings*, and cast Rita Hayworth as Salome, Charles Laughton as Herod, Judith Anderson as Herodias and Stewart Granger as a new character, Salome's lover Claudius. In a twist which may be seen as either audaciously inventive or simply ludicrous, Dieterle reversed Salome's motivation: instead of dancing to secure John the Baptist's death, in his film she danced as a favour to Herod in return for the prophet's life. During the dance, however, Herodias persuades Herod to proceed, so John dies anyway, and the film closes sickeningly with Salome and Claudius listening to the Sermon on the Mount – 'the beginning', as a caption reminds us.

Columbia attempted to justify this amazing rewriting of scripture by constructing a spurious historical controversy. 'What was the enigma of Salome, most seductive beauty of history? Innocent or guilty, should she have been stoned as a witch or crowned as a saint?' Anticipating controversy, they insisted that their script had been approved by (unnamed) 'representatives of the three great religious bodies [Protestant, Catholic and Jewish] generally concerned with the faith that sprang up in the Holy Land'.[97] Such sensibilities did not, however, inhibit Columbia from titillating the public with a lurid account of Rita Hayworth's 'glamorous transparencies', which 'range in color from black through purple and peacock to flame, orange and the ultimate flesh tone'.[98] (There were only six veils: the law, and the Breen Office, prohibited the removal of a seventh, a difficulty Dieterle negotiated by interrupting the action with a sword fight.) Hopelessly compromised between the demands of sex, appeasement, and the star system, Columbia's film serves only to underline the importance to any version of the story of the conflict between sexuality and order emphasised in Wilde's play.

It was to be many years before directors turned again to *Salome*. A Danish production of 1971, directed by Werner Schroeter, was adapted from Wilde's play. In 1972 the Italian director Carmelo Bene translated and adapted Wilde's text for his film of *Salome*. He gave to himself, as Herod, some additional lines from Wilde's poems, while Giovanni Davoli, playing Jokanaan, spoke his lines extemporaneously. In his notes for the Venice Film Festival's presentation, Bene described Herod as 'the truly historical antagonist to the figure of Christ' (who appears in the film, played by Franco Leo), and glossed the story as a parable of '[t]he impossibility of martyrdom . . . in a world such as the present which is no longer barbarian but just stupid . . . All that is left is survival.'[99] This existentialist reading of Wilde, and the disillusion with conventional religious and moral categories, places Bene's film firmly in the traditions of post-war Italian film-making, and accounts for the ironic reading of the past, not only in the reinterpretation of the crucifixion but in the colour-scheme (photography by Mario Masini; the scenic artist was Gino Marotta), which was intended to recall the world of *A Thousand and One Nights*, now emptied of significance. Similar ironies were encoded in the score, which included works by Schubert, Brahms and Puccini alongside Italian popular songs of the 1920s. As often in the films of Bene's Italian contemporaries, this feeling of emptiness – perhaps especially relevant here as hinting at a critique of decadence itself – is expressed paradoxically in a visual extravagance which in the case of Salome included 'a prolonged and bloody self-crucifixion, the skinning-alive of Herod, hermaphrodites in luminescent jockstraps, and an awful lot of male and female flesh'.[100]

Claude d'Anna's film of 1986 was equally extravagant, and based on a very loose adaptation of the Wilde–Strauss version. Twelve years before the story begins, Herod (Tomas Milian) and Herodias (Pamela Salem) had conspired in the murder of Herodias's first husband Philip, Salome's father; Salome herself was removed by the 'Emperor', Caesar, as a hostage to ensure their continued loyalty. One night, Herod and Herodias dream simultaneously of a huge black bird which flies ominously through the palace. Herod consults the prophet Jokanaan (Fabrizio Bentivoglio, pointedly cast against type on account of his youthful good looks), whom he has imprisoned in an attempt to deceive Caesar into thinking him loyal; but Jokanaan's words merely heighten Herod's sense of impending catastrophe. Soon the palace is visited by Caesar's emissary Nerva (Tim Woodward), accompanied by the beautiful, sixteen-year-old Salome (Jo Champa), whose return, Herodias soon realises, signifies Caesar's intention to displace herself and Herod, a political sub-plot which proceeds throughout the film in tandem with the more familiar sexual plot involving Herod, Salome and Jokanaan.

D'Anna then sets up a novel reading of the dance: Salome is tricked by the King and Queen into appearing at their banquet dressed in seven veils, which she and Nerva discover too late is the garb of a prostitute. Nerva reveals to Salome the truth about her father's murder, and it is at this point that she encounters and falls in love with Jokanaan, who is attracted to her but refuses her on the grounds that he longs only for death. Salome's subsequent dance before the King and Queen therefore becomes not merely an expression of rage directed against Herodias; it is an act of cleansing, simultaneously embracing and discarding the role of prostitute, and, in a twist which makes explicit the death instinct implicit in the motives of both Salome and Jokanaan in previous versions, a means of fulfilling Jokanaan's desire for death and eternal union with God. Choreographer Christopher Bruce drew on Indian and Balinese traditions in an attempt to capture a spontaneous, animalistic quality essential to the expression of Salome's antagonism towards Herodias. After the dance Herod is unable to refuse Salome and, after the execution, it is Nerva who orders the soldiers to crush her with their shields.

The most striking thing about d'Anna's treatment of the story itself is the manner in which it grafts together a number of chronologically distinct narrative tropes. To the biblical and decadent overtones fused in the received account, d'Anna has added recognisably Shakespearean motifs: the long-lost, sixteen-year-old daughter recalls Perdita in *The Winter's Tale*; the conspiratorial Herod and Herodias resemble Macbeth and Lady Macbeth; while there are gestures towards *Hamlet* in the emphasis on the murder of a king by his wife and the lover who will succeed him, and in the revelation of this truth to the murdered king's child during the performance of an entertainment before the court. These themes were already present in some versions of the Salome story, although Wilde had not emphasised them. More obviously and more problematically, d'Anna explored the imperialism in the relation of Rome to Judea by means of a much-ridiculed analogy with the then current *Star Wars* cycle, an analogy signalled explicitly in all manner of details of the visual design. Just as the screenplay incorporated material from various periods and genres, so the production designer, Giantito Burcheillaro, threw together jarringly incongruous iconographies: some figures appeared in biblical dress, but the outfits of a group of palace guards were unmistakably fashioned after Darth Vader, while the costumes of the Roman soldiers recalled those of the contemporary Soviet military, and Nerva wore a heavy winter overcoat over a shiny full-body garment. This device is so disorientating and persistent – one wit nicknamed the director Claude d'Annachronism[101] – as ultimately to detract from the narrative, which, perhaps in consequence, critics tended to dismiss, although d'Anna's treatment of the story line is the most interesting aspect of the film.

In an interview, d'Anna offered two explanations for this curious device. First, he explained that he was aiming to create 'a science fiction film set in the past', suggesting through the visual anachronisms the circularity of time, in a kind of voyage into the past reminiscent of Stanley Kubrick's *2001: A Space Odyssey*.[102] As noted, however, the design specifically recalls not *2001* but *Star Wars*, which automatically undermines this gesture towards philosophical speculation and invites the audience to view the film primarily as high-tech adventure, especially as the idea is not incorporated into the narrative, which unlike that of Kubrick's film is very easily reconstructed by the spectator into a linear sequence of events. More coherently, d'Anna hoped, by defamiliarising the audience's expectations of sartorial consistency, to underline the theme of imperial power: a modern, technologically superior force invades a weaker nation whose customs and dress have remained unchanged for centuries. The modern costumes worn by the Roman soldiers were intended to encourage the spectator to think of the Soviet invasion of Afghanistan.

There is a connection here with d'Anna's notion of *Salome* as a parable of terrorism:

> Herod is a rich man living in a palace who falls in love with a terrorist. That kind of thing happens often between the high bourgeoisie and terrorists – mutual fascination. Herod takes Yokanaan [*sic*] in, but he makes a real mess, cursing everyone, spitting on them, fucking the maids, pissing in the dining room, etc. And when the daughter of the owner comes home, naturally she falls in love with him. The terrorist is full of words, saying, we have to plant bombs, kill the middle class, but he never really does anything.
>
> So one day the girl says to him, 'Have you seen the papers? They bombed the train station.' He starts praising the bombing . . . And she says, 'I did it.' And he suddenly goes pale. I told this story to my co-writer, Aaron Barzman, and we adapted it to *Salome*.
>
> I wanted to invent this world before Catholicism took all the characters and the story and made a lovely, sweet version. When John

the Baptist lived, there were a thousand prophets out raving in the desert.[103]

These intriguing, inventive and rather avant-garde ideas raise the danger of creating two apparently separate political themes: the destruction of the state from within, by terrorism, and from without, by imperial force. The twin political plots, combined with the story of Salome's personal revenge, are not in themselves impossible to synthesise; indeed, all three of these elements are present in *Hamlet*, which as we have noted is intertextually related. What destroys the film is that it continually withdraws from developing these ambitious readings of a familiar story by reducing the construction to a disconnected series of superficially ambitious but actually defensive and merely titillating visual tropes. Although d'Anna's own accounts emphasise narrative, those narratives become contradictory, and compromised by visual and commercial temptations. He was making the film for Golan-Globus, a highly commercial production company which desperately needed box-office success to stabilise their increasingly precarious financial position. It is hard not to be cynical about the aping of popular contemporary films, the lashings of sex and nudity, and even d'Anna's own claims for the film. It is notable that even at the level of conception, he was not really engaging the political possibilities he had unearthed in the story, but instead resorting to the familiar practice of demonising the political in the twin threats of communism and terrorism, and so collapsing the tensions of the story back into the comfortable opposition of good and evil.

The most recent film of the Salome story is Ken Russell's *Salome's Last Dance* (1987), reputedly made in three weeks for less than a million pounds to win a bet.[104] This was the latest in a long line of films by Russell which propose a direct and crudely expressionistic relationship between an artist's life and his work: *The Music Lovers, Savage Messiah, Mahler, Gothic*, and many others.

One can see where this is heading. Russell's reading of *Salome* is infinitely more biographical, and of Wilde's life infinitely more teleological, than anything attempted since Billing's character assassination in 1918. This is achieved by telescoping a number of historically distinct episodes, and some purely invented ones, into a single night in 1892. Having suffered the disappointment of the censor's banning of *Salome*, Wilde (Nickolas Grace) is treated by his friends to a private performance of the play in a male brothel. The part of Herodias is taken by one Lady Alice (Glenda Jackson); Herod is played by the brothel-owner, Alfred Taylor (Stratford Johns in a bravura performance which, as one critic remarked, 'has to be seen to be disbelieved'[105]). Salome is performed by a prostitute, Rose (Imogen Millais-Scott), while, provocatively, the role of John the Baptist is taken by Alfred Douglas (Douglas Hodge). In a move presumably designed to parody the charges of self-indulgence invariably and rightly made against his films, Russell himself appears as a photographer present to record the proceedings.

The play within the film was newly translated by Vivian Russell. This was not, however, the signal for a daringly original interpretation; the director fell back on the witless bad taste which is often close to the surface of his films. So, for instance, when Herod mentions the wind – which directors have often used to suggest the power of hidden forces – the Roman ambassador, Tigellinus, farts loudly, several times. On receiving John's head, Salome masturbates on top of it. The gratuitousness of all this is confirmed by the historically inaccurate and wholly pointless presence of several nude women and a plethora of heterosexual acts, including a scene in which John the Baptist is whipped to orgasm by a group of leather-clad whores. Tellingly, while Russell's camera lingers titillatingly on the heterosexual acts, when the homosexual ones are to take place he cuts away.[106]

If the homophobia is apparent even in the shot selection and editing, it is still more evident in the conceit. By placing Bosie in the role of object of desire, Russell implies a parallel between Wilde and Salome, so imputing to the author an uncontrollable and self-destructive sexual desire, an identification strengthened by the sexual ambivalence of Rose. (There is some disagreement as to whether Rose is supposed to be male or female. Many have considered Rose to be exposed as a boy prostitute, but Imogen Millais-Scott saw herself as 'totally female all the way through. Some get muddled up because I have got rather a boyish figure, whereas normally Salome is rather curvaceous',[107] while the author of perhaps the most perceptive review of the film was angered that the role was taken by a woman, given Wilde's fondness for boy actors.[108] The confusion may be deliberate on Russell's part.) Furthermore, by bringing forward the date of Wilde's arrest to the same night in 1892, by showing the arrest just after Salome has been put to death, and by having Wilde accept his fate without demur, the ending comes with the force of a moral judgement all the more staggering at the conclusion of a film whose premise 'amounts to nothing but a license to humiliate at random'.[109] As usual, Russell had come not to praise the artist, but to bury him.

CONCLUSION

Oscar Wilde never saw *Salome* presented live on stage, and left frustratingly few explicit instructions as to its proper staging. One would have welcomed, for example, some indication of Wilde's notion as to the presumed age of his heroine; what precisely he had in mind for the Dance of the Seven Veils; and what status he would have accorded in production the strand of parody many have detected in the play, in view of the reprimand visited on Graham Robertson for his assumption that a humorous pastiche was intended. The comparative rarity of performances has meant that directors are still coming to terms with *Salome*'s peculiar demands, while wishing to open it up to innovative explorations, so that for better or worse both individual productions and the stage history of the play tend towards a series of uncoordinated impressions which fail to cohere into a graspable whole.

For example, problems in the stage presentation of sexuality in the play have only very recently been illuminated by the ground-breaking studies of Wilde in the wake of Ellmann's biography; as Ian Small remarked in 1993, '*Salome* is coming to be seen as a document which allows contemporary issues in the politics of gender to be glimpsed.'[1] Several early presentations shied away from the sexual implications of Wilde's treatment of the legend, although productions such as Evreinov's aborted endeavour of 1908 seemed in this respect to be far truer to the text. Pemberton-Billing's assault, too, even if it derived from a warped patriotic zeal, recognised *Salome*'s powerful sexual undercurrents. Nevertheless, the diversity of interpretation on this point indicates that the nature of that truth remains shifting and uncertain, changing in accordance with changes in socio-political and literary perceptions of sexuality.

Certainly, during the period preceding the First World War, the Salome figure became an embodiment of what anti-feminists viewed as the destructive male-crushing threat posed by a certain type of woman usually designated the *femme fatale*.[2] To what extent Wilde himself viewed her in this light is, perhaps, immaterial; his heroine may be viewed as modulating from the virginal if wilful princess of Stéphane Mallarmé's imagination to the ferocious Maenad of J. K. Huysmans, but it was the latter manifestation that identified her with the predatory female archetype whose goal was the ultimate act of symbolic castration, the severance of a man's head from his shoulders.

This was the predominant view of Salome in the years immediately following Wilde's imprisonment. For example, J. Arthur Symons in his poem 'The Daughters of Herodias' (1897), acting on hints gleaned from *Salome* as well as Mallarmé's 'Hérodiade', which Symons translated, enrols Wilde's princess within the ranks of the fatal dancers, though here their motivation is as much sexual as it is destructive:[3]

> They dance, the daughters of Herodias,
> With their eternal, white, unfaltering feet,
> And always, when they dance, for their delight,
> Always a man's head falls because of them.
> Yet they desire not death, nor would they slay
> Body or soul, no, not to do them pleasure:
> They desire love, and the desire of men;
> And they are the eternal enemy.[4]

Cast in the same mould is the figure of the princess created by Hermann Sudermann in his more ample treatment of the scriptural legend in his *Johannes*,[5] first staged in 1898 and routinely compared to Wilde's play by the Berlin critics attending Reinhardt's production of *Salome* in 1902. As Sylvia C. Ellis points out, this Salome, despite certain childlike traits, is the most sexually aware of all her sorority, and fearing no man, resolves to use her attractions to bring to his knees the stern unyielding Baptist, who as in Wilde resists her amorous advances. But in this version Salome's dance before Herod appears not to be motivated by a desire for vengeance or a desire to please her mother, but rather serves as an arbitrary act of total caprice, which is of course a complementary aspect of the conventional *femme fatale*. Further evidence of a comparatively conservative morality is found in the climax of Sudermann's play, as a second dance following the receipt of the head on its golden charger culminates in Salome's complete breakdown into madness.

But Wilde's assertive heroine can of course be seen in a much more affirmative way. Elaine Showalter has endeavoured to demonstrate that in several respects Salome encapsulates one aspect of the so-called 'New Woman' of the *fin de siècle*.[6] For this critic the rebellious princess represents an emancipated spirit akin to her real-life contemporaries, launching an attack on the male-dominated patriarchal society surrounding her, in which Herod ostensibly exercises arbitrary political sway, while Iokanaan delivers dogmatic pronouncements on issues of ethical substance, and jealously preserves his male inviolability. Salome may therefore be seen as challenging received patriarchal values in much the same way as did her actual late-Victorian and Edwardian counterparts.

Variants on a quite different reading, of *Salome* as a homosexual drama, have been prominent ever since Wilde's imprisonment. Direct internal evidence is largely confined to the Page's declaration of his attraction to the Young Syrian, an affection which Strauss masked operatically by scoring the role for contralto voice. (It might be intriguing to see the effect on the opera as a whole of having the part undertaken by a counter-tenor.) Wilde's reported dissatisfaction on hearing that the Page was played by a woman in the Parisian première in 1896 lends some slight support to the argument, while the qualified artistic success of Alla Nazimova's film of 1922 and Lindsay Kemp's presentation of 1977 show that the play is amenable to performances which lend themselves fully to a homo-sexual reading. Of course such performances, like all theatrical pro-ductions, depend on extra-textual sign-systems in framing a particular reading of the play (indeed, modern criticism is careful to distinguish a play's performance text from the written text). For Nazimova's film Natasha Rambova based her designs on those of Aubrey Beardsley, while Kemp's *Salome* made no pretence at fidelity to Wilde's script.

That *Salome* presents an encoded statement of its author's sexual predilections is of course plausible; but that it does so in terms which maintain the stability of such binary oppositions as masculine and feminine, homosexuality and heterosexuality, now seems dubious, although the issue continues to generate fierce debate.

It was Kate Millett's account of the play in *Sexual Politics* (1977) which perhaps did most to focus attention on these ques-tions, breathing new life into the criticism of a play which was in danger of finding itself buried under a mountain of source-studies. Her discussion gains much of its impact by conflating two familiar but apparently contradictory readings of the figure of Salome. Like Beardsley, Evreinov and others before, Millett first sees her as the castrating woman, 'an imperious *sexual will* . . . Nothing so passive as a vaginal trap, she is an irresistible force and is supposed to betoken an insatiable clitoral demand that has never encountered resistance to its whims before.'[7] But in a reading conducted throughout in remarkably unequivocal terms, Millett then asserts that Salome 'is Oscar Wilde too. The play is a drama of homosexual guilt and rejection followed by a double revenge. Salome repays the prophet's rebuttal by demanding his head, and then, in Wilde's uneasy vision of retribution, Salome is slain by Herod's guards.'[8] For this critic the play could be seen as an extreme reaction against the sexual revolution, but is better read as a coded expression of Wilde's own guilty homosexual desires.

Although this particular configuration of two possibilities is unusual, the ideas themselves have a long history, and indeed continue to inform the most interesting critical studies; but these studies have reoriented the terms in which the sexual identity of Wilde and his characters tend to be discussed, to the point at which the incipient essentialism of Millett's argument has become demonstrably too simplistic.

The most obvious difficulty with Millett's account is that it reads Wilde's homosexuality, and implicitly homosexuality itself, as something single, unproblematic and knowable. But as Alan Sinfield has recently shown, Wilde was not generally perceived as homosexual by his contemporaries until his prosecution in 1895, because in Wilde's lifetime homosexuality 'was in the process of becoming constituted. The concept was *emerging* around and through instances like . . . Wilde.' It was the trial, and events in the period immediately surrounding it, which solidified a range of practices into a single image which 'cohered at the moment when the leisured, effeminate, aesthetic dandy was discovered in same-sex practices, underwritten by money, with lower-class boys'.[9] In a related argument, Jonathan Dollimore has demonstrated that Wilde did not see the individual in essentialist terms, but as transgressive and, in Dorian Gray's words, 'a being with myriad lives and myriad sensations, a complex, multiform creature'.[10]

Such reorientations suggest that the sexual identities of Wilde's characters should be seen as fluid and unstable rather than fixed and easily definable. Sinfield amasses considerable evidence to show that contemporary critics and reviewers seemed largely unaware of homosexual implications in the works or in Wilde's own behaviour, and the point holds true for *Salome*. Although it received some hostile notices when published in 1893, the objections were to its pervasive atmosphere, rather than to any specific incident or connotation. *The Times* described it as 'an arrangement in blood and ferocity, morbid, *bizarre*, repulsive, and very offensive in its adaptation of scriptural phraseology to situations the reverse of sacred'; the *Pall Mall Gazette* implied that Wilde was merely 'a seeker after notoriety', found little of merit in the play's 'boldness' and 'voluptuous-ness', and considered that previous treatments of the story had already exhausted its power to shock.[11]

Indeed, the rather generalised unease indicated by such notices continued long after Wilde's imprisonment, even if the root cause of such unease appeared to have been identified. As long ago as 1913 essays were appearing in reputable psychoanalytical journals to demonstrate the 'polymorphous perversity' of the play, and such accounts have continued, so that we have readings which variously identify homosexuality, sadism, masochism, castration, a father–daughter complex, 'latent object doubling' and more;[12] and the Billing trial of 1918 added its own collection, including fetishism, clitoral stimulation and lunar fixation. Billing and his associates were paranoiacs, but this helped them to break the absurdly timid or narrow-minded responses to sexuality which characterised discussion of the play in England prior to the libel case of 1918. Albeit from a wholly different perspective, they were able to perceive in *Salome* the same richness of sexual possibilities which modern directors and critics have identified. It is that very richness which has contributed to the success of the play in a variety of productions, and this in itself suggests the poverty of attempts to reduce it to a single sexual signification.

If *Salome* reflected certain aspects of late-Victorian and Edwardian gender politics, its treatment of verbal and non-verbal communication had weighty literary and theatrical implications for W. B. Yeats, who, like Hugo von Hofmannsthal in Austria, suffered a loss of faith in the adequacy of the written word. In 'The Song of the Happy Shepherd', published in *Crossways* (1889), the youthful Yeats had his *alter ego* declare that 'Words alone are certain good', but by 1894 when writing his play *The Land of Heart's Desire* he was having recourse to dance when portraying the fatal allure of the Sidhe. As his dissatisfaction with language as a means of artistic expression increased, he came to share von Hofmannsthal's view that both actor and dancer were privileged to 'transcend words, circumstance, and personal identity'. In a review of 1895, the Austrian had observed that 'people are tired of listening to talk. They feel a deep disgust with words. For words have pushed themselves in front of things . . . This has awakened a desperate love for all those arts which are executed without speech: for music, for the dance, and all the skills of acrobats and jugglers.'[13]

In two of Yeats's plays in particular a general indebtedness to *Salome* in these respects is transcended by incidents which mirror those of Wilde's piece far more specifically. In *A Full Moon in March* and *The King of the Great Clock Tower* (both 1935) Yeats employs three of the Wildean *données*: a sexual encounter between a cruel royal personage and an unsubmissive ardent male commoner, albeit one now who dares to woo the indifferent Queen rather than resist her overtures; an act of violent revenge which terminates with the severance of a head; and a ritual dance (although in Yeats the Queen dances with the head rather than with the aim of obtaining it as her bloody trophy).[14]

In *A Full Moon in March* the parallels are notably close: leaving aside the link suggested by the title, the proud cold Queen courted by the coarse and importunate Swineherd may have closer affinities with the 'virgin cruelty' of Mallarmé's narcissistic princess, as Ellis points out, but there can be little doubt that her arbitrary decision to execute him for his insolent act of *lèse-majesté* brings to mind Salome's sadistic revenge on the man who, having aroused sexual desire in her, albeit unconsciously, failed to gratify it. Moreover, once the severed head is in her bloodstained hands the Queen makes love to it, singing over it much as Salome breathes out her frustrated desires to the head of the Baptist. Then Yeats's heroine performs a dance of adoration in honour of the head which sings to her in its turn, before the Queen again takes up the grim object and dances a final sequence with it, until as the stage-direction (far more explicit than Wilde's) specifies: '*As the drum-taps approach their climax, she presses her lips to the lips of the head. Her body shivers to very rapid drum-taps. The drum-taps cease. She sinks slowly down, holding the head to her breast.*' Many distinctions have to be drawn between Yeats's transformations of what is in many respects Wildean material and the older man's version of the Salome theme, and Sylvia Ellis has drawn most of them. But it remains true that Wilde in transmitting part of his dramatic message through the non-verbal medium of a dance (albeit one whose precise motivation he left obscure) blazed a trail for his fellow-countryman, even if Yeats affected to have a low opinion of his compatriot's piece. Once the principle of the efficacy of dance had gained currency, others would be certain to follow.

Recent decades have also seen fresh balletic treatments of the Salome story, none more significant than that presented in November 1978 in Copenhagen, where the Danish choreographer Flemming Flindt devised a work starring his wife Vivi and Johnny Eliasen, who danced to a score for a full symphony orchestra by Peter Maxwell Davies. But while the music was generally received with approbation, the ballet received mixed reviews. In Britain, the *Observer*'s music critic described the approach adopted as follows:

> This *Salome* has only the remotest connection with the story as embroidered by the decadents Moreau and Beardsley, or, in the theatre, Wilde and Strauss. True, Salome dances naked, clasps John the Baptist's severed head to her bosom, etc, etc. But this is only the culmination of a lengthy narrative of a highly moralistic character involving Salome (a basically sympathetic figure in love with John) in an allegorical struggle between good and evil, and ending in something very close to a redemptive *Liebestod*.[15]

Tom Sutcliffe in the *Guardian* was also hostile, accusing the Flindts of marketing their product on the presumed appeal of a naked Salome, whose nudity the critic found 'vulgar and pointless'. Sutcliffe found the venue (a circus-like enclosure) unhelpful to the choreography; the plot was 'a silly mixture of freedom themes (personal and national) and religious fable, spun out to inordinate length'. The set was 'sombre', the lighting 'heavy, unsubtle', the choreography 'a feeble and eclectic mixture of the expressive story-telling mime (full of ham gestures and much eye talk) . . . with the twisting bodies and busy floor-work of bad modern dance'.[16]

Sutcliffe's objections to the 'unintimate, unrevealing' nature of public nudity raised the question which many modern stagings provoke: how far is a dancer or choreographer wise to attempt a naturalistic presentation of Salome's performance before Herod? Of the ballet as a generic form Arthur Symons once wrote, '[it] is so entirely and beautifully artificial, so essentially conventional, that it can gain nothing by trying to become, what it never can and never should be, a picture of real life'.[17] This anticipates a number of W. B. Yeats's strictures on the drama of his day, from which he wished to distinguish his own brand of theatre; but for present purposes it serves to remind us that dance as 'self-expression', dance as an attempt to portray something in terms of a literal interpretation, is of comparatively recent origin and may be doomed to fail.

Many advocate utilising instead the power of suggestion, calling for a symbolic mediation of the emotion rather than the semi-naturalistic portrayal of the emotion itself. As we saw, Peter Brook believed once at least that music should do most of the work of the dancer, while Strauss himself advocated a minimum of histrionic display in Salome's dance, expressing support for an aristocratic, stylised routine. Interestingly, neither Stephanie Sundine in the Welsh National Opera's *Salome* in 1988 nor either of the Salomes in Steven Berkoff's presentation of the play the following year was required to perform a realistic erotic dance, Sundine supplying a minimum of movement, and the Berkoff heroines miming a striptease rather than being required actually to perform one.

However, such approaches and the 'thorough decency' Strauss recommended are often difficult to reconcile in performance with the impact the dance must be deemed to have on Herod. If the Tetrarch's granting of the reward is to be plausible, the dancer's movements and the final unveiling, however minimal, must have an effect on the audience too. The danger is rather that the very eroticism may create a sexual *frisson* which becomes the be-all and end-all of the entire portrayal: the dance should surely represent a high point in the action, not a premature conclusion to the piece.

In short, the impact of the work depends to a large extent on where the emphases are placed in the interaction of the various elements foregrounded in the play. Katharine Worth and others may have read more into Wilde's script than he ever intended by way of a grand gathering-together of the creative arts, but the opportunities *Salome* provides for the poet, the designers of sets, lighting and costumes, the choreographer, the composer and musician, the actor, the dancer, to amalgamate their talents in bringing the piece to life in the most satisfying and memorable way possible suggest that even in 1891 Wilde may have glimpsed his play's enormous future stage potential.

APPENDIX: CHRONOLOGICAL TABLE OF SELECTED PRODUCTIONS

9 February 1892. *La Bataille* announces *Salome* as part of forthcoming Théâtre d'Art (Paris) season. Never produced.

June 1892. Sarah Bernhardt plans to stage *Salome*, English Opera House, London. Licence refused.

11 February 1896. World première of *Salome*, Théâtre de l'Oeuvre, Paris. Director Aurélien Lugné-Poe. Lugné-Poe (Herod); Lina Munte (Salome); Max Barbier (Iokanaan).

15 November 1902. In double bill with *Bunbury*, Kleines Theater, Berlin. Supervisor: Max Reinhardt. Gertrud Eysoldt/Tilla Durieux (Salome); Emanuel Reicher/Ludwig Wüllner (Herod); Friedrich Kayssler/Max Eisfeldt (Iokanaan); Luise Dumont/Tilla Durieux (Herodias). (Various German productions follow, e.g. *c.* 25 August 1903, Munich; Lili Marburg (Salome).)

29 September 1903. Neues Theater, Berlin. Director: Max Reinhardt.

10 and 13 May 1905. New Stage Club, Bijou Theatre, Bayswater, London. 'Stage-Manager' (i.e. Director): Florence Farr. Robert Farquharson (Herod); Millicent Murby (Salome); Louise Salom (Herodias).

13 November 1905. Progressive Stage Society, Berkeley Lyceum Theatre, New York. Mercedes Leigh (Salome).

9 December 1905. Royal Opera House, Dresden. World première of Strauss's opera. Conductor: Ernst von Schuh. Marie Wittich (Salome); Karl Burian (Herod).

10 and 18 June 1906. Literary Theatre Society, King's Hall, Archer Street, Covent Garden, London. Robert Farquharson (Herod); Lewis Casson (Iokanaan); Letitia Darragh (Salome); Florence Farr (Herodias). Sets and costumes: Charles Ricketts.

26 December 1906. Vienna. Maud Allan in probable première of *The Vision of Salome*.

22 January 1907. Metropolitan Opera, New York. Strauss's opera given single

performance only. Olive Fremsted (Salome); Karl Burian (Herod). Closed due to public outcry.

November 1907. Théâtre des Arts, Paris. Loie Fuller in *La Tragédie de Salomé*. Music: Florent Schmitt.

1908. First cinematic version. Director J. Stuart Blackton for Vitagraph.

March 1908. Palace Theatre, London. Maud Allan in dance programme which includes *The Vision of Salome*; Music: Marcel Rémy.

27 October 1908. Nikolai Evreinov prepares to stage *Salome* as *Tsarevna*, Vera Kommissarzhevskaya Theatre, St Petersburg. N. Volkhova (Salome); A. Arkad'ev (Herod); A. Zakushnyak (Iokanaan). Sets and costumes: Nikolai Kalmakov. Banned by Holy Synod.

20 December 1908. Ida Rubinstein in a mimed performance at St Petersburg. Choreography: Fokine. Music: Glazunov. Set and costumes: Bakst.

8 December 1910. Covent Garden Opera House, London. Strauss's opera. Conductor: Thomas Beecham. Ainö Ackté/Signe Von Rappe (Salome); Ernst Krauss/Philip Brozel/Franz Costa (Herod); Clarence Whitehill ('The Prophet').

27 and 28 February 1911. The New Players, Royal Court Theatre, London. Producer: Harcourt Williams. Adeline Bourne (Salome); Herbert Grimwood (Herod); Arthur Wontner (Jokanaan); Edyth Oliver (Herodias).

1912. National Theatre, Prague. Olga Grovskaya (Salome).

12–19 June 1912. Théâtre du Châtelet, Paris. Ida Rubinstein appears as Salome in Wilde's play. Director: Alexandre Sanine. Eduoard de Max (Herod).

12 June 1913. Ballets Russes, Théâtre des Champs-Elysées, Paris. *La Tragédie de Salomé*. Tamara Karsavina (Salome). Choreography: Boris Romanov. Décor: Sergei Soudeikine. Music: Florent Schmitt.

August (?) 1917. Maly Theatre, Moscow. Director: Ivan Platon. Artistic Director: Konstantin Korovin. Olga Grovskaya (Salome); M. Lenin (Herod).

9 October 1917. Kamerny Theatre, Moscow. Director: Alexander Tairov. Décor: Alexandra Exter. Music: Jules Gyutel. Choreography: Mordkin. Alisa Koonen (Salome); Ivan Arkadin (Herod); Nikolai Tseretelli (Iokanaan).

12 April 1918. Royal Court Theatre, London. Sponsor: J. T. Grein. Director:

Mrs J. T. Grein. Maud Allan (Salome); George Relph (Herod); Ernest
Milton (Iokanaan); Alix Grein (Herodias). Music: Granville Bantock
and Howard Carr. Scenic design Guy de Gerald and H. W. Owen.

c. November 1918. Cinema film. Director: J. Gordon Edwards for William
Fox. Theda Bara (Salome); G. Raymond Nye (Herod); Albert Roscoe
(Iokanaan).

1919. Shochiku Company, Tokyo. Production of Wilde's play. Charles
Ricketts's designs impounded by US customs.

1 April 1919. Ida Rubinstein in *La Tragédie de Salomé.* Part of gala performance with Bernhardt and others at the Paris Opera. Choreography:
Nicola Guerra.

March 1922. Cinema film. Director Charles Bryant for Alla Nazimova.
Nazimova (Salome); Mitchell Lewis (Herod); Nigel de Brulier
(Iokanaan). Sets and costumes: Natasha Rambova (Mrs Rudolph
Valentino).

9 June 1929. Festival Theatre, Cambridge. Director: Terence Gray. Vivienne
Bennett (Salome); George Coulouris (Herod); Noel Iliff (Iokanaan);
Doria Paston (Herodias). Choreography: Ninette de Valois. Music:
Constant Lambert. Revived 23–28 November 1931 with Beatrix
Lehmann (Salome); Robert Morley (Herod).

May 1931. The Gate Theatre, Villiers Street, London. Director: Peter
Godfrey. Margaret Rawlings (Salome); Robert Speaight (Herod);
John Clements (Iokanaan); Flora Robson (Herodias). Design:
Joan Armstrong. Music: Constant Lambert.

5–10 October 1931. People's National Theatre, Savoy Theatre, London.
Producer: Nancy Price. Joan Maude (Salome); Robert Farquharson
(Herod); Lawrence Anderson (Iokanaan); Nancy Price (Herodias).
Transferred 21 October 1931 to the Duke of York's Theatre, London, as
part of triple bill. As for 5–10 October 1931, but with Austin Trevor
(Iokanaan).

October 1933. Vice-Chancellor of Oxford University refuses the Oxford
Repertory Company permission to stage the play at the Oxford
Playhouse.

1 May 1947. The Centaur Theatre Company, Rudolph Steiner Theatre,
London, in double bill with *Sweeney Agonistes.* Director: Peter Zadek.

Bernice Rubens (Salome); Michael Yannis (Herod); Neville Bewley
(Iokanaan); René Goddard (Herodias).

11 November 1949. Royal Opera House, Covent Garden. Strauss's opera.
Director: Peter Brook. Ljuba Welitsch (Salome); Kenneth Schon
(Jokanaan). Design: Salvador Dali.

1953. Cinema film. Director: William Dieterle for Columbia. Rita Hayworth
(Salome); Charles Laughton (Herod); Alan Badel (John); Judith
Anderson (Herodias).

15 June 1954. 'Q' Theatre, Kew Bridge, London. Director: Frederick Farley.
Agnes Bernelle (Salome). Transferred to St Martin's Theatre, 20 July.

21 February 1977. Lindsay Kemp Company, Roundhouse, London. Director,
designer, etc.: Lindsay Kemp. Kemp (Salome); Vladek Sheybal
(Herod); The Incredible Orlando (Herodias); David Haughton
(Jokanaan).

1986. Cinema film. Director: Claude d'Anna. Jo Champa (Salome); Tomas
Milian (Herod); Fabrizio Bentivoglio (Jokanaan).

1987. Cinema film, *Salome's Last Dance*. Director: Ken Russell. Imogen
Millais-Scott (Salome); Glenda Jackson (Herodias); Stratford Johns
(Herod).

February 1989. New York Metropolitan Opera. Strauss's opera. Director:
Nikolaus Lehnhoff. Eva Marton (Salome).

14–19 August 1989. Royal Lyceum Theatre, Edinburgh. Transferred from
Gate Theatre, Dublin. Director: Steven Berkoff. Olwen Fouere
(Salome); Alan Stanford (Herod); Joe Savino (Jokanaan); Barbara
Brennan (Herodias). Set: Robert Ballagh. Music: Roger Doyle.

7 November 1989. Lyttelton Theatre, National Theatre, London. As at
Edinburgh (14–19 August), but with Katharine Schlesinger (Salome);
Rory Edwards (Jokanaan); Steven Berkoff (Herod); Carmen du Sautoy
(Herodias).

NOTES

INTRODUCTION

1 The English version of *Salome* was issued in 1894, with a dedication to Lord Alfred Douglas, 'the translator of my play', and in *De Profundis* Wilde speaks of quarrels arising from his pointing out 'the schoolboy faults' of Douglas's rendering. However, few today believe that Wilde had no hand in the translation which appeared in print.

2 Notably by Katharine Worth in her *Oscar Wilde*, Macmillan Modern Dramatists, London, 1983, p. 7.

3 *Ibid.*, pp. 36–38, 47–49.

4 See *The Artist as Critic: Critical Writings of Oscar Wilde*, ed. Richard Ellmann, New York, 1969, pp. 341–71.

5 Richard Aldington (ed.), *Oscar Wilde: Selected Works*, London, 1946, p. 23.

6 Edmund Wilson, *Axel's Castle: A Study in the Imaginative Literature of 1870–1930*, New York, 1931; reprinted London, 1961, pp. 9–27. For a fuller definition, see Charles Chadwick, 'The French Symbolists', in *The Encyclopedia of Literature and Criticism*, eds. Martin Coyle et al., London, 1990, pp. 296–97.

7 See Katharine Worth, *Maeterlinck's Plays in Performance*, Theatre in Focus, Cambridge, 1985.

8 J. T. Grein, *Dramatic Criticism*, 5 vols., London, 1899–1905, vol. 1, p. 71.

9 See, in particular, Mario Praz, *The Romantic Agony*, trans. Angus Davidson, Oxford, 1933; reprinted London, 1970, p. 298.

10 Peter Raby, *Oscar Wilde*, British and Irish Authors, Cambridge, 1988, p. 105.

11 *Ibid.*

12 For the Théâtre d'Art, see John A. Henderson, *The First Avant-Garde*

1887–1894, London, 1971, pp. 90–103; Raymond Rudorff, *Belle Epoque*, London, 1972, pp. 139–46.

13 For a detailed comparison of the diction of *Salome* and that of the Song of Songs, see Ewa Kuryluk, *Salome and Judas in the Cave of Sex*, Evanston, Ill., 1987, pp. 223–27. Kuryluk also draws attention to the way the language of the Baptist derives in some measure from that of the Book of Revelation.

14 *Hugo Von Hofmannsthal Harry Graf Kessler Briefwechsel, 1898–1929*, ed. Hilde Burger, Frankfurt am Main, 1968, p. 177.

15 Quoted in Katharine Worth, *The Irish Drama of Europe from Yeats to Beckett*, London, 1978, p. 114.

16 See *The Letters of Oscar Wilde*, ed. Rupert Hart-Davis, London, 1962, p. 348: 'for the only artist who, besides myself, knows what the dance of the seven veils is, and can see that invisible dance'.

BEGINNINGS

1 See Mario Praz, *The Romantic Agony*, trans. Angus Davidson, Oxford, 1933; reprinted London, 1970, p. 312; Richard Ellmann, 'Overtures to Wilde's *Salome*', *Tri-Quarterly*, 5:1 (Spring 1969), pp. 45–64. Ellmann's essay and extracts from Praz are reproduced in Derek Puffett (ed.), *Richard Strauss: Salome*, Cambridge Opera Handbooks, Cambridge, 1989, pp. 11–35. For an invaluable discussion of the entire sequence, see Helen Grace Zagona, *The Legend of Salome and the Principle of Art for Art's Sake*, Geneva, 1960. See also Sylvia C. Ellis, *The Plays of W. B. Yeats: Yeats and the Dancer*, London, 1995, and Brad Bucknell, 'On "Seeing" Salome', *English Literary History*, 60 (1993), pp. 503–26.

2 Katharine Worth, *The Irish Drama of Europe from Yeats to Beckett*, London, 1978, p. 99.

3 See Kerry Powell, *Oscar Wilde and the Theatre of the 1890s*, Cambridge, 1990, pp. 33–54.

4 See *The Letters of Oscar Wilde*, ed. Rupert Hart-Davis, London, 1962, pp. 330–31. Hereafter referred to as *Letters*.

5 *Oscar Wilde: Interviews and Recollections*, ed. E. H. Mikhail, 2 vols., London, 1979; vol. 1, pp. 186–89.

6 Richard Ellmann, *Oscar Wilde*, London, 1987, pp. 321–22.

7 Mikhail (ed.), *Interviews*, vol. 1, pp. 200–203.

8 W. Graham Robertson, *Time Was*, London, 1931, p. 136.

9 *The Decorative Art of Leon Bakst*, trans. Harry Melvill, London, 1913; reprinted 1972, p. 51.

10 See Praz, *Romantic Agony*, p. 312; Powell, *Theatre of the 1890s*, pp. 52–53. Elliot L. Gilbert, '"Tumult of Images": Wilde, Beardsley, and *Salomé*', *Victorian Studies*, 26 (1983), pp. 133–59, advances a similar argument to defend the relevance of Beardsley's illustrations.

11 Wilfrid Scawen Blunt, *My Diaries*, vol. 1 (1880–1900), New York, 1931, p. 58.

12 Mikhail (ed.), *Interviews*, vol. 1, pp. 192–95.

13 For Lorrain, see Raymond Rudorff, *Belle Epoque*, London, 1972, pp. 226–28. Lorrain himself had written a poem on Herodias contained in *La Forêt Bleue* (1883); another was to appear in a later collection, *Lunaires* (see Ellis, *The Plays of W. B. Yeats*, pp. 38–40).

14 Vincent O'Sullivan, *Aspects of Wilde*, London, 1936, p. 33.

15 Ellmann, *Oscar Wilde*, p. 324.

16 See Ian Small, *Oscar Wilde Revalued: An Essay on New Materials and Methods of Research*, Greensboro, N.C., 1993, p. 106, for a brief account of the *Salome* manuscripts.

17 *Letters*, pp. 305–306.

18 Clyde de L. Ryals, 'Oscar Wilde's *Salomé*', *Notes and Queries*, 204 (January 1959), pp. 56–57.

19 Ellmann, *Oscar Wilde*, p. 353.

20 *Letters*, pp. 324–25.

21 *La Plume*, Paris, 1903, pp. 107–15.

22 *Letters*, pp. 305–306, n.1.

23 Mikhail (ed.), *Interviews*, vol. 1, pp. 190–91.

24 Ellmann, *Oscar Wilde*, pp. 342–43.

25 *Ibid.*, p. 324.

26 For Fort and the Théâtre d'Art, see John A. Henderson, *The First Avant-Garde 1887–1894*, London, 1971, pp. 90–103; Rudorff, *Belle Epoque*, pp. 139–46.

27 Jacques Robichez, *Le Symbolisme au Théâtre*, Paris, 1957, p. 127; for the background, see pp. 110–41.

28 Ellmann, *Oscar Wilde*, p. 350.

29 *Ibid.*, pp.350–51.

30 Details in *The London Stage 1890–1899: A Calendar of Plays and Players*, ed. J. P. Wearing, Metuchen, N.J., 1976.
31 Robertson, *Time Was*, pp. 125–26. Wilde's notion for the exhaled perfumes probably derived from the Théâtre d'Art's experiment on 11 December 1891, staged during Wilde's stay in Paris, to accompany Paul-Napoléon Roinard's *Cantique de Cantiques*, based on the Song of Solomon (see Rudorff, *Belle Epoque*, pp. 143–45).
32 Robertson, *Time Was*, p. 126.
33 *Ibid.*, p. 127.
34 *Letters*, p. 336.
35 *Ibid.*, p. 392.
36 *Ibid.*, p. 834.

EARLY STAGE PRODUCTIONS IN EUROPE

1 See David Whitton, *Stage Directors in Modern France*, Manchester, 1987, pp. 18–48; John A. Henderson, *The First Avant-Garde 1887–1894*, London, 1971; Jean Chothia, *André Antoine*, Cambridge, 1991.
2 *Max Beerbohm's Letters to Reggie Turner*, ed. Rupert Hart-Davis, Philadelphia, 1965, p. 53; quoted in Kerry Powell, *Oscar Wilde and the Theatre of the 1890s*, Cambridge, 1990, p. 50.
3 Aurélien Lugné-Poe, *Acrobaties*, Paris, 1932, pp. 148–53.
4 *Ibid.*, pp. 148–49.
5 Gertrude Rathbone Jasper, *Adventure in the Theatre: Lugné-Poe and the Théâtre de l'Oeuvre to 1899*, New Brunswick, 1947, p. 207.
6 Achille Segard, *La Plume*, 8 (1896), p. 164.
7 Jean de Tinan, *Mercure de France*, 17 (March 1896), p. 416.
8 *Ibid.*, p. 416.
9 Robert Ross, letter to Mrs Gwendolen Bishop, 6 April 1905, Mander and Mitchenson Collection.
10 Philippe Jullian, *Oscar Wilde*, trans. Violet Wyndham, London, 1969, p. 347.
11 *Journal des Débats*, 13.2.1896.
12 Jasper, *Adventure in the Theatre*, p. 209.
13 Tinan, *Mercure de France*, 17, p. 417.
14 Segard, *La Plume*, 8, p. 164.
15 *Journal des Débats*, 13.2.1896.

16 *The Letters of Oscar Wilde*, ed. Rupert Hart-Davis, London, 1962, pp. 683, 695.

17 On Reinhardt, see J. L. Styan, *Max Reinhardt*, Directors in Perspective, Cambridge, 1982; Oliver M. Sayler (ed.), *Max Reinhardt and His Theatre*, New York, 1924; Huntly Carter, *The Theatre of Max Reinhardt*, London, 1914.

18 *Allgemeine Zeitung* (Munich), 18.11.1902.

19 On Wagner, see Arthur Symons, 'The Ideas of Richard Wagner', in Eric Bentley (ed.) *The Theory of the Modern Stage*, Harmondsworth, 1968, pp. 283–326.

20 *Berliner Boersen Courier*, 16.11.1902.

21 *Neues Wiener Tageblatt*, 17.11.1902.

22 *Vorwaerts*, 18.11.1902.

23 *Deutsche Zeitung*, 24.2.1903.

24 *Neue Freie Presse* (Vienna), 30.9.1903.

25 *Rheinisch-Westfälische Zeitung*, 8.2.1903.

26 *Berliner Zeitung*, 30.9.1903; *Bonner Zeitung*, 4.10.1903.

27 *Der Reichsbote*, 1.10.1903.

28 *Berliner Zeitung*, 15.9.1904.

29 *Berliner Tageblatt*, 15.9.1904; *Das Kleine Journal*, 15.9.1904.

30 *Die Welt am Montag*, 19.9.1904.

31 *Deutscher Reichsanzeiger*, 15.9.1904.

32 *Berliner Neueste Nachrichten*, 15.9.1904.

33 *Täglische Rundschau*, 15.9.1904.

34 *Berliner Morgenpost*, 15.9.1904.

35 *Leipziger Tageblatt*, 17.9.1904.

36 *Das Kleine Journal*, 30.9.1903.

37 *Berliner Morgenpost*, 10.10.1903.

38 *Berliner Tageblatt*, 15.9.1904.

39 *Berliner Tageblatt*, 15.9.1904.

40 *Berliner Morgenpost*, 10.10.1903.

41 Margery Ross (ed.), *Robert Ross: Friend of Friends*, London, 1952, pp. 83–84.

42 *Berliner Tageblatt*, 24.5.1905.

43 *Berliner Lokal Anzeiger*, 16.11.1902.

44 *Berliner Lokal Anzeiger*, 4.10.1903.

45 *Neues Wiener Journal,* 4.10.1903.

46 *Der Reichsbote,* 1.10.1903.

47 *Der Tag,* 1.10.1903.

48 *Volkszeitung,* 30.9.1903.

49 *Neues Wiener Journal,* 4.10.1903.

50 *Berliner Zeitung,* 30.9.1903.

51 Styan, *Max Reinhardt,* p. 25.

52 *Bremer Nachrichten,* 1.10.1903.

53 Styan, *Max Reinhardt,* p. 25.

54 Charles Ricketts, 'On the Art of Stage Decoration', in *Pages on Art,* London, 1913, p. 244.

55 *Der Reichsbote,* 1.10.1903.

56 *Die Welt am Montag,* 17.11.1902.

57 *Breslauer Nachrichten,* 17.11.1902.

58 *Berliner Zeitung,* 30.9.1903.

59 *Berliner Tageblatt,* 16.11.1902.

60 Correspondence in the archives of the Mander and Mitchenson Collection.

61 Margery Ross, *Robert Ross,* p. 115.

62 Unidentified review, Mander and Mitchenson Collection.

63 The *Daily Chronicle,* 11.5.1905; quoted in Leonard Creswell Ingleby, *Oscar Wilde,* London, 1907, pp. 190–92.

64 Unidentified review, Mander and Mitchenson Collection.

65 Publicity still, Mander and Mitchenson Collection.

66 Unidentified review, Mander and Mitchenson Collection.

67 Max Beerbohm's review is reprinted in his *Around Theatres,* London, 1953, pp. 377–79.

68 Unidentified review, Mander and Mitchenson Collection.

69 *Ibid.*

70 Ricketts, 'Stage Decoration', pp. 243–44.

71 Jean Paul Raymond [Charles Ricketts] and Charles Ricketts, *Oscar Wilde: Recollections by Jean Paul Raymond and Charles Ricketts,* London, 1932, p. 53.

72 Richard Allen Cave, 'Wilde Designs: Some Thoughts about Recent British Productions of His Plays', *Modern Drama,* 37:1 (Spring 1994), pp. 175–91.

73 Cecil Lewis (ed.), *Self Portrait: Taken from the Letters and Journals of Charles Ricketts, R.A.*, London, 1939, p. 52.

74 Ricketts, 'Stage Decoration', pp. 232–33.

75 Margery Ross, *Robert Ross*, p. 124.

76 Robert Ross, 'The Drama of *Salome*', *Morning Post*, 8.12.1910.

77 Margery Ross, *Robert Ross*, pp. 124–25.

78 Ricketts, 'Stage Decoration', p. 247.

79 Lewis (ed.), *Self Portrait*, p. 137.

80 Quoted in Ingleby, *Oscar Wilde*, p. 193.

81 Margery Ross, *Robert Ross*, p. 127.

82 Charles Delaney, *Charles Ricketts: A Biography*, Oxford, 1990, p. 200.

83 Margery Ross, *Robert Ross*, p. 127.

84 *Works and Days: Extracts from the Journal of Michael Field*, eds. T. and D. C. Sturge Moore, London, 1933, p. 250.

85 Beerbohm's review is reprinted in his *Last Theatres*, London, 1970, pp. 249–52.

86 Denys Sutton (ed.), *Letters of Roger Fry*, London, 1972, vol. I, p. 267.

87 Delaney, *Charles Ricketts*, p. 201.

88 Quoted in Ingleby, *Oscar Wilde*, p. 193.

89 Field, *Works and Days*, pp. 250–51.

90 Charles Ricketts's diary for 1906, Ricketts and Shannon papers, British Library MS 58104. The review is pasted into the space allotted to 22 and 23 June. Sandow was a popular exponent of health and fitness routines.

91 Quoted in Ingleby, *Oscar Wilde*, p. 193.

92 Richard Allen Cave, *Charles Ricketts' Stage Designs*, Theatre in Focus, Cambridge, 1987, p. 27.

93 Lewis (ed.), *Self Portrait*, p. 319.

94 Quoted in Eric Binnie, *The Theatre Designs of Charles Ricketts*, Ann Arbor, Mich., 1986, p. 27.

95 Laurence Senelick, '*Salome* in Russia', *Nineteenth Century Theatre Research*, 12 (1984), p. 93.

96 Karina Dobrotvorskaya, 'Russkiye Salomeii', *Teatr*, (1993), p. 135.

97 C. Moody, 'Nikolai Nikolaevich Evreinov 1879–1953', *Russian Literature Triquarterly*, 13 (Fall 1975), p. 664.

98 Nikolai Evreinov, 'Apologia Teatral 'nosti', *Utro* (Morning), 8 September 1908; cited and trans. Tony Pearson, 'Evreinov and

Pirandello: Twin Apostles of Theatricality', *Theatre Research International*, 12 (1987), p. 157. In 'The Decay of Lying' (1889) Wilde stated that 'Life imitates Art far more than Art imitates Life.'

99 Dobrotvorskaya, 'Russkiye Salomeii', p. 136.
100 See Pearson, 'Evreinov and Pirandello', pp. 147–67; Spencer Golub, *Evreinov: The Theatre of Paradox and Transformation*, Ann Arbor, Mich., 1984.
101 For Evreinov's disputes with Meyerhold, see Tony Pearson, 'Meyerhold and Evreinov: "Originals" at Each Other's Expense', *New Theatre Quarterly*, 8 (1992), pp. 321–32.
102 Pearson, 'Evreinov and Pirandello', p. 161.
103 Moody, 'Evreinov 1879–1953', pp. 668–69.
104 Dobrotvorskaya, 'Russkiye Salomeii', p. 137.
105 *Ibid.*, p. 136.
106 Spencer Golub, *The Recurrence of Fate: Theatre and Memory in Twentieth-Century Russia*, Iowa City, 1994.
107 See Elaine Showalter, *Sexual Anarchy: Gender and Culture at the Fin de Siècle*, London, 1991, pp. 144–68.
108 Golub, *Evreinov*, pp. 178–79.
109 Moody, 'Evreinov 1879–1953', p. 664.
110 Golub, *Evreinov*, p. 179.
111 *Ibid.*, p. 24.
112 Moody, 'Evreinov 1879–1953', p. 670.
113 M. Vaikone, 'Salome: Review of Dress Rehearsal', *Teatr i Isskustvo*, 44 (1908), p. 769.
114 Moody, 'Evreinov 1879–1953', pp. 669–70, provides a substantial account of the circumstances leading up to the banning of the production.
115 A. A. Mgebrov, *Zhizn' v Theatr* (Life in the Theatre), vol. I: *Moscow Arts Theatre*, Leningrad, 1929, pp. 375–80.
116 Senelick, '*Salome* in Russia', p. 94.
117 We are indebted to Karina Dobrotvorskaya's article, 'Russkiye Salomeii', for the following account of Grovskaya's performances.
118 Senelick, '*Salome* in Russia', p. 94.
119 Nick Worrall, *Modernism to Realism on the Soviet Stage*, Cambridge, 1989, p. 29.

120 Alexander Tairov, *Notes of a Director*, trans. William Kuhlke, Coral Gables, Fla., 1969, p. 65; italics in the original.

121 *Ibid.*, p. 120; italics in the original.

122 Worrall, *Modernism to Realism*, p. 29.

123 Oliver M. Sayler, *The Russian Theatre*, London, 1923, p. 154.

124 Tairov, *Notes*, p. 103.

125 Worrall, *Modernism to Realism*, p. 27.

126 Edward F. Fry, *Cubism*, London, 1966, pp. 14, 20.

127 Sayler, *The Russian Theatre*, p. 160.

128 *Ibid.*, pp. 155–56.

129 *Ibid.*, p. 155.

130 *Ibid.*, p. 160.

131 Tairov, *Notes*, p. 120.

132 This and the following quotations are from Sayler, *The Russian Theatre*, pp. 153–62.

133 Exter's model for the set is illustrated in Tairov, *Notes*, p. 121; additional details of the set are in Sayler, *The Russian Theatre*, p. 154.

'SALOME' ON THE ENGLISH STAGE, 1911–1990

1 *The Times*, 28.2.1911, p. 10.

2 Michael Orme, *J. T. Grein: The Story of a Pioneer, 1862–1935*, London, 1936, pp. 197–98.

3 For a full account of the trial and the events leading up to it, see Michael Kettle, *Salome's Last Veil: The Libel Case of the Century*, London, 1977, pp. 7–9; also Orme, *J. T. Grein*, pp. 257–62.

4 Kettle, *Salome's Last Veil*, p. 17.

5 *Ibid.*, pp. 18–19.

6 *Ibid.*, p. 145.

7 *Ibid.*, pp. 156–57.

8 Orme, *J. T. Grein*, p. 260.

9 Margery Ross (ed.), *Robert Ross: Friend of Friends*, London, 1952, p. 332.

10 *Ibid.*, p. 333.

11 *Ibid.*, p. 331.

12 *Ibid.*, p. 334.

13 Quoted in Orme, *J. T. Grein*, p. 258.

14 *Ibid.*, p. 262.

15 *The Stage*, 18.4.1918, p. 14.

16 *The Era*, 17.4.1918, p. 8.

17 Ross, *Robert Ross*, p. 335.

18 Michel Foucault, *The History of Sexuality*, vol. 1: *An Introduction*, trans. Robert Hurley, Harmondsworth, 1981.

19 See Alan Sinfield, *The Wilde Century: Effeminacy, Oscar Wilde and the Queer Moment*, London, 1994, ch.6, esp. p. 132.

20 On the Festival, see Richard Allen Cave, *Terence Gray and the Cambridge Festival Theatre*, Theatre in Focus, Cambridge, 1980; Norman Marshall, *The Other Theatre*, London, 1947, pp. 53–71; Ernest Reynolds, *Modern English Drama: A Survey of the Theatre from 1900*, Norman, Okla., 1951, pp. 42–46.

21 Programme for the Festival Theatre's production of *Salome*, 9 June 1929.

22 Richard Allen Cave, *Terence Gray*, p. 62.

23 Max Beerbohm, *Last Theatres*, London, 1970, pp. 251–52.

24 The details in this paragraph are taken from Marshall, *The Other Theatre*, pp. 45–47.

25 *Daily Express*, ? May 1931; Mander and Mitchenson Collection.

26 Photographs of the production were printed in *The Sketch*, 3.6.1931, p. 386.

27 *The Times*, 28.5.1931, p. 10.

28 A number of reviews of this production are held in the Mander and Mitchenson Collection.

29 Programme for the Centaur Theatre Company's production of *Salome* and *Sweeney Agonistes*, Mander and Mitchenson Collection.

30 *Illustrated*, 24.5.1947.

31 Reviews of the production are held in the Mander and Mitchenson Collection.

32 David Haughton, *Lindsay Kemp and Company*, p. 10; quoted in Paul Raven, '*Salome* by Oscar Wilde: A Stage History', diss., University of Warwick, 1994, p. 40.

33 Irving Wardle, *The Times*, 22.2.1977.

34 Michael Coveney, *Financial Times*, 22.2.1977.

35 Christopher Innes, *Avant Garde Theatre*, p. 123; cited in Raven, '*Salome* by Oscar Wilde', p. 29.

36 Richard Ellmann, *Oscar Wilde*, London, 1987, p. 68.

37 Alexander Bland, *Observer*, 27.2.1977.

38 Coveney, *Financial Times*, 22.2.1977.

39 *Sunday Telegraph*, 27.2.1977.

40 Coveney, *Financial Times*, 22.2.1977.

41 See, in particular, Kate Millett, *Sexual Politics*, London, 1977, pp. 152–56.

42 Charles Ricketts, 'On the Art of Stage Direction', in *Pages on Art*, London, 1913, pp. 243–44; Jean Paul Raymond [Charles Ricketts] and Charles Ricketts, *Oscar Wilde: Recollections by Jean Paul Raymond and Charles Ricketts*, London, 1932, p. 53.

43 Quoted in Ellmann, *Oscar Wilde*, p. 283.

44 Neil Bartlett, *Who Was That Man?: A Present for Mr Oscar Wilde*, Harmondsworth, 1993, p. 50.

45 *Ibid.*, pp. 46–50.

46 Quoted in Raven, '*Salome* by Oscar Wilde', p. 32.

47 Irving Wardle, *The Times*, 22.2.1977.

48 Quoted by Michael Church, *Independent*, 3.7.1989; cited in Raven, '*Salome* by Oscar Wilde', p. 33.

49 John Gross, *Sunday Telegraph*, 12.11.1989.

50 Michael Billington, 'Acted to the Hilt', *Country Life*, 16.11.1989.

51 *Ibid.*

52 Steven Berkoff, Introduction to Oscar Wilde, *Salome*, London, 1989, p. xiii. (Berkoff's own adaptation is held by the National Theatre.)

53 *Ibid.*, pp. xi–xii.

54 Angela Lambert, 'Dramatic Passions of a Beverley Hills Cop', *Independent*, *Living* section, 13.11.1989, p. 16.

55 Michael Coveney, *Financial Times*, 16.8.1989, p. 13.

56 Michael Coveney, *Financial Times*, 8.11.1989.

57 Kate Kellaway, *Observer*, 12.11.1989.

58 Jack Tinker, *Daily Mail*, 8.11.1989.

59 Berkoff, Introduction, p. xii.

60 Kevin Myers, 'An Irishman's Diary', *The Irish Times*, 24.8.1989.

61 Quoted in *Stage*, 7.9.1989.

62 *Ibid.*, 21.9.1989.

63 Irving Wardle, 'Licence under Discipline', *The Times*, 18.8.1989.

64 John Gross, 'Dream Peacocks on a Bare Stage', *Observer*, 20.8.1989.

TRANSFORMATIONS

1 Richard Ellmann, *Oscar Wilde*, London, 1987, p. 290.
2 Holbrook Jackson, *The Eighteen Nineties*, London, 1913, p. 290.
3 William Gaunt, *The Aesthetic Adventure*, Harmondsworth, 1957, p. 169.
4 See Simon Wilson, *Beardsley*, London, 1972, plate 12. For a full listing of Beardsley's known work, see A. E. Gallatin, *Aubrey Beardsley: Catalogue of Drawings and Bibliography*, New York, 1945.
5 *The Letters of Oscar Wilde*, ed. Rupert Hart-Davis, London, 1962, pp. 318n., 302n. Hereafter referred to as *Letters*.
6 *Ibid.*, p. 344, n. 3.
7 *The Early Works of Aubrey Beardsley*, New York, 1967, plates 139–57. See also Gallatin, *Catalogue*, items 875–89.
8 See Elliott L. Gilbert, '"Tumult of Images": Wilde, Beardsley, and *Salome*', *Victorian Studies*, 26 (1983), pp. 133–59.
9 *Ibid.*, p. 147.
10 Linda Gertner Zatlin, *Aubrey Beardsley and Victorian Sexual Politics*, Oxford, 1990, p. 94.
11 Ewa Kuryluk, *Salome and Judas in the Cave of Sex*, Evanston, Ill., 1987, pp. 189, 235–36.
12 *The Early Works*, plate 157.
13 *Letters*, p. 348n.
14 Zatlin, *Aubrey Beardsley*, p. 95.
15 *Letters*, p. 353.
16 *More Letters of Oscar Wilde*, ed. Rupert Hart-Davis, London, 1985, p. 177.
17 Sir Thomas Beecham, *Frederick Delius*, 1959; rev. edn. London, 1975, p. 122.
18 Barbara Tuchman, *The Proud Tower*, London, 1966, p. 291.
19 On Strauss, see Norman Del Mar, *Richard Strauss: A Critical Commentary on his Life and Works*, 3 vols., London, 1962–72; Alan Jefferson, *Richard Strauss*, London, 1975; Kurt Wilhelm, *Richard Strauss: An Intimate Portrait*, London, 1989. For the operas, see Alan Jefferson, *The Operas of Richard Strauss in Britain, 1910–1963*, London, 1963; William Mann, *Richard Strauss: A Critical Study of the Operas*, London, 1964; Charles Osborne, *The Complete Operas of Richard*

Strauss, London, 1988. For *Salome*, see Gary Schmidgall, *Literature as Opera*, New York, 1977, ch. 8; Nicholas John (ed.), *Salome/Elektra*, English National Opera Guide series 37, London, 1988; Derek Puffett (ed.), *Richard Strauss: Salome*, Cambridge Opera Handbooks, Cambridge, 1989.

20 Wilhelm, *Richard Strauss*, p. 101.

21 Richard Aldrich, *Concert Life in New York 1902–1923*, ed. Harold Johnson, Freeport, N.Y., 1971, pp. 172–79.

22 Quoted in Puffett, *Salome*, p. 132.

23 *Ibid.*, p. 133.

24 Quoted in Del Mar, *Critical Commentary*, vol. 1, p. 283.

25 Wilhelm, *Richard Strauss*, p. 102.

26 Quoted in L. C. Ingleby, *Oscar Wilde: Some Reminiscences*, London, 1912, p. 107.

27 Sir Thomas Beecham, *A Mingled Chime*, London, 1944, pp. 104–105.

28 Quoted in Puffett, *Salome*, p. 162.

29 Peter Brook, *Observer*, 4.12.1949; reprinted in *The Shifting Point*, London, 1988, pp. 170–71.

30 Puffett, *Salome*, pp. 165–67.

31 Quoted in Wilhelm, *Richard Strauss*, pp. 103–104.

32 See Jefferson, *Operas of Strauss in Britain*, pp. 53–54; James Laver, 'Setting the Scene', in *The Year's Work in the Theatre 1949–1950*, British Council, 1950, p. 49.

33 Brook, *Observer*, 4.12.1949.

34 Elaine Showalter, *Sexual Anarchy: Gender and Culture at the Fin de Siècle*, London, 1991, p. 168. See also *Opera News*, 53:12 (1989), pp. 18–24.

35 Edward J. Dent, *Opera*, Harmondsworth, 1940; rev. edn., 1949, pp. 142–43.

36 Wilhelm, *Richard Strauss*, p. 101.

37 Quoted in Jefferson, *Operas of Strauss in Britain*, p. 48.

38 *Ibid.*, p. 52.

39 *The Penguin Guide to Compact Discs and Cassettes*, ed. Ivan March, new edn., Harmondsworth, 1992, p. 1016.

40 *Ibid.*

41 Robin Holloway, '"Salome": Art or Kitsch?', in Puffett, *Salome*, pp. 145–60.

42 Christopher Nassaar, *Into the Demon Universe*, New Haven, 1974, p. 107.

43 This section owes a particular debt to Richard Bizot, 'The Turn-of-the-Century Salome Era: High-and-Pop-Culture Variations on the Dance of the Seven Veils', *Choreography and Dance*, 2:3 (1992), pp. 71–87.

44 Sally R. Sommer, 'Loie Fuller', *The Dream Review*, 19 (1975), pp. 53–67; M. H. Harris, *Loie Fuller: Magician of Light*, Richmond, Va., 1979; Susan Au, *Ballet and Modern Dance*, London, 1988, pp. 87–89; Bizot, 'Salome Era', pp. 72–73. See also Loie Fuller, *Fifteen Years of a Dancer's Life*, London, 1913.

45 Bizot, 'Salome Era', pp. 72–73.

46 Sommer, 'Loie Fuller', p. 64.

47 Roger Marx, *La Revue Dramatique*, 1.4.1895, p. 127.

48 Translated in Bizot, 'Salome Era', p. 73.

49 Pierre-Octave Ferroud, *Autour de Florent Schmitt*, Paris, 1927, p. 93. For an outline of the scenario, see the booklet accompanying the recording of Schmitt's score by the Rheinland-Pfalz Philharmonic under Patrick Davin (Marco Polo 8.22 3448).

50 *The Daily Telegraph*, quoted in Bizot, 'Salome Era', p. 77.

51 See Suzanne Shelton, *Divine Dancer: A Biography of Ruth St-Denis*, New York, 1981, esp. pp. 76–78; Ruth St-Denis, *An Unfinished Life*, New York, 1939.

52 *Hugo von Hofmannsthal Harry Graf Kessler Briefwechsel 1898–1929*, ed. Hilde Burger, Frankfurt am Main, 1968, pp. 135–36.

53 For Allan, see Felix Cherniavsky, *The Salome Dancer*, Toronto, 1991; J. E. Crawford Flitch, *Modern Dancing and Dancers*, London, 1912, pp. 103–20; Amy Koritz, 'Dancing the Orient for England: Maud Allan's "The Vision of Salome"', *Theatre Journal*, 46 (1994), pp. 63–78; and Allan's own memoir, *My Life and Dancing*, London, 1908.

54 The dance is described in Allan, *My Life*, pp. 120–28.

55 Sir Frederick Ponsonby, *Recollections of Three Reigns*, London, 1951, p. 242.

56 *Times Literary Supplement*, 26.3.1908, p. 102.

57 Quoted in Bizot, 'Salome Era', p. 79.

58 See Sam Waagenaar, *The Murder of Mata Hari*, London, 1964.

59 Michel Fokine, *Fokine: Memoirs of a Ballet Master*, trans. Vitale Fokine, ed. Anatole Chujoy, London, 1961, p. 137.

60 Boris Kochno, *Diaghilev and the Ballets-Russes*, Paris, 1970, p. 36.

61 Richard Buckle, *Diaghilev*, London, 1979, p. 130.

62 Quoted by Karina Dobrotvorskaya, 'Russkiye Salomeii', *Teatr*, 5 (1993), p. 138.

63 Showalter, *Sexual Anarchy*, p. 159.

64 Michael de Cossart, *Ida Rubinstein: A Theatrical Life*, Liverpool, 1987, p. 14.

65 Jean Cocteau, *The Decorative Art of Leon Bakst*, trans. Harry Melvill, London, 1913; reprinted New York, 1972, p. 52.

66 Dobrotvorskaya, 'Russkiye Salomeii', pp. 138–39.

67 Cocteau, *The Decorative Art*, p. 52.

68 Nesta Macdonald, *Diaghilev Observed by Critics in England and the United States 1911–1929*, New York, 1975, p. 95; see also Buckle, *Diaghilev*, pp. 245, 256.

69 Richard Buckle, *Nijinsky*, London, 1971, pp. 232–33.

70 Buckle, *Diaghilev*, p. 256.

71 *Ibid.*, pp. 304–305.

72 Serge Lifar, *Diaghilev*, London, 1940, p. 287.

73 Macdonald, *Diaghilev Observed*, p. 95.

74 De Cossart, *Ida Rubinstein*, pp. 75–76.

75 *Moving Picture World*, 30:9 (29 August 1908), pp. 163–64.

76 For the Brockliss production, see *Bioscope*, 169 (6 January 1910), p. 45; for Pathé, see *Bioscope*, 195 (7 July 1910), p. 31.

77 *Bioscope*, 18:325 (2 January 1913), pp. 65, 69.

78 See Alexander Walker, *Sex in the Movies: The Celluloid Sacrifice*, Harmondsworth, 1968, pp. 21–30.

79 See Bram Dijkstra, *Idols of Perversity: Fantasies of Feminine Evil in Fin-de-Siècle Culture*, Oxford, 1987.

80 *Bioscope*, 41:651 (3 April 1919), p. 74.

81 Susannah Radstone, 'Theda Bara', in Annette Kuhn and Susannah Radstone, eds., *The Women's Companion to International Film*, London, 1990, pp. 35–36.

82 Neil Bartlett, *Who Was That Man?: A Present for Mr Oscar Wilde*, Harmondsworth, 1993, p. 40.
83 National Film Theatre programme notes on *Salome*, n.d.
84 *Ibid.*
85 Raymond Rohauer, Program for the Gallery of Modern Art screenings, February 1967.
86 Quoted in David Robinson, review of *Salome*, *Financial Times*, 3.6.1966.
87 Showalter, *Sexual Anarchy*, p. 163.
88 *Ibid.*
89 Robinson, *Financial Times*, 3.6.1966.
90 Showalter, *Sexual Anarchy*, p. 163.
91 *Ibid.*, pp. 163–64.
92 Robinson, *Financial Times*, 3.6.1966.
93 *Photoplay*, 22:3 (August 1922), p. 61.
94 Kenneth Anger, *Hollywood Babylon*, London, 1986, p. 113.
95 Robert I. Sherwood, *The Best Moving Pictures of 1922–23*, New York, 1923, p. 103; quoted in Showalter, *Sexual Anarchy*, p. 163.
96 James Monaco, *How to Read a Film: The Art, Technology, Language, History, and Theory of Film and Media*, rev. edn., Oxford, 1981, pp. 230–31.
97 Columbia publicity release, 16.7.1953.
98 Columbia publicity release, n.d.
99 National Film Theatre programme notes, n.d.
100 Jack Babuscio, 'Daughter of Sodom', *Gay News*, 198 (5–8 May 1977).
101 Richard Mayne, *Sunday Telegraph*, 11.1.1987, p. 15.
102 Cannon 'Production Notes' for *Salome*, Cannes Film Festival, 1986, p. 9. Our factual information about the production is derived from this source.
103 Cannon 'Notes', pp. 8–9.
104 Dennis Barker, *Guardian*, 18.6.1988.
105 Charles Osborne, *Daily Telegraph*, 30.6.1988, p. 12.
106 Neil Bartlett, 'Inside Eye', *Independent*, 30.6.1988, p. 13.
107 *Guardian*, 18.6.1988.
108 Bartlett, 'Inside Eye'.
109 Michael Feingold, *Village Voice*, 17.5.1988, p. 23.

CONCLUSION

1 Ian Small, *Oscar Wilde Revalued: An Essay on New Materials and Methods of Research*, Greensboro, N.C., 1993, p. 197.

2 See Bram Dijkstra, *Idols of Perversity: Fantasies of Feminine Evil in Fin-de-Siècle Culture*, Oxford, 1987.

3 Sylvia C. Ellis, *The Plays of W. B. Yeats: Yeats and the Dancer*, London, 1995, pp. 56–58.

4 J. Arthur Symons, *Poems*, 2 vols., London, 1906; reprinted 1924, vol. II, p. 36.

5 See Ellis, *The Plays of W. B. Yeats*, pp. 58–63.

6 Elaine Showalter, *Sexual Anarchy: Gender and Culture at the Fin de Siècle*, London, 1991, pp. 144–68; see also Linda Gertner Zatlin, *Aubrey Beardsley and Victorian Sexual Politics*, Oxford, 1990.

7 Kate Millett, *Sexual Politics*, London, 1977, p. 152.

8 *Ibid.*, p. 153.

9 Alan Sinfield, *The Wilde Century: Effeminacy, Oscar Wilde and the Queer Moment*, London, 1994, pp. 8, 121.

10 Quoted in Jonathan Dollimore, *Sexual Dissidence: Augustine to Wilde, Freud to Foucault*, Oxford, 1991, p. 16.

11 *The Times*, 23.2.1893, p. 8; *Pall Mall Gazette*, 27.2.1893, p. 3; both reprinted in Karl Beckson (ed.), *Oscar Wilde: The Critical Heritage*, London, 1970, pp. 133–37.

12 For a convenient summary of such accounts, see Ian Fletcher and John Stokes, 'Oscar Wilde', in Richard J. Finneran (ed.), *Anglo-Irish Literature: A Review of Research*, New York, 1976, p. 103.

13 Quoted in Michael Hamburger, 'Art as Second Nature', in Ian Fletcher (ed.), *Romantic Mythologies*, London, 1967, pp. 226–27.

14 Ellis, *The Plays of W. B. Yeats*, pp. 66–68.

15 Stephen Walsh, 'New Dances for Salome', *Observer*, 17.12.1978.

16 Tom Sutcliffe, 'A Serving of Spiced Salome', *Guardian*, 18.12.1978.

17 *The Sketch*, 4.10.1893, p. 488; quoted in Ellis, *The Plays of W. B. Yeats*, p. 169.

SELECT BIBLIOGRAPHY

For reasons of space we have listed only books we feel to be of central importance to the genesis and composition of Wilde's *Salome*, the history of its presentation in the theatre, its treatment in art, opera, ballet and the cinema, and its present-day significance for critics and artists. Newspapers and journal articles are cited only in the notes. All quotations from Wilde are taken from Vyvyan Holland (ed.), *The Complete Works of Oscar Wilde*, London, 1966, apart from 'The Truth of Masks', taken from Richard Ellmann (ed.), *The Artist as Critic: Critical Writings of Oscar Wilde*, New York, 1969, and, for the letters, Rupert Hart-Davis (ed.), *The Letters of Oscar Wilde*, London, 1962, and *More Letters of Oscar Wilde*, London, 1985.

WORKS OF REFERENCE
Gallatin, A. E., *Aubrey Beardsley: Catalogue of Drawings and Bibliography*, New York, 1945.
Mason, Stuart (C. S. Millard) (ed.), *Bibliography of Oscar Wilde*, London, 1914; reprinted London, 1967.
Mikhail, E. H. (ed.), *Oscar Wilde: An Annotated Bibliography of Criticism*, London, 1978.
Small, Ian, *Oscar Wilde Revalued: An Essay on New Materials and Methods of Research*, Greensboro, N.C., 1993.

MEMOIRS AND REMINISCENCES
Allan, Maud, *My Life and Dancing*, London, 1908.
Beecham, Thomas, *A Mingled Chime*, London, 1944.
Fokine, Michel, *Fokine: Memoirs of a Ballet Master*, trans. Vitale Fokine, ed. Anatole Chujoy, London, 1961.

Fuller, Loie, *Fifteen Years of a Dancer's Life*, London, 1913; reprinted
New York, n.d.

Lugné-Poe, Aurélien, *Souvenirs de Théâtre: La Parade sous les Etoiles,
1903–1912*, Paris, 1933.

Mikhail, E. H. (ed.), *Oscar Wilde: Interviews and Recollections*, 2
vols., London, 1979.

O'Sullivan, Vincent, *Aspects of Wilde*, London, 1936.

Robertson, W. Graham, *Time Was*, London, 1931.

BIOGRAPHIES

Buckle, Richard, *Nijinsky*, London, 1971.

Diaghilev, London, 1979.

Cherniavsky, Felix, *The Salome Dancer* [Maud Allan], Toronto,
1991.

De Cossart, Michael, *Ida Rubinstein: A Theatrical Life*, Liverpool,
1987.

Ellmann, Richard, *Oscar Wilde*, London, 1987.

Harris, M. H., *Loie Fuller: Magician of Light*, Richmond, Va.,
979.

Jefferson, Alan, *Richard Strauss*, London, 1975.

Orme, Michael, (Mrs J. T. Grein), *J. T. Grein: The Story of a Pioneer
1862–1935*, London, 1936.

Read, Charles, *Thomas Beecham: An Independent Biography*,
London, 1961.

Shelton, Suzanne, *Divine Dancer: A Biography of Ruth St-Denis*,
New York, 1981.

Wilhelm, Kurt, *Richard Strauss: An Intimate Portrait*, trans. Mary
Whittall, London, 1989.

CRITICISM

Beckson, Karl (ed.), *Oscar Wilde: The Critical Heritage*, London,
1970.

Brook, Peter, Interview, *Observer*, 4.12.1949, reprinted in *The
Shifting Point*, London, 1988, pp. 170–71.

Calloway, Charles, *Charles Ricketts: Subtle and Fascinating Decorator*, London, 1979.

Cave, Richard Allen, *Terence Gray and the Cambridge Festival Theatre*, Theatre in Focus, Cambridge, 1980.

Charles Ricketts' Stage Designs, Theatre in Focus, Cambridge, 1987.

Chadwick, Charles, 'The French Symbolists', in *The Encyclopedia of Literature and Criticism*, eds. Martin Coyle et al., London, 1990, pp. 295–307.

Del Mar, Norman, *Richard Strauss: A Critical Commentary on his Life and Works*, 3 vols., London, 1962–72.

Dijkstra, Bram, *Idols of Perversity: Fantasies of Feminine Evil in Fin-de-Siècle Culture*, Oxford, 1987.

Ellis, Sylvia C., *The Plays of W. B. Yeats: Yeats and the Dancer*, London, 1995.

Flitch, J. E. Crawford, *Modern Dancing and Dancers*, London, 1912.

Hamburger, Michael, 'Art as Second Nature', in Ian Fletcher (ed.), *Romantic Mythologies*, London, 1967, pp. 225–41.

Henderson, John A., *The First Avant-Garde 1887–1894*, London, 1971.

Jackson, Holbrook, *The Eighteen Nineties*, London, 1913.

Jefferson, Alan, *The Operas of Richard Strauss in Britain, 1910–1963*, London, 1963.

John, Nicholas (ed.), *Salome/Elektra*, English National Opera Guide series 37, London, 1988.

Kuryluk, Ewa, *Salome and Judas in the Cave of Sex*, Evanston, Ill., 1987.

Mann, William, *Richard Strauss: A Critical Study of the Operas*, London, 1964.

Nassaar, Christopher, *Into the Demon Universe: A Literary Exploration of Oscar Wilde*, New Haven, 1974.

Osborne, Charles, *The Complete Operas of Richard Strauss*, London, 1988.

Powell, Kerry, *Oscar Wilde and the Theatre of the 1890s*, Cambridge, 1990.

Praz, Mario, *The Romantic Agony*, trans. Angus Davidson, Oxford, 1933; reprinted London, 1970.

Puffett, Derek (ed.), *Richard Strauss: Salome*, Cambridge Opera Handbooks, Cambridge, 1989.

Raby, Peter, *Oscar Wilde*, British and Irish Authors, Cambridge, 1988.

Robichez, Jacques, *Le Symbolisme au Théâtre*, Paris, 1957.

Rudorff, Raymond, *Belle Epoque*, London, 1972.

Sayler, Oliver M., *The Russian Theatre*, London, 1923.

Schmidgall, Gary, *Literature as Opera*, New York, 1977.

Showalter, Elaine, *Sexual Anarchy: Gender and Culture at the Fin de Siècle*, London, 1991.

Styan, J. L. *Max Reinhardt*, Directors in Perspective, Cambridge, 1982.

Walker, Alexander, *Sex in the Movies: The Celluloid Sacrifice*, Harmondsworth, 1968.

Wilson, Edmund, *Axel's Castle: A Study in the Imaginative Literature of 1870–1930*, New York, 1931; reprinted London, 1961.

Wilson, Simon, *Beardsley*, London, 1972.

Worrall, Nick, *Modernism to Realism on the Soviet Stage: Tairov-Vakhtangov-Oklopkov*, Cambridge, 1989.

Worth, Katharine, *The Irish Drama of Europe from Yeats to Beckett*, London, 1978.

  Oscar Wilde, Macmillan Modern Dramatists, London, 1983.

  Maeterlinck's Plays in Performance, Theatre in Focus, Cambridge, 1985.

Zagona, Helen Grace, *The Legend of Salome and the Principle of Art for Art's Sake*, Geneva, 1960.

Zatlin, Linda Gertner, *Aubrey Beardsley and Victorian Sexual Politics*, Oxford, 1990.

INDEX

Lightning Source UK Ltd.
Milton Keynes UK
24 April 2010

153250UK00001B/25/P